Implementation and Benefits of Digital Twin on Decision Making and Data Quality Management

Florian Blaschke

Implementation and Benefits of Digital Twin on Decision Making and Data Quality Management

Springer Gabler

Florian Blaschke
Bietigheim-Bissingen, Germany

Ph.D. Thesis Hungarian University of Agriculture and Life Sciences Kaposvár Campus
2023

ISBN 978-3-658-44452-5 ISBN 978-3-658-44453-2 (eBook)
https://doi.org/10.1007/978-3-658-44453-2

This Springer Gabler imprint is published by the registered company Springer Fachmedien Wiesbaden GmbH, part of Springer Nature.
The registered company address is: Abraham-Lincoln-Str. 46, 65189 Wiesbaden, Germany

Foreword by Atilla Wohllebe

In most cases, the term digital twin is probably associated primarily with the manufacturing industry. The understanding ranges from a specific object, which is mapped as a digital twin, to entire systems and processes. The ultimate goal is to digitally replicate the corresponding entity with all its properties as accurately as possible so that manipulations of the digital twin provide information about how the entity will behave in reality. In fact, most publications on digital twins come from the secondary sector—as outlined by Florian Blaschke in his dissertation. But how can digital twins be used in such a fast-growing sector as e-commerce—and therefore in the tertiary sector? In general, it is conceivable that they could be used along the entire e-commerce value chain. This includes modeling processes in logistics or customer service as well as modeling IT systems in order to carry out testing in software development or simulate cyber attacks.

However, the use of digital twins for consumers, i.e. online shoppers, has hardly been developed to date. If you ask Google how digital twins can be used in e-commerce, the results are essentially limited to 3D models that enable products to be displayed using augmented reality (AR) or virtual reality (VR). There is no doubt that 3D models can be seen as digital twins, but this view seems too simplistic. It would be much more exciting to also capture the physical properties of products, such as the properties of the materials used, model them in the digital twin and make them available in the online store. This could take potential use cases for AR and VR to a whole new level. The virtual fitting room, which today essentially projects a 3D model onto a human body, would then become a real customer experience if the digital twin of an evening dress moved authentically with the movements of the body, depending on the fabric used. In combination with the knowledge of the material a wall is made of, the right screws for the wall mount could also be recommended based on the weight of a TV. And if the

TV is to be placed on a sideboard, the knowledge of the weight of the TV and the load-bearing capacity of the sideboard could be used to recommend a more stable piece of furniture.

Whatever the specific use cases of digital twins in e-commerce will look like for consumers, I would like to emphasize four things at this point: Firstly, 3D models of products are just the beginning—if ever. Secondly, it will be the task of e-commerce to discover and implement value-adding use cases. Thirdly, digital twins will support e-commerce companies and online shoppers alike in their decisions, provided that—fourthly—the necessary data is available in the required quality and the systems involved communicate with each other. Digital twins therefore represent an important field of research that must and will receive even more attention in e-commerce in the coming years.

Until then, Florian Blaschke's dissertation is a contribution to research into digital twins from the perspective between management and IT. He deliberately leaves the context of the technical performance required to create a digital twin. Instead, he looks at the digital twin in the context of decision support and at the same time emphasizes the relevance of data quality management.

I would like to take this opportunity to congratulate my friend and former fellow student on the completion and publication of his dissertation. I wish the readers of his work many new insights and inspiration for the use of digital twins.

In January 2024 Prof. Dr. Atilla Wohllebe

Foreword by Stefan Waitzinger

In today's rapidly evolving manufacturing landscape, the ability to make informed decisions based on data is of paramount importance. Digital twins have emerged as powerful tools that can provide manufacturers with a virtual representation of their physical systems, enabling them to monitor, analyse, and optimize their operations with unprecedented efficiency. Florian Blaschke's dissertation "Implementation and Benefits of Digital Twin on Decision Making and Data Quality Management" delves into the intricacies of this technology and its transformative potential for manufacturing companies.

In today's competitive environment, manufacturers are constantly seeking ways to improve their processes, increase productivity, and reduce costs. Data, when harnessed effectively, can provide valuable insights into the performance of production lines, identify potential bottlenecks, and guide decision-making processes. Digital twins play a pivotal role in unlocking the power of data not only but foremost in manufacturing and other core value creation processes. These virtual replicas of physical systems capture real-time data from sensors, allowing manufacturers to monitor and analyse their operations in unprecedented detail.

By creating a digital representation of their production processes, manufacturers can simulate various scenarios, test potential improvements, and optimize their operations before implementing changes in the real world. Florian Blaschke's dissertation highlights the specific benefits that digital twins offer in the context of decision making. The technology enables e.g. manufacturers to gain a holistic view of their operations. Digital twins provide a comprehensive picture of the entire production process, from raw material inputs to finished product outputs. This holistic view allows manufacturers to identify potential inefficiencies and optimize their operations across the entire value chain.

They also become essential in the prediction of potential failures and disruptions: Digital twins can analyse historical data and real-time sensor data to predict potential failures and disruptions in production lines. This predictive capability enables manufacturers to take proactive measures to prevent downtime and minimize disruptions to their operations. By capturing and analysing real-time data from sensors, digital twins help manufacturers identify and eliminate data quality issues. This, in turn, ensures that the data used for decision making is accurate, reliable, and actionable. Regarding the ongoing decline in available qualified work force especially in industrialized countries the optimization of resource allocation becomes vital. Digital twins can simulate various scenarios and optimize resource allocation, such as machine utilization, manpower deployment and inventory management. This optimization can lead to significant improvements in productivity and cost savings.

Additionally digital twins can be used to personalize products and services based on individual customer preferences and usage patterns. This personalization can enhance customer satisfaction and loyalty. All of the above needs high end data quality management as a basis, and the approach proposed indicates this hypothesis is clearly true.

Florian Blaschke's dissertation provides a comprehensive and insightful examination of the implementation and benefits of digital twins in decision making and data quality management for companies. The findings of this research have the potential to improve corporate decision making not only in theory but to lead to enhanced efficiency, improved product quality, and increased competitiveness. I would like to extend my heartfelt congratulations to my friend Florian on the successful completion and publication of his valuable dissertation. I wish him all the best in his future endeavours!

In January 2024 Prof. Dr.-Ing. Stefan Waitzinger

Acknowledgment

This book is the revised version of my dissertation, which was accepted at the Hungarian University of Agriculture and Life Sciences (MATE) in 2023 under the title "Implementation and Benefits of Digital Twin on Decision Making and Data Quality Management".

The dissertation was written to investigate the technology of the digital twin, which is one of the most important technologies and research directions for the realization of Industry 4.0 using cyber-physical systems (CPS) and information technology. CPS form the backbone to support the creation of a network for decentralized and autonomous decision-making. The design principles for Industry 4.0 serve as guidelines for virtualization concepts that are virtual copies of the physical world and provide a link between the real and virtual worlds in order to collect data and monitor processes.

Here, technology has evolved into what is known as "digital twin technology". Gartner's "hype cycle" predicts that digital twins will be deployed in most large industrial organizations by 2021, increasing effectiveness by 10%. The industry implications of digital twins have not gone unnoticed. Siemens AG, PTC Inc, Dassault Systèmes, IBM, Microsoft Azure, SAP and General Electric are all currently building a corresponding industrial IoT-platform, which is a clear indication of the importance of digital twins. In short, digital twin technology is crucial for the future development of an organization. Therefore, the objective of this dissertation is to show differences within and across management level, company size and industry, focusing on the automotive, healthcare, retail, transport, construction, computer and food industries. Furthermore, it develops a theoretical digital twin-driven decision-making model (DTDDMM) by combining corporate data quality management, a process digital twin, and model-driven decision support systems.

The benefits of digital twins are transparency, new insights, the facilitation of what-if analyses, a reduced time-to-market, process monitoring, process diagnosis, time reduction, cost reduction, predictive maintenance and product improvement, which all lead to an improvement in operational effectiveness. The model creates, tests, and builds a process in the virtual world to support decision-making by combining data, analytics, and visualization of insights. These results will help managers understand and appreciate the differences between data quality management, digital twins, decision support systems for strategic positioning, the 14 prioritized implementation requirements, the 10 benefits, and the 11.13% improvement in operational effectiveness achieved with the model.

I could not have carried out this research without the tireless support of my family, my friends and my doctoral supervisor. I would like to take this opportunity to express my special thanks to them.

I would like to dedicate this book to my dad Udo Blaschke (24.02.1966-23.11.2021), who unfortunately passed away unexpectedly. **Dad**, my life began with you. Together, we took my first steps, and I spoke my first words to you. We were a great family. With your words, you guided me, with your deeds, you set standards. I want to thank you for everything I experienced with you and for what you made possible for me. With great sadness, I let you go. This dedication is my last greeting to you. I love you. I miss you. We will meet again.

I would like to thank my dear wife, **Saskia** Blaschke, and my dear daughters, **Emilia** and **Sophie** Blaschke, for their unconditional support in my personal life, my professional life and my academic career. For kicking my ass and making me finish this dissertation, and for the countless weeks, evenings, and weekends you had without me as a result. I love you.

Furthermore, and for the same reason, I would like to extend my thanks to my mother **Susanne** Blaschke, father-in-law **Dieter** Lorenz, mother-in-law **Silke** Lorenz, family and friends for their support.

I would also like to thank my esteemed PhD supervisor, **Prof. Dr. Zoltán Gál**, for his patience and the unyieldingness with which he accompanied me to the finished dissertation.

I must also mention the following with gratitude for their support: my fellow students and the great time I experienced in Hungary; various publications; and finally the Hamburger Fern-Hochschule and Hungarian University of Agriculture and Life Sciences (MATE) Kaposvár Campus for setting up this PhD program.

Contents

Abbreviations

AI	Artificial Intelligence.
BA	Business Analytics.
BD	Big Data.
BDA	Big Data Analytics.
BI	Business Intelligence.
CAGR	Compound Annual Growth Rate.
CPS	Cyber-Physical system.
DTDDMM	Digital Twin-Driven Decision-Making Model.
IoT	Internet of Things.
ISO	International Organization for Standardization.
Mdn	Median.
PRISMA	Preferred Reporting Items for Systematic Reviews and Meta-Analyses.
RQ	Research Question.

List of Figures

List of Tables

Introduction 1

"By 2021, half of large industrial companies will use digital twins, resulting in those organizations gaining a 10% improvement in effectiveness."(Gartner, 2017b)

Digital transformation is becoming a very important issue, and companies that are not able to adapt to digital transformation will fall victim to "digital Darwinism" (Helmy Ismail et al., 2018). Some companies will disappear, and only the most adaptable that respond to technological trends will survive (Schwartz, 2001). Therefore, digital transformation requires a company to develop a wide range of capabilities that vary in importance depending on the business context and the specific needs of the company (Reis et al., 2018; Stolterman et al., 2004; Yoo et al., 2010). Digital transformation at industrial level began with Industry 4.0, which includes transformation based on the use of cyber-physical systems (CPS) and the support of information and communication technology such as the Internet of Things (IoT), big data (BD), cloud computing and artificial intelligence (AI) (Pires et al., 2019). All of these technologies are based on data, the amount of which will increase from 26 in 2017 to 180 zettabytes by 2025 (Roy et al., 2018; Vassakis et al., 2018).

The quality of this data directly determines the value of these technologies as well as the quality of decisions (Pavlovich et al., 2020). For the implementation of Industry 4.0, CPS are the backbones that support the creation of a network of components with cyber and physical counterparts capable of making decentralized and autonomous decisions (E. Lee, 2008). The design principles for Industry 4.0 serve as guidelines for implementation and include decentralization, interoperability, virtualization, real-time capability, service orientation, and modularity (Pires et al., 2019). An important role is played by virtualization concepts. These are virtual copies of physical systems, creating a link between real and virtual systems (Hermann et al., 2015). The concept has evolved into a new technology, namely the digital twin (Rodič, 2017) which has received increasing attention in

F. Blaschke, *Implementation and Benefits of Digital Twin on Decision Making and Data Quality Management*, https://doi.org/10.1007/978-3-658-44453-2_1

the development of industrial IoT-platforms (3DS, 2021; GE, 2021; IBM, 2021; Microsoft, 2021; PTC, 2021; SAP, 2021; Siemens, 2021). Digital twins have a critical role to play in the evolution of Industry 4.0, and this has been confirmed by Gartner's "hype cycle" (Gartner, 2017a,b).

Gartner rated the digital twin as one of the top 10 strategic technology trends for 2017 (Gartner, 2017a), 2018 (Gartner, 2018), 2019 (Gartner, 2019) and 2020 (Gartner, 2020). Indeed, Gartner's 2018 hype cycle predicted that hundreds of millions of objects, machines or systems would have a digital twin by 2023 (Gartner, 2018). For these reasons, the digital twin is critical to the future development of an organization and therefore should be explored. A **digital twin** is a digital representation of an entity that meets the needs of a number of use cases (Platenius-Mohr et al., 2020) through a combination of data, analytics, and visualization of insights to support decision-making (Meierhofer et al., 2020). It can be used to address three high-level priorities in industry: (1) **sustainability**, the reduction of energy consumption, and the development of green alternatives (Biewendt et al., 2020); (2) **smart innovations**, such as smart cars (Blaschke et al., 2021); and (3) health care and safety, for disease diagnosis and treatment, and occupational health and safety concepts (Apte et al., 2021). Digital twins are equipped with technologies such as IoT, BD, cloud computing, and AI that rely on data, the quality of which directly determines the value of these technologies and the quality of the digital twins (Pavlovich et al., 2020).

It may be useful to begin by defining a few terms. **Data** is a collection of facts or information from various sources that influence the quality of decision-making (Sulistyo et al., 2020). **Data quality** provides data suitable for use by data consumers (Fürber, 2016). **Data quality management** defines, collects, stores, processes, and manipulates data (Glowalla, Balazy, et al., 2014). In this context, **decision-making** consists of a course of action, action strategy, or goal achievement strategy (Rashidi, Ghodrat, et al., 2018), where **decision support systems** help managers to understand **unstructured decisions** (Hosack et al., 2012) that cannot be solved with standard procedures (E. Turban et al., 2007). Here, a **process digital twin**, as a maximum expansion stage of the digital twin, could support unstructured decision-making with end-to- end process digitization (Raj et al., 2020) as **information technology** (Meierhofer et al., 2020) in the input-process-output model shown in Figure 1.1 (Raghunathan, 1999) to improve **operational effectiveness**.

However, managers should not only pay attention to effectiveness but also to strategic positioning, as strategic and basic management processes are indispensably linked (Sadun et al., 2017). **Strategic positioning** (making decisions) means doing things differently by creating a unique value proposition that is the

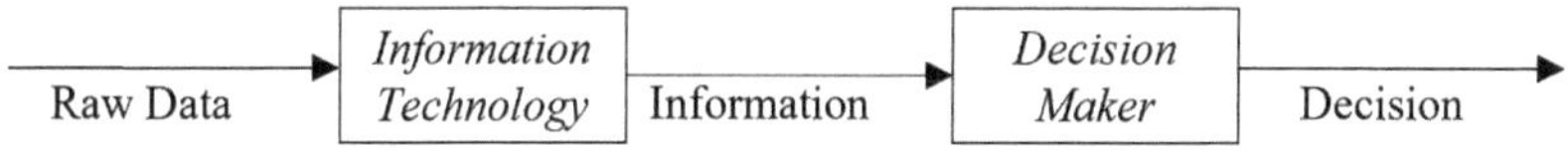

Figure 1.1 Input-process-output model with the digital twin. (Source: Own Figure, derived from Raghunathan, 1999)

key competitive opportunity. **Operational effectiveness** (validation and execution) means adopting, acquiring, and extending best practices by doing things increasingly better (Porter, 1996). For strategic positioning, the knowledge of data quality, the digital twin, and decision support across **management levels**, **company sizes** and **industries** is essential for understanding the current state and progress of competitors. For operational effectiveness, leveraging the **benefits** of the digital twin is particularly important. To conclude, the end product of a manager's efforts is a quality decision (Drucker, 1963), where the knowledge of strategic positioning leads to a competitive opportunity as shown in Figure 1.2.

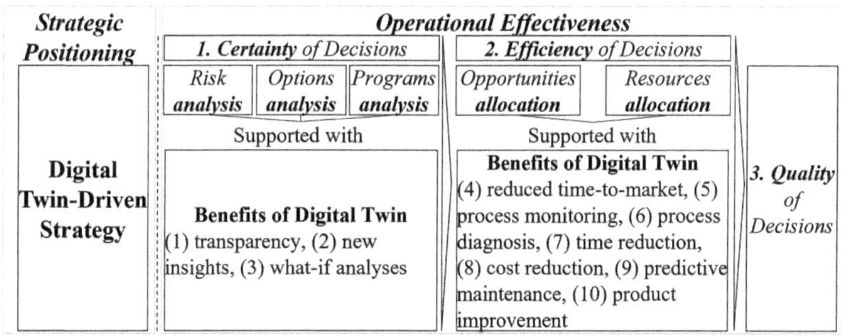

Figure 1.2 Model of quality decision-making process with the digital twin. (Source: Own Figure, modified and derived from Negulescu et al., 2014)

In order to verify the potential of the digital twin and its use in decision-making, the following research questions (RQ) should be answered:

- **RQ 1** Are there differences in data quality, digital twins and decision support in terms of management level, company size and industry for strategic positioning?
- **RQ 2** What could a theoretical model look like that relies on a digital twin for decision making while focusing on data quality?

- **RQ 3** Does the theoretical model, using digital twins for decision-making and focusing on data quality, increase operational effectiveness?

This dissertation is organized as follows (Figure 1.3): **Chapter 1** presents the connection and importance of the topic to Industry 4.0, introduces the input-process-output model and model of quality decision-making process, discusses the potential of the digital twin and introduces the research questions (RQ). **Chapter 2** introduces the theoretical foundations of data quality management, the digital twin and decision support systems to answer RQ 1, and establishes the theoretical digital twin-driven decision-making model (DTDDMM). Subsequently, **Chapter 3** reveals the research gap and defines the objectives, focusing on strategic positioning, DTDDMM and operational effectiveness to derive the hypotheses from the theoretical foundations of **Chapter 2**.

Chapter 4 describes the research design, the data from the preliminary (N = 144) and main study (N = 122) focusing on the automotive, healthcare, retail, transport, construction, computer and food industries. Additionally, the Wilcoxon signed-rank test is used to show differences within each industry, the Kruskal–Wallis test is used to show the differences across the industries and percentage points are allocated to show the operational effectiveness. The results and the evaluation within each industry and across the seven industries are then discussed in **Chapter** 5 to answer the research questions (RQ) and test the hypotheses. The results are presented in **Chapter 6** along with three recommendations focusing on strategic positioning, the DTDDMM and its operational effectiveness. **Chapter 7** discusses the results and summarizes six new scientific results showing the theoretical DTDDMM (Figure 7.1). **Chapter 8** summarizes and concludes the dissertation and provides an outlook for future research.

1. Introduction	By 2021, half of large industrial companies will use digital twins, resulting in those organizations gaining a 10% improvement in effectiveness
2. Literature Review	1. PRISMA - Data quality management (DQM): **67** publications 2. PRISMA - Digital twin (DT): **117** publications 3. PRISMA - Decision support system (DSS): **28** publications
3. Objectives	1. *Strategic Positioning:* Determination of differences (management level, company size and industry) of DQM, DT and DSS in industries 2. DTDDMM*:* Elaboration of a theoretical model for the industries 3. *Operational Effectiveness:* Elaboration and analysis of the effects of DTDDMM for industries
4. Materials & Methods	1. Preliminary Study: **N=144**; *Standardized quantitative questionnaire* with **15 questions** 2. Main Study: **N=122**; *Standardized quantitative questionnaire* with **50 questions** **Industry:** Automotive, healthcare, retail, transport, construction, computer and food **Methods:** Kruskal-Wallis, Wilcoxon and Percentage Points
5. Results & Evaluation	1. Preliminary Study: N=144; **H_1, H_2, H_3, H_4 accepted** ✓ Differences btw. industry awareness level for DT and company sizes, but no differences btw. management level 2. Main Study: N=122; **H_1, H_2, H_3, H_4, H_5 accepted** ✓ Differences btw. and company sizes , but no differences btw. industries and management levels
6. Conclusion & Recommendations	1. *Strategic Positioning:* Addition of DT as part of the **digitization strategy.** 2. *DTDDMM:* **Full implementation** of DQM, DT and DSS, if necessary, with new and consistent organizational structures, processes and methods, architectures and application systems 3. *Operational Effectiveness:* **Integration** of the **Digital Twin-Driven Decision-Making Model** to the existing information systems and digitization and linking of processes
7. New scientific results	1. **Theoretical DTDDMM** 46 potential industries 2. **Identification and analysis of differences** between the industries. (1) lower awareness level in the retail industry and a (2) higher acceptance level in companies with 250 or more employees regarding some questions 3. **Identification and analysis** of the implementation level of digital twins, data quality management and decision support systems already or would do so within the next three years 4. **Identification and definition** of the DTDDMMs top five **requirements** - timeliness, consistency, accuracy, integration, and update - and the top five benefits - process monitoring, time savings, process diagnostics, new insights, and transparency. 5. Identification of a potential **increase of 11.13% in operational effectiveness** by combining and using the **benefits of digital twins**. 6. **The identification of 65% average data quality score** in automotive, healthcare, retail, transport, construction, computer and food industry.
8. Summary	**Implementation of DTDDMM for strategic positioning and increased operational effectiveness by 11.13%**

Figure 1.3 Structure of the dissertation. (Source: Own Figure)

2 Literature Review

This chapter is based on the systematic literature review approach shown in Figure 2.1.

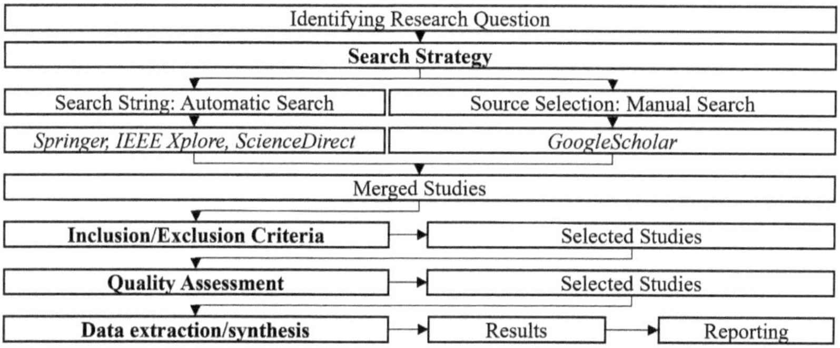

Figure 2.1 Process of the systematic literature review. (Source: Own Figure)

The literature was derived from Springer, IEEE Xplore, ScienceDirect and Google Scholar on 04 January 2021 using the PRISMA scheme (Moher et al., 2009). *"Digital Twin"*, *"Data Quality Management"* and *"Decision Support System"* in connection with *"Decision Making"* were searched, focussing on the titles and abstracts of the publications. Subsequently, the identified publications were merged with the **inclusion and exclusion criteria** (The corresponding data

---

Supplementary Information The online version contains supplementary material available at https://doi.org/10.1007/978-3-658-44453-2_2.

F. Blaschke, *Implementation and Benefits of Digital Twin on Decision Making and Data Quality Management*, https://doi.org/10.1007/978-3-658-44453-2_2

can be viewed in Appendix Table 1 in the electronic supplementary material) to form the basis for more detailed analyses and to provide a multidisciplinary perspective.

As the total results of the *"Data Quality Management"* and *"Decision Support System"* were >40,000 and those of the *"Digital Twin"*, were >3,000, it was unlikely that all were related to the RQ. For this reason, **quality assessment** judged the overall quality of the research by focussing on the first 10 pages (Springer: 200; IEEE Xplore: 250; ScienceDirect: 250 results sorted by relevance). Additionally, GoogleScholar was used to get a holistic scientific view, focusing on the first 10 pages (100 results sorted by relevance) to remove duplicates. Once an article met the quality requirements, it was included in the **data extraction and synthesis** (Figure 2.2).

2.1 Basic Definitions

2.1.1 Data and Big Data

According to ISO 9000:2015 3.8.1, *"data are facts about an object"* (ISO, 2015). Furthermore, data are a collection of facts or information gathered from various sources and used to make decisions in an organization (Sulistyo et al., 2020) and describe certain events (Subbalakshmi et al., 2018). In this respect, the IoT is a data streaming environment where a large deployment of smart things continuously report readings and then are consumed by pervasive applications (Karkouch et al., 2016). Data are a valuable resource, which is reflected in the increased spending on data management (Hao Jiang et al., 2013). They are the source for business transactions or decisions (Fürber and Hepp, 2010) and are divided into four types (Otto and Oesterle, 2015):

- **Master data**: Basic information representing the main business objects. This information must be referenced for transactions and has a low frequency of change.
- **Inventory Data**: Warehouse information concerning the stock of inventory and exhibits. This information has a high frequency of change.
- **Transaction Data**: Information about contracts, deliveries, invoices and payments, with a high frequency of change.
- **Meta Data**: Data containing definitions, value lists and access rights, specifying data properties and data meaning.

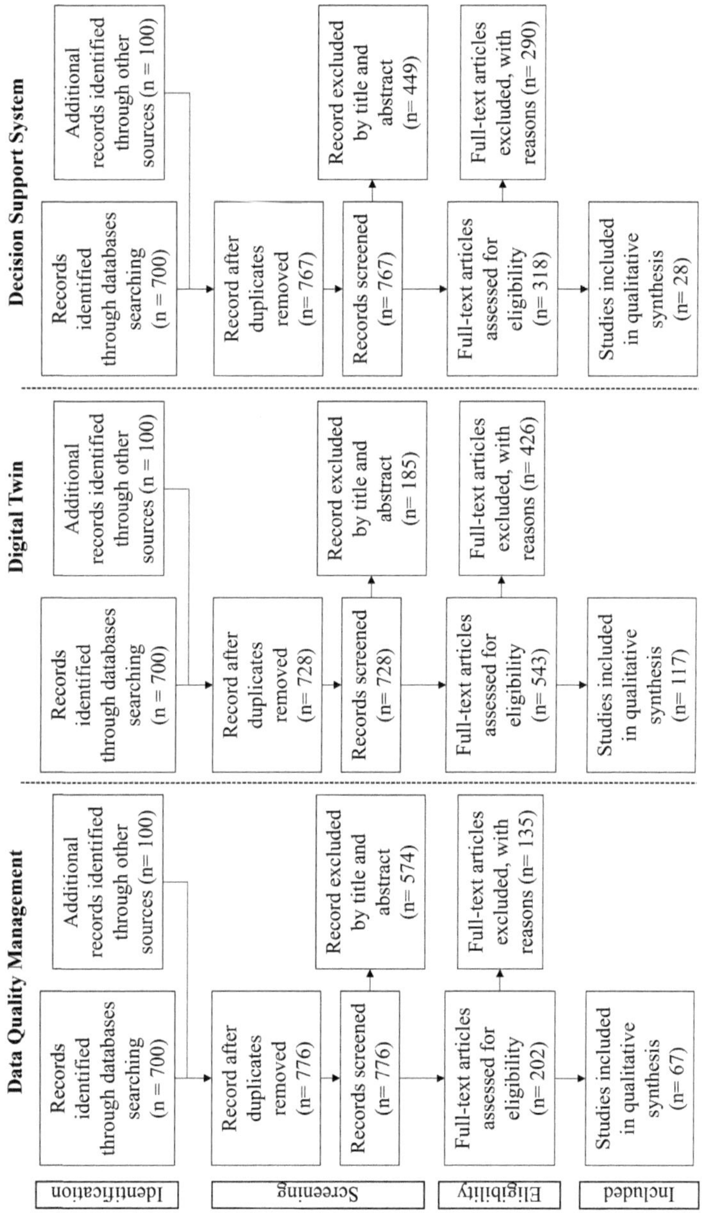

Figure 2.2 PRISMA statement of the dissertation. (Source: Own Figure)

Data consists of structured, unstructured and semi-structured data (Avison et al., 2006; Batini, Cappiello, et al., 2009). Structured data are elementary attributes within a domain defined by generalization or aggregation of elements (Fatimah et al., 2012). Structured data are improved by data cleansing technology (Rahm et al., 2000) and abnormal, missing, inconsistent and duplicate data detection (Dong et al., 2018). Unstructured data are generic sequences of symbols encoded in natural language from a variety of sources, such as online networks, text messages, images, and audio documents (Jaya et al., 2017). Furthermore, these data focus on entity detection with algorithms and error detection based on rules and main data by modifying or adding incorrect data, including rule-based/machine learning repair and true value discovery (Dong et al., 2018).

Semi-structured data are data that have a structure with some degree of flexibility, starting from a wide range of basic combinations of organized and informal information and using various data frameworks (Subbalakshmi et al., 2018). Because these data are collected from multiple sources, they are heterogeneous and of low quality, which hinders the decision-support capability (Mao et al., 2019). Data consumers access data through the following interfaces (Fürber, 2016):

- **Data layer**: Pure data, i.e., values composed of characters according to syntactic rules.
- **Data model layer**: Context information of data and schema, i.e., formally described data structure, constraints, rules, classifications and metadata.
- **Presentation layer**: Presentation of the data in designed user interfaces containing transformations of data and schema objects.
- **Access layer**: Permissions, i.e., user access rights to view, modify, create, or delete specific data.

In general, all components of these layers can be sources of their own quality issues. As a result, when using intermediaries to access data, data quality can be affected by factors other than by data values (T. C. Redman, 2001). **Big data** (BD) are a collection of large data sets that require a scalable architecture for efficient storage, manipulation, and analysis (Volk et al., 2019). The extraction of high-quality and real data when using and processing BD from massive, variable and complicated datasets is a challenging issue (L. Cai et al., 2015). These volumes of data exceed the time required by current software tools to capture, manage and process them (Babu et al., 2014; Ongsulee et al., 2018). However, capturing and analysing the vast amount of information from multiple sources has benefits for understanding customer needs, predicting risks, and improving quality (L. Cai et al., 2015). Therefore, BD is used as a term for the field of analysis of large data sets (Geerdink, 2013). Enabling **decision-making** and process automation, BD requires specific forms of information processing (Mccarthy et al., 2019), taking the following factors into account:

- **Volume**: The volume is determined by size, the amount of data generated, and stored.
- **Velocity**: The speed at which data is generated and processed to meet the demands and challenges of growth and development.
- **Variety**: The type and state of the data in order to effectively use the resulting insights and fill in missing pieces through data fusion.
- **Value**: The quality of data collected can vary widely, affecting accurate analysis.

To conclude, BD are used to analyse large data sets to find correlations and statistical patterns (Persson et al., 2017) to encourage decision-making (Gupta et al., 2017).

2.1.2 Analytics

Business analytics (BA) developed in the late 2000 s to outline the main analytical elements in business intelligence (BI) (Vassakis et al., 2018). BA can be considered part of BI. However, it focuses on future forecasts for planning and decision-making, while BI focuses on reporting and analysing historical data (Wadan et al., 2019). Therefore, BI systems are data-driven decision-making systems, while BA are the data analysis techniques used to support the decision-making process (Vassakis et al., 2018). BA creates analytical models and simulations to build scenarios, understand realities, and predict future states (Mccarthy et al., 2019). It consists of three parts (Kumar, 2017):

- Descriptive: *What is happening?* Business problems and opportunities.
- Predictive: *What will happen?* Accurate projections of the future state.
- Perspective: *Why should we do it?* Decision based on predictions.

Subsequently, big data analytics (BDA) was developed to analyse large and complex data sets that require advanced technologies for data storage, management, analysis and visualization (Vassakis et al., 2018). It helps to analyse BD against a wider range of useful data and optimizes the effectiveness of prediction (Lim et al., 2020). BDA plays a vital role in BD (Ganguli et al., 2020; Raj et al., 2020). It predicts future volumes, gains insights, and takes proactive measures to pave the way for better strategic decision-making (Husamaldin et al., 2020). BDA is a data-driven technology that uses machine learning algorithms to analyse large amounts of data to discover patterns, uncover opportunities, predict outcomes (Oo et al., 2019), identify and correct problematic relationships and make decisions about incomplete underlying data (Anagnostopoulos, 2016).

2.1.3 Digital Twin

There are many different definitions of digital twins depending on their purpose. However, there is **no definitive definition** (Adamenko et al., 2020). Many publications explicitly avoid defining the concept of a digital twin, assuming that its set of capabilities and characteristics makes it difficult to form a precise definition (Sjarov et al., 2020). However, most definitions agree on the basic idea that a digital twin enables physical system-specific storage and provision of models used for specific application purposes (Löcklin et al., 2020) with IoT, BD, cloud computing and AI (Qianzhe et al., 2019) (Figure 2.3).

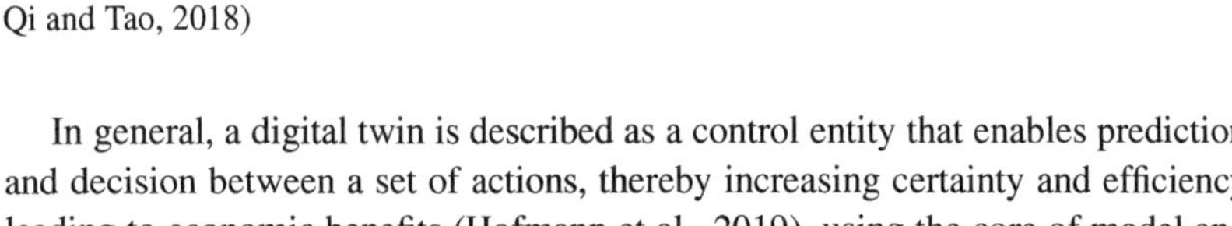

Figure 2.3 Information technology for the digital twin. (Source: Own Figure, derived from Qi and Tao, 2018)

In general, a digital twin is described as a control entity that enables prediction and decision between a set of actions, thereby increasing certainty and efficiency leading to economic benefits (Hofmann et al., 2019), using the core of model and data (Z. Liu et al., 2019). Additionally, a digital twin can be both model-based and data-driven (Jaensch et al., 2018). Most publications refer to component, asset or system digital twins (Qianzhe et al., 2019) and do not mentioned process digital twins (Vijayakumar, 2020). However, it is important to differentiate them depending on the stage of expansion (Raj et al., 2020):

- A **Component Digital Twin** is single individual component used for operations and maintenance through data-driven decisions.
- An **Asset Digital Twin** is an entire asset that gives a holistic view of how something works and enables predictive maintenance.
- A **System Digital Twin** is system that provides data showing how various assets interact with each other.
- A **Process Digital Twin** is an enterprise-level view to measure operational aspects and provide end-to-end visibility to optimize quality, performance and simulate alternative approaches for process transformation.

Grieves introduced the digital twin in 2002 as a *"set of virtual information constructs that fully describes a potential or actual physical manufactured product from the micro atomic level to the macro geometrical level"* (Grieves, 2016), shown in Figure 2.4.

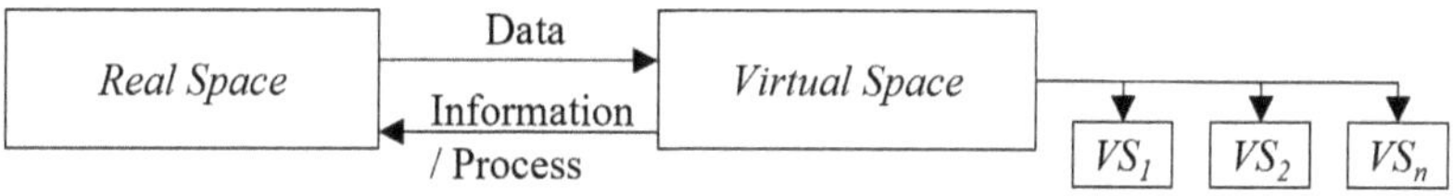

Figure 2.4 Conceptual idea of the digital twin. (Source: Own Figure, derived from Grieves, 2015)

"Twin" implies in this context that the digital information is connected to the physical system throughout its life cycle (Shao et al., 2020). Since Grieves introduced the digital twin and NASA (Glaessgen et al., 2012) gave the first specific definition, a large body of literature has been published (M. Liu et al., 2020) and it has been used for many applications (Wright et al., 2020). Zhifeng mentions that a digital twin is an *"intelligent, interdisciplinary and multi-model based technology that gathers big data"* (Z. Liu et al., 2019). Boschert states that a digital twin is a *"physical and functional description of a component, product or system, which includes more or less all information which could be useful in all lifecycle phases"* (Boschert and Rosen, 2016). Parmar states that a digital twin *"enables firms to better understand, predict, and optimize the performance of an individual asset, an integrated system of assets, or a fleet of assets"* (Parmar et al., 2020). To conclude, a digital twin is a virtual representation of an entity to satisfy the requirements of different use cases (Platenius-Mohr et al., 2020).

2.1.4 Decision Making

A decision is defined as the choice of a course of action, a strategy for action, or a strategy for achieving a goal (Rashidi, Ghodrat, et al., 2018). Decision-making is a non-random activity that leads to the selection of a course of action considering multiple strategies, and a "decision support system" is a system that facilitates decision-making (Burstein et al., 2008). Decisions can be classified as highly structured, semi-structured, completely unstructured, and single or multi-step with risky, certain, or uncertain outcomes (Rashidi and Lemass, 2011):

- **Structured decisions**: These are standard solutions for repetitive problems in all phases of decision-making, characterized by unambiguous decision criteria and a limited number of precise alternatives, and whose consequences are without complexity.
- **Semi-structured decision**: These are decisions in which some standard solution procedures are applicable and some phases of decision-making are structured. However, the rest are supplemented by human judgment, and the decisions are adaptively developed.
- **Unstructured decisions**: With these decisions there is a lack of clear decision criteria and none of the phases of decision-making are structured since there is a finite set of alternatives, leading to a high degree of uncertainty about the consequences of the known alternatives.

Activities to identify potential solutions and alternatives to address unstructured problems (Fielder et al., 2016) take a top-down approach with provisions and steps to return to earlier levels (Hogenboom et al., 2016) based on the decision-making process in Figure 2.5 with the (1) information, (2) design, (3) selection (Simon, 1977), and (4) implementation phase, executed by a decision support system (Efraim Turban et al., 2001).

The **intelligence or problem identification phase** is concerned with identifying discrepancies between the current and target states, diagnosing the problems that need to be addressed and/or options that need to be pursued (Srinivasan et al., 2000). In the **design phase**, alternatives are developed and options are analysed to gain insight into relevant implications so that it can be determined whether additional knowledge is needed, which would lead to a return to the intelligence phase (Burstein et al., 2008). The **selection phase** selects the proposed alternatives that were explored in the design phase, which depends heavily on the nature of the decision context and the idiosyncrasies of the decision maker, but

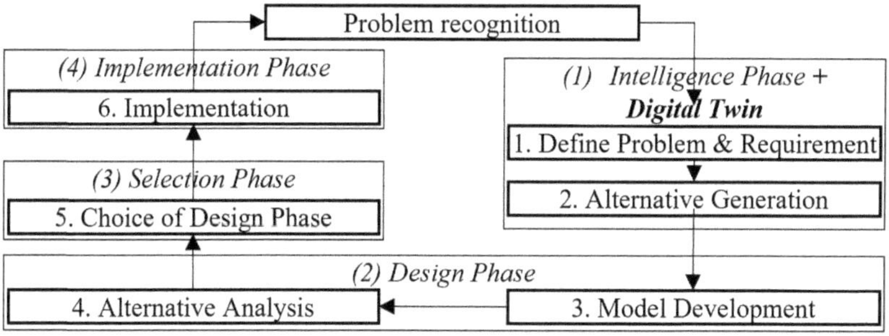

Figure 2.5 Process of decision-making with the digital twin. (Source: Own Figure, modified and derived from Aqel et al., 2019)

one option must be selected (Rashidi, Ghodrat, et al., 2018). The **implementation phase** involves a set of selected solutions that have been approved and must be put into practice over time, which requires planning and sensitivity to constructively involve stakeholders (Srinivasan et al., 2000). The solution must then be monitored to ensure that the problem has been resolved, which completes the decision-making process (Rashidi, Ghodrat, et al., 2018). Thus, the result of a successful implementation is the problem solution (Efraim Turban et al., 2001).

In this context, **decision analysis** (Keefer et al., 2004), which deals with the complexity of decision-making in the context of uncertainty, dynamics, and the numerous factors that influence value, are important (Spetzler et al., 2016). It is assumed that the decision maker makes his decision based on the information produced by information technology. Equation 2.1 measures **decision quality** (Spetzler et al., 2016) by the absolute differences between probability (P_0) and belief (B_0) which are equal to 1 (or 0) (Raghunathan, 1999).

$$(1 - |B_0 - P_0|) \tag{2.1}$$

In summary, the steps of decision-making can be reduced by digital twins to the simplified form of describing a set of possible actions or alternatives, evaluating these actions, and selecting the preferred action (Meierhofer et al., 2020).

2.2 Data Quality Management

Altogether, 67 papers were selected as a result of the data extraction and synthesis. Some 12 of these papers stated different frameworks (The corresponding data can be viewed in Appendix Table 2 in the electronic supplementary material), as well as 29 papers stated 23 different data quality dimensions (The corresponding data can be viewed in Appendix Table 3 in the electronic supplementary material).

2.2.1 Data Quality

According to ISO 9000:2015 3.6.2 *"quality is defined as the degree to which a set of inherent characteristics satisfies requirements"* (ISO, 2015). Quality dimensions are divided into schema quality (representation of the data = schema) and data quality (representation of the data = value) (Avison et al., 2006) and express the characteristics that data must have (Bellatreche et al., 2020). Data quality is the degree to which data meets the requirements of various individuals or groups, standards, laws, regulations, business policies, or data processing application expectations (Fürber, 2016). Data quality requires strategic focus by establishing a culture of quality and tactical focus by identifying data quality areas to conduct data quality projects, in addition to strong business and information technology collaboration (Allen et al., 2015). The issue of data quality is therefore becoming increasingly important since information in new information systems is ubiquitous, diverse and uncontrolled (Batini, Cappiello, et al., 2009).

In this context, data quality reflects the degree of satisfaction of data for specific applications that help managers make optimal decisions efficiently, while low data quality will detrimentally affect decision makers' judgement (Dong et al., 2018). Common to all definitions of data quality is the assumption that data quality are relatively formally or informally defined quality expectations, such as consumer expectations and intentions, specifications, or requirements imposed by the use of the data (Fürber, 2016). There is no agreement on the set of dimensions that characterize data quality nor on their meaning (Batini and Scannapieco, 2016), although various authors have proposed a variety of possible data quality dimensions. However, a comprehensive list is not available (Batini, Cappiello, et al., 2009), and therefore the choice depends on the type of application, task, and user requirements (Bellatreche et al., 2020). The level of data quality is determined by comparing the current state with a target state (Fürber, 2016) using the following two strategies (Jaya et al., 2017):

- **Data-driven**: This improves data quality by directly modifying the data value, capturing, standardizing or normalizing new data, locating and correcting errors, linking data sets, integrating data and schema, checking source trustworthiness and optimizing costs.
- **Process-driven**: This redesigns the process that produces or changes data to improve its quality, through process control where the data is reviewed and managed, the causes of low quality are removed, and a new process is added to produce high quality.

However, it should be noted that process-driven methods work better over a long period of time because they completely eliminate quality problems, while data-driven methods are more expensive but more efficient over a short period of time (Fatimah et al., 2012). To conclude, data quality is defined as the degree to which data meets the requirements of various individuals or groups, standards, laws, regulations, business policies, or data processing application expectations (Fürber, 2016). The DTDDMM uses this definition.

2.2.2 Data Quality Management

According to ISO 9000:2015 3.3.3, management is defined as *"the coordination of activities for the direction and control of an organization"* (ISO, 2015), so data quality management is the management of quality. Data quality management has a wide range of tasks and techniques used by companies and organizations to evaluate and improve data quality (Otto and Oesterle, 2015). Therefore, data quality management improves data quality by including and establishing data quality policies, data cleansing, and correcting and improving data quality processes (Shankaranarayanan et al., 2006; Sulistyo et al., 2020). It reports on the data quality measured against defined data quality dimensions and requirements (Yang et al., 2006) and corrects the data if necessary (Brüggemann et al., 2009). Data quality management has been examined from a variety of technical, functional, and organizational perspectives (Even et al., 2010) and is a knowledge-intensive discipline (Fürber and Hepp, 2013). It relies on domain knowledge to detect and correct erroneous data since data without definition cannot be interpreted as information and is meaningless (Brüggemann et al., 2009). So, data quality management enables the improvement of an information system (Glowalla, Balazy, et al., 2014) and consists of the following (Hernes et al., 2020; L. Jiang et al., 2012):

- **Data profiling**: The process of analysing and understanding the existing data to determine whether the data is complete and correct.
- **Assigning the quality of acquired data**: These are rules for the correctness of data, which result in data exclusion, data acceptance, data correction and the insertion of a default value.
- **Data integration**: Data about the same object stored in different databases may differ. To integrate these, negotiation and consensus can be used.
- **Data augmentation**: Data is converted into a form that enables deeper business analysis.

For this reason, data quality management must have measurable goals as well as clearly defined policies and technologies (Allen et al., 2015; Shi et al., 2019). In terms of data, this means making data **"fit for use"** through planning, implementation and control (Mao et al., 2019). Faulty data has always existed in systems, but the effects of incorrect data have become much more visible and the consequences more severe (Marsh, 2005). As a result, data quality management should occur throughout the whole information system: from the structure of data resources, to the system's position in the data process, to data evaluation and processing to the final data product (Glowalla and Sunyaev, 2013; Hao Jiang et al., 2013) see Figure 2.6.

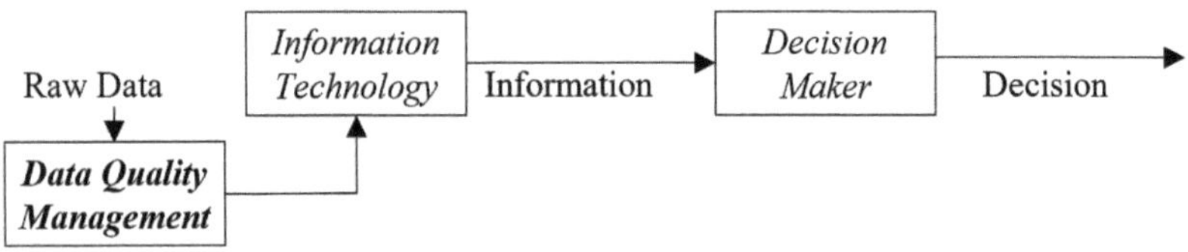

Figure 2.6 Input-process-output model—Data quality management. (Source: Own Figure, modified and derived from Raghunathan, 1999)

To conclude, data quality management can be defined as a management system for data that ensures high quality by defining, collecting, storing, and processing or manipulating data (T. Redman, 2013). **The DTDDMM use this definition**.

2.2.3 Corporate Data Quality Management

In 1995, Wang introduced the concept of *"total quality management"* (R. Y. Wang, Reddy, et al., 1995). This was expanded in 1998 to *"total data quality management"* (R. Y. Wang, 1998), after which ten other data quality management frameworks identified in this dissertation (The corresponding data can be viewed in Appendix Table 2 in the electronic supplementary material). In 2007, *"corporate data quality management"* (The corresponding data can be viewed in Appendix Figure 1 in the electronic supplementary material) was developed by Otto (Otto, Weber, et al., 2007), added in 2015 by applying the business engineering approach to enterprise-wide management of data quality and is now known industry-wide by Allianz, Bayer CropScience, Beiersdorf, Bosch, Festo, Hilti, Johnson&Johnson, Lanxess, Shell, Syngenta (Otto and Oesterle, 2015). The corporate data quality management framework addresses business (organizational alignment) and technical issues (implementation of data architectures). It helps define the tasks for implementing data quality management as well as identify relevant design objects and organizational responsibilities (Otto, Weber, et al., 2007) with requirements like definition, transparency, prevention, automation, flexibility, uniformity and law-abidance (Otto and Oesterle, 2015). Here, consistency at all levels is important for a digital twin, as is a top down strategy to ensure access to the right data, quality, provenance and security (Apte et al., 2021). **The DTDDMM has adopted corporate data quality management**.

2.2.4 Data Quality Dimensions

A variety of possible data quality dimensions for data quality management have been proposed in the literature, but a universally accepted list is not available (Batini, Cappiello, et al., 2009). However, managing data quality dimensions and improving them through a process is important to ensure high data quality (Jaya et al., 2017). The choice of data quality dimensions depends on the type of application, the task, and the requirements of the users (Bellatreche et al., 2020). Data quality requirements have changed to reflect the changing context of use, and information management has evolved, requiring more organized planning, monitoring, and control of data quality (Avison et al., 2006). According to these definitions, the level of data quality is determined by comparing the actual state of the data with a target state (Fürber, 2016). Wang and Strong identified **179 data quality** dimensions in 1996 by interviewing data consumers (R. Y. Wang and Strong, 1996), which must be viewed with caution (Kahn et al., 2002) for the following reasons:

- Typically, data consumers do not distinguish between data, application, and hardware when assessing data quality.
- Data quality dimensions (The corresponding data can be viewed in Appendix Table 3 in the electronic supplementary material) are difficult to measure because they are based on highly user-and context-specific assumptions and requirements.
- Data producers, custodians and providers also have data requirements that may differ from data consumer requirements.
- Considering only the perspective of the data consumer is not sufficient when developing artifacts for practical data quality management because this may ignore important data quality dimensions and neglect potential quality issues in the data.

However, the identified five major data quality dimensions mentioned (The corresponding data can be viewed in Appendix Table 3 in the electronic supplementary material) can serve as a **starting point** for structuring data quality assessment (Fürber, 2016) by focusing on the early definitions of the dimensions. **The DTDDMM uses (1) accuracy, (2) completeness, (3) consistency, (4) timeliness and (5) accessibility as data quality dimensions**. The dimensions derived are theoretically described below in Table 2.1.

Table 2.1 Major data quality dimensions

Category	Dimension	Description
Intrinsic	Accuracy	Data are correct, reliable and certified as error-free
Contextual	Completeness	Data are of sufficient depth, breadth and scope
	Timeliness	Age of the data is appropriate
Representational	Consistency	Data are in the same format and compatible with previous data
Accessibility	Accessibility	Data are available or easily and quickly retrievable

Source: Own Table, derived from Batini and Scannapieco, 2006

(1) **Accuracy:** *"The extent to which data are correct, reliable and certified free of error"* (R. Y. Wang and Strong, 1996). This focuses on the question: *"Is*

the information correct, objective and can it be validated?" (Marsh, 2005). Accuracy is defined as the closeness between a data value v and v0, distinguishing between temporal and structural accuracy (Batini and Scannapieco, 2006). The weak accuracy error is a Boolean variable β (.) equal to 1 if the condition TRUE and 0 otherwise, and $q_i = \sum_{i=1}^{n} q_{ij}$ accounts for the case where accuracy errors ($q_i > 0$) occur for a tuple t_i, but do not affect the identification ($s_i = 0$) defined in Equation 2.2 (Batini and Scannapieco, 2006).

$$\sum_{i=1}^{n} \frac{\beta((q_i > 0)(s_i = 0))}{N} \tag{2.2}$$

The strong accuracy error, where β (.) and q_i have the same meaning as above, consider the case where accuracy errors ($q_i > 0$) occur for a tuple t_i and actually affect the identification ($s_i = 1$) defined in Equation 2.3 (Batini and Scannapieco, 2006).

$$\sum_{i=1}^{n} \frac{\beta((q_i > 0)(s_i = 1))}{N} \tag{2.3}$$

The percentage of exact tuples matching the reference table is expressed by the degree of syntactic accuracy of the relational instance r by considering the percentage of exact ($q_i = 0$) matching ($s_i = 0$) tuples given in Equation 2.4 (Batini and Scannapieco, 2006).

$$\sum_{i=1}^{n} \frac{\beta((q_i > 0)(s_i = 0))}{N} \tag{2.4}$$

To conclude, inaccuracy is a distorted representation of a false state in information system from which a false state of the real world is inferred (Wand et al., 1996). **(2) Completeness:** *"The extent to which data are of sufficient depth, breadth, and scope for the task at hand"* (R. Y. Wang and Strong, 1996). This focuses on the question: *"Do they provide all the information required?"* (Marsh, 2005). Completeness differs by schema, column, or population and is measured for a relation r in a model without zero values as the proportion of tuples actually represented in relation r and their size with respect to the total number of tuples in ref(r), defined in Equation 2.5 (Batini and Scannapieco, 2006):

$$C(r) = \frac{|r|}{|ref(r)|} \tag{2.5}$$

To conclude, completeness is the ability of an information system to represent any state of the real system without incomplete representations (Wand et al., 1996). **(3) Consistency:** *"The extent to which data are always presented in the same format and are compatible with previous data"* (R. Y. Wang and Strong, 1996). This focuses on the question: *"Are the data consistent and easily understood?"* (Marsh, 2005). Consistency captures the violation of semantic rules for data elements, where the elements can be records in a file or tuples of relational tables (Batini and Scannapieco, 2006):

- Key dependency: Relational instance r is defined over a set of attributes, where there is a key dependency in r for a subset K of the attributes unless two rows of r have the same K values.
- Inclusion Dependency: Relational instance r says that some columns of r are contained in other columns of r or in another relational instance.
- Functional Dependency: Relational instance r, X and Y are two nonempty sets of attributes in r and r satisfies the functional dependence $X \rightarrow Y$ for each pair of tuples t1 and t2 in Equation 2. 6:

$$[If \quad t_1 X = t_2 X; \quad then \quad t_1 Y = t_2 Y] \tag{2.6}$$

To conclude, inconsistency of data values is when there is more than one state of information system corresponding to a state of the real system (Wand et al., 1996). **(4) Timeliness:** *"The extent to which the age of the data is appropriate for the task at hand"* (R. Y. Wang and Strong, 1996). This focuses on the question: *"Is it available whenever required?"* (Marsh, 2005). Timeliness expresses not only how current the data are for the task at hand but also how timely the events that correspond to their use are, so the measurement of timeliness is linked to currency and volatility, where age measures the age of receipt, delivery time is the time at which the information product is delivered to the customer, and input time is the time at which the data are received as defined in Equation 2.7 (Batini and Scannapieco, 2006):

$$curreny = age + (deliverytime - arrivaltime). \tag{2.7}$$

Timeliness ranges from 0 poor timeliness to 1 good timeliness where the relevance of timeli ness depends on volatility which is the period over which the data remains valid, as defined in Equation 2.8 (Batini and Scannapieco, 2006):

$$Timeliness = max\left\{0, 1 - \frac{\text{currency}}{volatility}\right\} \tag{2.8}$$

To conclude, untimeliness is related to the delayed change in the real world and information system, leading to a past state of the real world (Wand et al., 1996). **(5) Accessibility:** *"The extent to which data are available or easily and quickly retrievable"* (R. Y. Wang and Strong, 1996). This focuses on the question: *"Can the data be easily accessed and exported to other applications?"* (Marsh, 2005). Accessibility measures the user's ability to access the data-based culture, physical status, characteristics, available technologies, and security level (Batini and Scannapieco, 2006).

2.3 Digital Twin

Altogether, 117 papers were selected as a result of the data extraction and synthesis. A total of 16 papers stated a definition of digital twin in relation to decision-making, 14 papers stated a definition of process digital twin, 28 papers stated a generic model (Table 2.2), 33 papers stated requirements (The corresponding data can be viewed in Appendix Table 4 in the electronic supplementary material), and 46 potential industries (The corresponding data can be viewed in Appendix Figure 2 in the electronic supplementary material).

2.3.1 Digital Twin for Decision Making

Due to the focus on **decision-making**, only definitions of the digital twin that mention decision-making are discussed. **Meierhofer** provides the basic definition of the digital twin, which is *"a combination of data, analytics, and the visualization of insights to support decision-making"* (Meierhofer et al., 2020), although Liu added the time period by *"managing the whole lifecycle"* (M. Liu et al., 2020). Mathupriya and Madni mentioned the visualisation and real-time decision-making possibilities of a digital twin as the *"digital specification of a physical item continuously updated and visualized"* (Mathupriya et al., 2020) for *"real-time decision-making"* (Madni et al., 2019). In order to establish the importance and connection to the subject of data quality, Perno, Datta, Wu and Tao mention that digital twins are *"virtual representations of physical assets"* (Perno et al., 2020) created by *"different sources, approved by cognitive supervisors, and connected by secure systems"* (Datta, 2017) with *"analysis through the data"* (Wu et al., 2020) to make *"proactive and data-driven decisions"* (Tao, M. Zhang, and Nee, 2019b).

Conejos Fuertes and Kunath mention the competitive opportunity and the implementation status, so that the digital twin *"will be an essential support system in the near future for decision-making"* (Conejos Fuertes et al., 2020) and the *"main tool for decision support, once the Digital Twin is fully integrated"* (Kunath et al., 2018). Another important component is the topic of analytics. Haag and Fuller have believe that digital twins ensure *"information continuity throughout the entire product life cycle [as] decision support and system behavior predictions"* (Haag et al., 2018) with *"rapid analysis and real-time decisions made through accurate analytics"* (Fuller et al., 2020). The monitoring and control function of the digital twin is noted by Errandonea, Lu and Kong as the *"replica of a physical process for control"* (Errandonea et al., 2020) for *"monitoring and prediction purposes"* (Lu et al., 2019) to *"solve the insufficiencies in decision-making"* (Kong et al., 2020). Wanasinghe mentions that digital twins are *"virtual replicas of physical assets to make more informed decisions and "what-if" scenario analysis"* (Wanasinghe et al., 2020). **The DTDDMM uses Meierhofer's definition**.

2.3.2 Process Digital Twin

The process digital twin, Figure 2.7, is a concept designed to reach several industries.

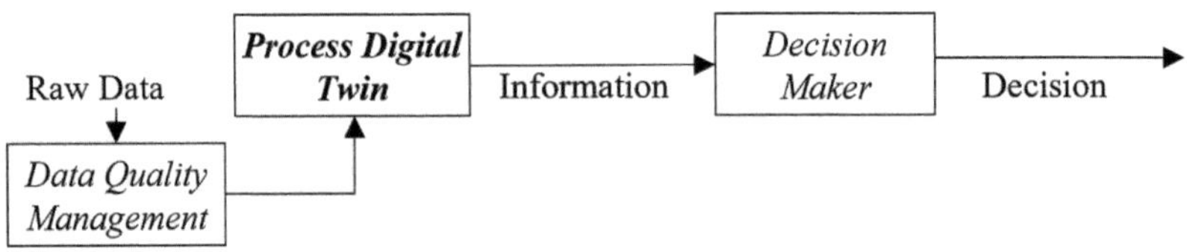

Figure 2.7 Input-process-output model—Process digital twin. (Source: Own Figure, modified and derived from Raghunathan, 1999)

Raj has provided an appropriate definition of the process digital twin as a concept that provides a *"business-level view to measure operational aspects across the enterprise with end-to-end visibility to optimize throughput, quality and performance of the process and enables organizations to visualize and simulate alternative approaches to re-engineer entire processes"* (Raj et al., 2020). In general, Feldt and Qiuan mention that the process digital twin is a *"concept of Industry 4.0 or IoT applying a set of CPS in order to create a precise digital replica of processes"* (Feldt geb. Wagner et al., 2020), to *"map the process completely"* (Chen et al., 2020).

Durão, Barricelli, Waschull, Deryabin, Madni, Kamath and Makarov are more specific, defining the process digital twin as a *"current state and behavior in interaction with the real world"* (Durão et al., 2018), *"a living, intelligent and evolving model"* (Barricelli et al., 2019), a *"virtual and computerized counterpart"* (Waschull et al., 2020), a *"real physical object"* (Deryabin et al., 2020), a *"process"* (Kamath et al., 2020; Madni et al., 2019) *"present[ing] a service"* (Makarov et al., 2019). Another important component is the topic of analytics and optimization where Lu and Wärmefjord define the process digital twin as a *"mirror of the real world predicting and optimizing processes"* (Lu et al., 2019), is used to *"perform real-time optimization of a process"* (Wärmefjord et al., 2017). The control function of the process digital twin is noted by Rajratnakharat and Zheng, it is a concept *"that models the entire process as a virtual model and enables bidirectional control with the physical process"* (Rajratnakharat et al., 2018) and *"can simulate, monitor, calculate, regulate, and control the process"* (P. Zheng, Sang, et al., 2018). **The DTDDMM uses Raj's definition.**

2.3.3 Five-Dimensional Digital Twin

Grieves created a three-dimensional (3D) digital twin (20/28) with physical entities, virtual entities, connections (Grieves, 2016) while Tao extended it to five-dimensional (5D) digital twin (8/28) with service and digital twin data (Tao, M. Zhang, and Nee, 2019c) (Table 2.2).

The five-dimensional digital twin consists of physical entities (PE), virtual entity (VE), dig ital twin data (DD), services (Ss) and connection (CN) shown in Equation 2.9:

$$M_{DT} = (PE; VE; Ss; DD; CN) \tag{2.9}$$

Table 2.2 Frameworks of the digital twin

	Grieves (2016)	Schleich et al. (2017)	Jaensch et al. (2018)	Stojanovic et al. (2018)	Kunath et al. (2018)	H. Cai et al. (2019)	Qi, Tao, Hu, et al. (2019)	Qianzhe et al. (2019)	Silva Souza et al. (2019)	Stark et al. (2019)	**Tao, M. Zhang, and Nee (2019c)**	Wagner et al. (2019)	Y. Zheng et al. (2019)	Z. Liu et al. (2019)
3D	X	X	X	X	X	X				X		X		X
5D							X	X	X		X		X	

	Agostino et al. (2020)	AlaLaurinaho et al. (2020)	Chen et al. (2020)	Fuller et al. (2020)	Haifan Jiang et al. (2020)	Kong et al. (2020)	X. Liu et al. (2020)	Shao et al. (2020)	Sjarov et al. (2020)	Sundharam et al. (2020)	Y. Wang et al. (2020)	W. Xu et al. (2020)	C. Zhang et al. (2020)	X. Zheng et al. (2020)
3D		X	X	X	X	X	X	X		X	X		X	X
5D	X								X			X		

Source: Own Table

Tao give a very illustrative example of Figure 2.8: *"If the five-dimension digital twin is compared to a person, its components can be considered as important tissues or organs. PE plays a role as the skeleton, which forms the supporting structure of the digital twin. VE is the heart, as it pumps simulation results/strategies to other components. Ss is the sense organ, which interacts with users directly. DD is the blood, which feeds the digital twin with valuable* ***information*** *continuously. Accordingly, CN is the blood vessel, carrying the data to different components of the digital twin"* (Tao, M. Zhang, and Nee, 2019c). Where digital twin data (DD) plays plays the central role shown in Figure 2.8.

Figure 2.8 Generic framework of the five-dimensional digital twin. (Source: Own Figure, modified and derived from Tao, M. Zhang, and Nee, 2019c)

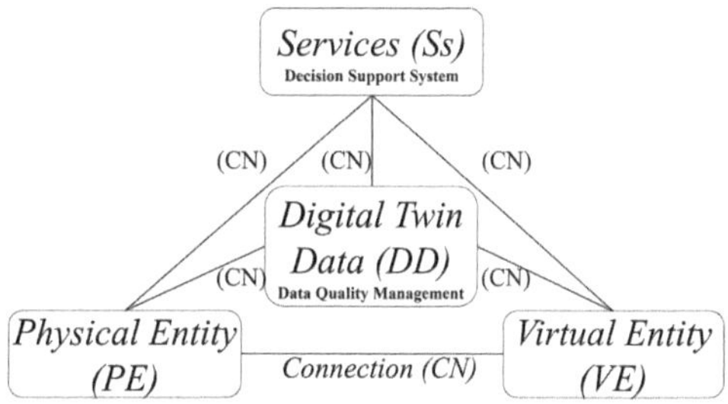

Physical entities (PE) are created digitally as virtual entities to simulate their behaviour, and consist of products, systems, processes, or organizations (Tao, Cheng, et al., 2018) and perform activities according to physical laws, deal with uncertain environments, and can be divided into unit levels, system levels, and system of system levels (Tao, Qi, et al., 2019). **Virtual entities** (VE) are faithful replicas of physical entities that reflect physical geometries, properties, behaviors, and rules by following the rules extracted from historical data or obtained from experts (Tao and M. Zhang, 2017). **Digital Twin Data** (DD) are multitemporal, / -dimensional, /-source, and heterogeneous data generated from physical entities, simulation results, services, knowledge, and fusion data (Qi, Tao, Hu, et al., 2019) (Figure 2.9), why **data quality management** is important. For Figure 2.9, data quality management plays an important role in data acquisition, preprocessing, analysis, mining and fusion, including databases processed by rule-based data cleansing, structuring and clustering to enhance **data quality** for analysis and processing through mining, classification, advanced clustering and outlier detection to achieve data fusion for decision-making (Y. Zheng et al., 2019). **Service** (Ss) provides application services in simulation, verification, monitoring, optimization, diagnosis, and prediction (Tao and Qi, 2019) to enable simulation, operation, and analysis, so that **connection** (CN) enables information and data sharing (Tao, M.

Zhang, Yushan Liu, et al., 2018), supported by **decision** support systems. The DTDDMM proposes Tao's five-dimensional digital twin.

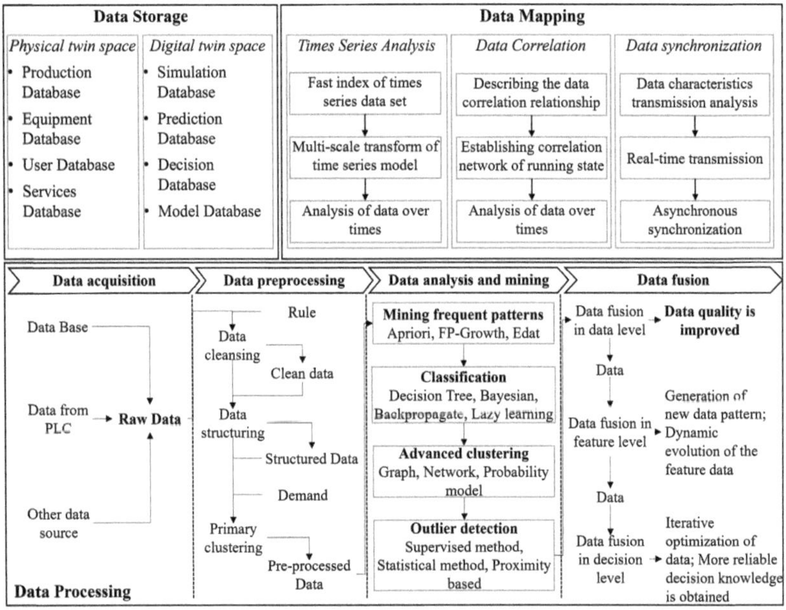

Figure 2.9 Information processing layer of digital twin data. (Source: Own Figure, derived from Y. Zheng et al., 2019)

2.3.4 Requirements

According to ISO 9000:2015 3.6.4, requirement is defined as "the need or expectation that is stated, generally implied or obligatory" (ISO, 2015). The digital twin is required to do a number of things (Durão et al., 2018). As shown in the corresponding data can be viewed in Appendix Table 4 in the electronic supplementary material, the digital twin must be able to analyse, convert, match information at different scales and establish equivalence between representation models, integrate models, and match physical entities (Schleich et al., 2017). **The DTDDMM lists (1) real-time, (2) integration, (3) interaction, (4) communication, (5) connectivity, (6) update and (7) scalability as requirements**. These seven major requirements are described in detail below. However, when focusing on a particular digital twin use case, more specific requirements may emerge. Generally, the following are the main requirements: **Real-time (1)** is necessary to optimize products and processes (Hao Zhang et al., 2017), to detect the state of the product (Canedo, 2016), or to monitor the process through data analysis to manage and optimize (Konstantinov et al., 2017). The physical entities must respond to the changes according to the optimized scheme, continuously send real-time data describing new states, and respond to new optimizations (Boschert, Heinrich, et al., 2018). To enable real-time synchronization and closed-loop optimization, feature extraction and selection are important for dealing with BD (Tao, M. Zhang, Yushan Liu, et al., 2018). Currently, there are no universally accepted standards to combine data from different sources with different interfaces and data formats in real-time (Adamenko et al., 2020). **Data integration (2)** is required to represent physical entities using different subgraphs of nodes and edges. The integration of the different nodes is essential for the creation of valuable data (Durão et al., 2018) used to create a virtual model that represents the anatomy of the digital twin (DebRoy et al., 2017).

Dynamic, historically static, and descriptively static exchanged data must be stored in a data storage system (Kiritsis, 2011). The continuous **interaction (3)** of data between physical entities and virtual entities is necessary for closed-loop optimization to understand, analyse, predict, estimate, and continuously optimize the physical entities (Barricelli et al., 2019). Through closed-loop optimization, digital twin technology enables process performance improvement (Boschert and Rosen, 2016). Since a digital twin constantly receives data from different sources, an appropriate ontology for understanding and formalizing the data should provide a common, machine-understandable vocabulary for information interaction between dispersed agents (Schroeder et al., 2016). Therefore, **communication (4)** between the physical entities and the virtual entities, different digital twins in the environment, and domain experts through usable and accessible interfaces is required (Barricelli et al., 2019). Digital twins have self-adaptation and self-parameterization capabilities that enable the physical entities to be connected throughout the lifecycle through modularization and parameterization (T. Uhlemann et al., 2017). To enable this **connectivity (5)**, a seamless and continuous data exchange through direct physical communication or indirect cloud-based connections, physical entities and virtual entities must be equipped with network devices that describe the state of the physical entities as well as the environment and send predictions and forecasts (Barricelli et al., 2019). To deal with **uncertainty**, digital twins use descriptive, predictive, and prescriptive analytics for decision-making by identifying a set of alternative actions and applying optimization algorithms to achieve a given outcome (Guo et al., 2019). Descriptive data must be continuously exchanged and **updated (6)** by real-time data and short-term memory, so that physical entities and virtual entities can always be kept up to date, synchronized, or changed, with the change affecting the properties of the mirrored physical entities (Barricelli et al., 2019). Through pattern recognition, unsupervised/supervised learning, and statistical applications, digital twins characterize, understand, group, and classify input data (T. H.-J. Uhlemann et al., 2017). **Scalability (7)** is the competence to analyse different scales of information (Durão et al., 2018). Therefore, the collection of high-dimensional complex process spaces (Stojanovic et al., 2018) of the best available physical entities, sensor data, and historical data is important to represent one or more real systems during their life cycle (Kunath et al., 2018). Digital twins process high-dimensional data with (de)coding and analysis techniques, data fusion algorithms, AI, and access through interfaces (Barricelli et al., 2019).

2.3.5 Industry Dissemination

The importance of the digital twin is reflected in the fact that many companies have built a industrial IoT-platform (3DS, 2021; GE, 2021; IBM, 2021; Microsoft, 2021; PTC, 2021; SAP, 2021; Siemens, 2021) showing the importance of digital twin. Infiniti Research has estimated a market growth of 24.81 billion USD by 2025 (a compound annual growth rate (CAGR) of 39.48%) (Infiniti, 2021). MarketsandMarkets Research assume a growth from 3.1 billion in 2020 to 48.2 billion USD in 2026 (CAGR of 58%) (MarketsandMarkets, 2020). Prescient & Strategic Intelligence assume a growth from 3.6 billion in 2019 to 73.2 billion USD in 2030 (CAGR of 31.9%) (Prescient et al., 2020). Research and Markets assume a growth from 5.1 billion in 2020 to 115.1 billion USD in 2035 (CAGR of 23.2%) (Research et al., 2020). This proves the importance of digital twins and makes it important to increase efforts in the industry to generate a viable solution (Pires et al., 2019). Some 164[1] (The corresponding data can be viewed in Appendix Figure 2 in the electronic supplementary material) publications have identified 46 industries (Figure 2.10).

Table 2.3 shows the 46 industries classified into industry sector I–III.

[1] The delta of 47 publications results from a pure search for potential industrial applications of the digital twin, including papers that were not relevant for the research questions and were therefore excluded.

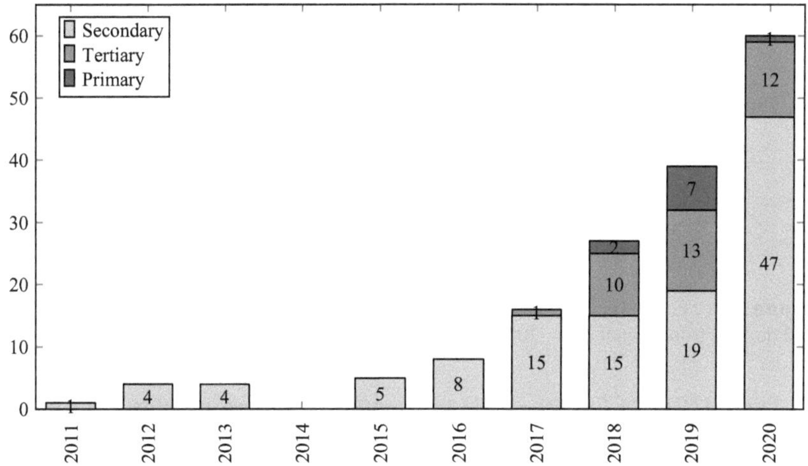

Figure 2.10 Digital twin publication timeline with industry sectors. (Source: Own Figure, modified and derived from Barricelli et al., 2019)

Table 2.3 Industries for the digital twin in literature

Sector	Industry
2. Secondary	Aerospace, **Automotive**, Chemical, **Computer**, **Construction**, Defense, Electric power, Electronics, Energy, **Food**, Industrial robot, Low technology, Meat, Mining, Petroleum, Pulp and paper, Semiconductor, Shipbuilding, Steel, Telecommunications, Textile, Water
3. Tertiary	Advertising, Cultural, E-Commerce, Education, Fashion, Film, Financial services, Floral, Healthcare, Hospitality, Insurance, Leisure, Mass Media, Professional services, Real estate, **Retail**, Software, Sport, **Transport**, Video game
1. Primary	Fishing, Horticulture, Tobacco, Wood

Source: Own Table

2.3.6 Benefits

The benefits of digital twin are described in detail below and assigned to the areas of certainty, efficiency and the quality of decision-making (Awino, 2013). Figure 2.11 illustrates the link between inputs, outputs and outcomes, where **efficiency** is the ratio of monetary and non-monetary resources (Section 2.3.6.1 and

2.3.6.2) used to produce outputs and **effectiveness** between outputs produced to the goals (Section 2.3.6.3) or interact with the environment (Mandl et al., 2008).

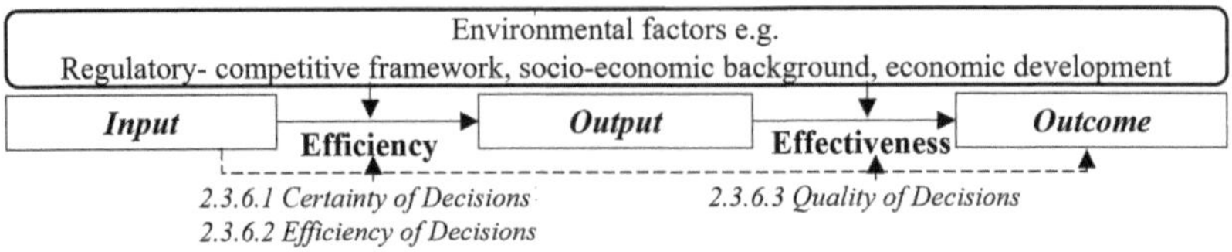

Figure 2.11 Framework of efficiency and effectiveness. (Source: Own Figure, modified and derived from Mandl et al., 2008)

The DTDDMM focuses on (1) transparency, (2) new insights, (3) what-if analyses, (4) reduced time-to-market, (5) process monitoring, (6) process diagnosis, (7) time reduction, (8) cost reduction, (9) predictive maintenance and (10) product improvement.

2.3.6.1 Certainty of Decisions

In this context, it is important to establish the link between digital twin and decision uncertainty (Lipshitz et al., 1997; Spetzler et al., 2016). Decision makers distinguish between three types of uncertainty: insufficient understanding (requiring transparency), incomplete information (requiring new knowledge), and undifferentiated alternatives (requiring what-if analyses) (Lipshitz et al., 1997). Li give an example of a digital twin in the aircraft industry, in which *"a digital model that virtually flies through the same loading history as the actual aircraft wing reduces* ***uncertainty*** *in model parameters, tracks time-dependent system states using measured data, and predicts the evolution of damage states when no data are available"* (Li et al., 2017; Tao, M. Zhang, and Nee, 2019b). To increase **decision certainty**, transparency, new insights and what-if analyses are projected onto decision-making. Regarding **Transparency (1)**, the virtual entities, which always have up-to-date information, facilitate monitoring, and the information is presented in such a way that the user can simulate different scenarios (Melesse et al., 2020) and see the current status directly and transparently (Adamenko et al., 2020; Waschull et al., 2020). For this reason, digital twin should provide a transparent user interface for all relevant variables (Papanagnou, 2020), allowing increased transparency of processes to detect errors for optimization (Feldt geb. Wagner et al., 2020; Haijun Zhang et al., 2020). As a result, the consequences of each decision are more transparent without causing disruption in the physical entities (Kunath et al., 2018), while improvements in virtual entities enable transparency during processes (Lim et al., 2020). This is achieved by true mapping between the virtual entities and the actual data to enable transparent monitoring (Zhuang, Gong, et al., 2020). To summarize, digital twin continuously integrates and completes data and knowledge to enable visualization and transparency (Nikolaev et al., 2018; Tao, M. Zhang, and Nee, 2019a). Regarding **new insights (2)**, the ability to quickly simulate how performance will respond to a given decision can increase business agility through rapid or automated decisions based on data insights (Parmar et al., 2020) 2020) by applying BD insights in real-time to not only map but also optimize the entire lifecycle (Papanagnou, 2020).

By combining real-time data with virtual entities, data can be used to new insights in places that are not normally accessible and offer entirely new perspectives (Adamenko et al., 2020; Augustine, 2019). Digital twin provides meaningful access to tools, methods, and collected data, and provides an informed basis for decision-making for all perspectives and stakeholders involved (M. Liu et al., 2020; Lutters et al., 2019) for the purpose of creating smart products with self-knowledge (Lim et al., 2020). Real-time data from multiple sources are used to enable inference and actionable insights (Raj et al., 2020), with virtual entities remaining connected to physical entities throughout the lifecycle to reflect real-time states (Tao, M. Zhang, and Nee, 2019b) and provide insights for prediction (Tao, M. Zhang, and Nee, 2019a). In addition, artefacts created in previous digital twin projects can serve as additional supports for decisions, as current project specifications can be compared to previous ones and insights can be gained (Azevedo et al., 2020). To sum up, the digital twin provides insight into current environmental conditions and internal and/or external data (Khan et al., 2020). Regarding **what-if-analyses (3)**, with ever-increasing computing power, digital twins and algorithms are able to simulate and predict complex environments with what-if scenarios (Cortés et al., 2020). What-if scenarios can be run with the digital twin to test changes in environmental conditions or settings to intentionally allow potential errors in the virtual entities to generate predictions (Adamenko et al., 2020). Simulations can be used to test what might happen in the real world (Lu et al., 2019), where virtual entities become the link between the actual and target model (Lutters et al., 2019), simulate the future through what-if scenarios and determine optimal performance metrics for situations with the highest probability (Raj et al., 2020). A what-if analysis enables the optimization of the performance of the physical entities and provides visibility and transparency (Makarov et al., 2019; Melesse et al., 2020). A digital twin is highly adaptive because it not only performs what-if analyses to control physical entities, it also validates and acts on data (Papanagnou, 2020). To summarize, a what-if analysis from a digital twin is used for hypothetical process simulations (Stojanovic et al., 2018).

2.3.6.2 Efficiency of Decisions

A digital twin concept enables linking BD to fast simulations through realistic process models, allowing the early and efficient evaluation of the impact, performance, and quality of decisions on processes (Tao, M. Zhang, and Nee, 2019b; Hao Zhang et al., 2017). To increase the **efficiency** (Howard, 1988; Rashidi and Lemass, 2011) of decision-making, reduced time-to-market, process monitoring, process diagnosis, time reduction, cost reduction, predictive maintenance and product improvement are all projected onto the decision-making process. Regarding **reduced time-to-market (4)**, in today's fast-moving markets, the digital twin is used to shorten the all-important time-to-market (Schleich et al., 2017; Sjarov et al., 2020) and create other benefits along the entire lifecycle (Durão et al., 2018). A digital twin enables an increase in sales by improving innovation, shortening the time to market for new products, and providing service for existing products (Tao, M. Zhang, and Nee, 2019b). In this regard, the use of behaviour prediction simulations eliminates weaknesses and potential failure sources with minimal effort. Furthermore, high-resolution virtual entities for customer feedback enable further adjustments to directly optimize the product and shorten time-to-market (Adamenko et al., 2020). Therefore, shortening time-to-market is a key aspect, which means that the interweaving of simulation models must be forced across different levels of detail, across all disciplines involved, and across lifecycle phases (Boschert and Rosen, 2016). To sum up, the digital twin shortens the time-to-market (Erol et al., 2020; Park et al., 2019). Regarding **process monitoring (5)**, there must be continuous monitoring of processes within the organization (Lim et al., 2020; Parmar et al., 2020) through data collection, analysis, and simulation to improve quality (Adamenko et al., 2020) and process efficiency (Afazov et al., 2020; Zhuang, Gong, et al., 2020). The digital twin helps in real-time process optimization and monitoring by forming a closed loop between physical entities and virtual entities (Tao, M. Zhang, and Nee, 2019a). Therefore, real-time data is of great importance for managing and optimizing processes through monitoring and data analysis (Durão et al., 2018) to keep up with rapidly changing constraints and develop optimal operational control strategies (Qi and Tao, 2018). By using digital twin for process control and monitoring, process control uses real-time and historical data to feed the virtual decision support system, which helps users make strategic or operational decisions or directly implement operational adjustments (Pires et al., 2019). Thus, not only processes in a factory can be monitored in real time, but they can also be compared with processes in other factories (Grieves, 2015) to discover new business opportunities, make future improvements and plan new developments (Madni et al., 2019).

To summarize, the digital twin can realize dynamic visual process monitoring in real-time (Wu et al., 2020). Regarding **process diagnostics (6)**, industrial companies should take a step beyond digitization and adopt a more granular approach to virtual entities for monitoring, diagnosing and troubleshooting process problems in the form of digital twin (Papanagnou, 2020). Having a digital twin for all physical objects can be useful for monitoring, diagnostic and predictive purposes (Alam et al., 2017). A digital twin is based on real-time data derived from the physical counterpart and can be used for monitoring, control, diagnosis and prediction (Lu et al., 2019). It is used in various stages of product development, such as design, simulation, testing, production, and prediction and diagnosis (Haijun Zhang et al., 2020), where observations can be visualized by 3-D visualization of parameters and simulations can add unobservable data (Raj et al., 2020). As a result, a digital twin promotes improved decision support through detailed diagnosis (Kritzinger et al., 2018; Tao, M. Zhang, and Nee, 2019a) and an analysis of unforeseen disturbances (Kunath et al., 2018). When an unforeseen fault occurs on the virtual entities, the fault is visually diagnosed and analysed, showing the user the location and cause of the fault (Kaur et al., 2020; Qi and Tao, 2018). This information from complex or disparate sources is processed, real-world conditions are monitored, and prediction results can be inserted into the virtual entities (Qianzhe et al., 2019). In data-based fault diagnosis, the amount of data is not sufficient to train a reliable model because these physical entities only work for anomalies that are already known. By contrast, a digital twin can tackle unforeseen anomalies (M. Liu et al., 2020). Digital twin performs fault diagnosis and fault localization of the physical product based on the obtained data and historical data (Wu et al., 2020). In short, most decision support systems are developed to provide monitoring and predictive functions. Very few of them include direct or autonomous feedback control provided by the digital twin (Lu et al., 2019). Regarding **reduction of time (7) and cost (8)**, a further advantage of a digital twin is that when planning and developing an object or a process, simulations can predict whether the desired properties and functions can be fulfilled, and thus an optimization of the design or performance can be carried out in advance, resulting in cost and time reduction (Adamenko et al., 2020; Boschert and Rosen, 2016).

Here, the digital twin has the potential to have a major impact on reducing resource waste in the life cycle (Grieves and Vickers, 2017; Pires et al., 2019).

This improves product life and maintenance efficiency, reducing maintenance time and cost (Qi and Tao, 2018), and impacts the resource model with benefits such as cost reduction (Lim et al., 2020). If the digital twin is effectively used in product development, the discrepancy between the expected behaviour and the design behaviour can be reduced, design cycles can be shortened (Qi, Tao, Zuo, et al., 2018), and the costs of verification and testing can be reduced (Madni et al., 2019). Regarding **predictive maintenance (9)** digital twin-based simulations (Tao, M. Zhang, and Nee, 2019a) or data-driven approaches (Adamenko et al., 2020) are the most popular applications (M. Liu et al., 2020; Park et al., 2019; Zhuang, J. Liu, et al., 2018). However, using Digital Twin with predictive simulation capabilities (Chatti et al., 2019; Z. Liu et al., 2019) detects anomalies by simulating the results of engineering interventions such as repairs and upgrades (Bruynseels et al., 2018; Tao, Sui, et al., 2019). Therefore, the digital twin enables predictive maintenance by connecting and interacting with the physical entities and enables real-time human-machine collaboration by seamlessly connecting the physical and virtual entities (J. Wang et al., 2019) to optimize operations (Ala-Laurinaho et al., 2020). This includes creating a model of one physical entity that continuously adapts to changes in the environment or operation by using real-time data to predict the future for predictive maintenance (Kaur et al., 2020). In addition, the identification of failure modes can be combined with the results of simulations from digital twin models, paving the way for predictive maintenance (Arrichiello et al., 2020). To sum up, the digital twin's visualization techniques help to understand whether a certain machine is reliable by using the existing data representation and computational model for predictive maintenance (P. Zheng and Lim, 2020). Regarding **improvement of products (10)**, the digital twin also influences the design and development of new products by analysing objects already in use and the user behaviour or operation to identify improvement opportunities for new products (Adamenko et al., 2020; Lim et al., 2020). For product improvement, information must be consistently available and evaluable so that existing models can be used and easily modified for product modifications (Boschert and Rosen, 2016; Qi and Tao, 2018), which is enabled by revealed and visualized data (Parmar et al., 2020).

Therefore, there is a need for product lifecycle management to integrate all lifecycle data artefacts into a comprehensive management system that can be used by different stakeholders (Schleich et al., 2017) to track process performance, analyse real-world data, and simulate potential improvements (Mabkhot et al., 2018). In addition, communication between customers and designers enables transparent and faster decisions by using real-time transmission data and customer feedback (Tao, Cheng, et al., 2018). For existing products, a digital twin can record and analyse product behaviour in real time to reflect user habits and encourage improvements and product innovation (Arrichiello et al., 2020; Tao, M. Zhang, and Nee, 2019b). To summarize, virtual verification integrates product characteristics into a fully virtual model to evaluate product performance and detect defects while realizing optimization (M. Liu et al., 2020).

2.3.6.3 Quality of Decisions

The quality of decision-making is affected by slow decision-making, the wrong people in the wrong part of an organization, or the wrong information (Blenko et al., 2010). However, the quality and speed of decision-making are the decisive factors for success or failure (McGregor, 2001). Identifying goals, providing alternatives to solve problems, and balancing values and interests are critical to the quality of decision-making (Negulescu et al., 2014). This is achieved through **programs**, **options** and **risk avoidance** to distinguish alternatives using transparency, new insights, and what-if analyses. The benefits are a more efficient allocation of **resources** and **opportunities**, using reduced time-to-market, process monitoring, process diagnosis, time reduction, cost reduction, predictive maintenance and product improvement. To sum up, the quality of decision-making is essential for operational effectiveness and is therefore responsible for the (future) success of a company.

2.4 Decision Support System

Altogether, 28 papers were selected as a result of the data extraction and synthesis, from which five different frameworks were derived (The corresponding data can be viewed in Appendix Table 5 in the electronic supplementary material). Additionally, the foundation of the theoretical DTDDMM is shown in Figure 2.13.

2.4.1 Decision Support System

The decision support system has been developed over the last four decades to help managers (D. Power, 2008; Sprague, 1980). It includes a variety of decision analysis tools (Efraim Turban et al., 2001) supporting decision-making activities (see Figure 2.12).

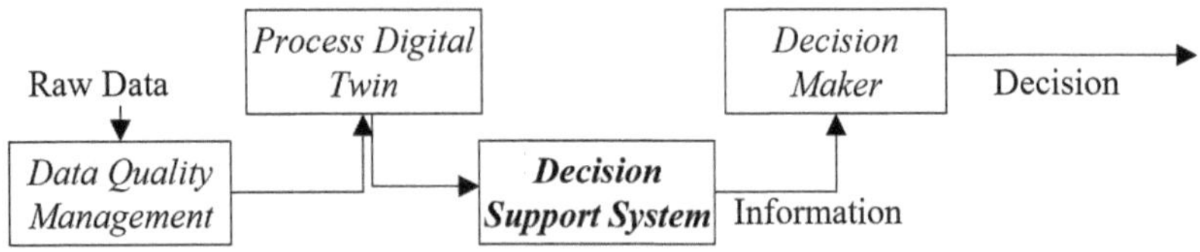

Figure 2.12 Input-process-output model—Decision support system. (Source: Own Figure, modified and derived from Raghunathan, 1999)

Power defines a decision support system as *"an interactive computer-based system or sub-system intended to help decision makers use communications technologies, data, documents, knowledge and/or models to identify and solve problems, complete decision process tasks, and make decisions"* (Hosack et al., 2012; D. J. Power, 2003). Because information systems are constantly changing and developing as technology continues to grow, there are many types of information systems (Ada et al., 2015). However, there is no clear consensus concerning which hierarchical level the decision support system serves. Shurrab believes it is intended for top management (Shurrab, 2014), while Ada believe the management level (Ada et al., 2015) would benefit the most. Decision support systems, thus cover a wide range of leadership levels and support both individuals and groups (Efraim Turban et al., 2001) by providing a view of data content (Hosack et al., 2012) to provide insight and advice (Bousquet et al., 2011). Hosack mentions that decision support systems *"facilitate better decision-making to understand a large number of parameters and relationships that are stable but nevertheless limit the decision maker's ability to process all aspects of the decision"* (Hosack et al., 2012). To summarize, decision support systems improve decision-making regarding speed, quality and difficulty (Morana et al., 2017). **The DTDDMM use the definition from Power**.

2.4.2 Model-Driven Decision Support System

There are several decision support system frameworks: communication-driven, data-driven, model-driven, knowledge-driven and document-driven (D. J. Power, 2002) (The corresponding data can be viewed in Appendix Table 5 in the electronic supplementary material). Model-driven decision support systems focus on accessing and manipulating models, such as statistical, financial, optimization, and/or simulation models, to provide decision support (D. J. Power, 2003) shown in Figure 2.13 (Ada et al., 2015). These models are used to analyse problems because modeling allows experimentation with different strategies under different configurations (Efraim Turban et al., 2001). The focus is on accessing and editing models through user interfaces provided to decision makers to help them analyse a situation using data and parameters (Kopácˇková et al., 2006). This supports decision makers and gives them control over all levels of the process (Efraim Turban et al., 2001). However, it doesn't replace them. In addition, a model-driven decision support system is designed to allow the user to manipulate the model parameters to explore the sensitivity of the results or to perform a what-if analysis (D. J. Power and Sharda, 2007). To sum up, a decision support system facilitates interdependent and/or sequential decisions, which can be made once, several times, or repeatedly (Efraim Turban et al., 2001). **The DTDDMM uses Power's definition of a model-driven decision support system.**

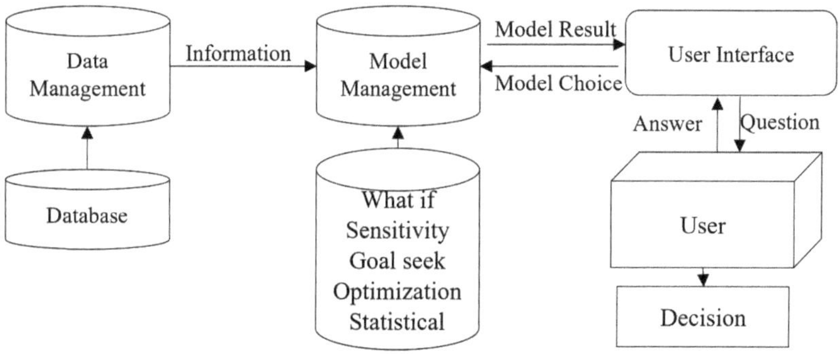

Figure 2.13 A simple view of a decision support system. (Source: Own Figure, modified and derived from Ada et al., 2015)

2.4.3 Characteristics

According to ISO 9000:2015 3.10.1, a feature is a "distinguishing characteristic" that is theoretically required for decision-making in the context of the digital twin (ISO2015). Therefore, it is not possible to define the standard features of decision support systems (Turban2001). Model-driven decision support systems are distinguished from computer support systems by a model that is accessible to a non-expert through an easy-to-use and flexible interface that is configurable for the same or similar decision situations (D. J. Power and Sharda, 2007). **The DTD-DMM focuses on (1) accessibility, (2) flexibility, and (3) configurability**. Since there is no way to define standard features of decision support systems, the most important features for the DTDDMM are explained by Efraim Turban (Efraim Turban et al., 2001). Decision support systems improve the effectiveness and efficiency of decision-making by defining difficult problems earlier, finding feasible solutions quicker, comparing the consequences of each solution fairly, designing an interface for presentation, and performing sensitivity analysis to validate model assumptions (Rashidi, Ghodrat, et al., 2018). Decision support systems need to be user-friendly, with graphical interfaces that provide user-friendly **access (1)** to data sources and formats (Efraim Turban et al., 2001). They should provide access to a knowledge repository and be able to define, control, and document actions or address unforeseen needs. Furthermore, the results should be presented in formats adapted to the needs of decision makers (Holsapple et al., 2003). In addition, they should be **flexible (2)** and adaptable, allowing decision makers to add, change, delete, reorganize, or manipulate elements (Efraim Turban et al., 2001). They should also provide flexibility in determining the timing of queries through a knowledge store that creates new knowledge through automated computation, analysis, or inference and accepts queries that meet decision makers' needs (Holsapple et al., 2003). Moreover, they should be easy to **configure (3)**—to create, change, and modify systems that can be integrated with other systems or applications and distributed via network and web technologies (Efraim Turban et al., 2001). However, mechanisms should be provided for the configuration of the tasks by individual or multiple decision makers within or outside the organization (Holsapple et al., 2003). To sum up, the efficiency of decision-making is influenced by data quality, but knowledge of a domain, constraints, and the design of decision tools are also factors that influence how well decision makers base their decisions on the information presented to them (Samitsch, 2015).

2.5 Summary—Digital Twin-Driven Decision-Making Model

Based on the 212 publications the DTDDMM definition was as follows: **A process digital twin, with usable data through data quality management, analytics and the visualization in decision support systems** and summarized in Table 2.4.

Table 2.4 Summary of the literature review results

(1) Data Quality Management	(2) Digital Twin	(3) Decision Support System
1. Definition of T. Redman (2013) and Fürber (2016). 2. Corporate Data Quality Management framework of Otto, Weber, et al. (2007). 3. Data Quality dimensions: Accuracy, Completeness, Consistency, Timeliness, accessibility.	1. Definition of Meierhofer et al. (2020) and Raj et al. (2020). 2. Five-dimensional framework of Tao, M. Zhang, and Nee (2019c). 3. Requirements: Real-time, Integration, Interaction, Communication, Connectivity, Update, Scalability. 4. Benefits: Transparency, Gain new insights, What-if analyses (decision certainty); Reduced time-to-market, Process monitoring, Process diagnosis, Time/Cost reduction, Predictive maintenance, Product improvement (decision efficiency)	1. Definition of D. J. Power (2003). 2. Model-Driven Decision Support System framework of D. J. Power (2003). 3. Characteristics: Accessibility, Flexibility, Configurablility.

Soruce: Own Table

In connection with the **theoretical DTDDMM**, it is important to mention that the elaborated dimensions, requirements, characteristics are theoretical recommendations, which may vary in importance from use case to use case and from company to company.

3 Objectives

Based on the 212 publications, the **research gap**, the **objectives** and the **hypothesis** were derived. In examining the research areas, the focus was primarily on the **overlap** between the research areas, and a *lack of decision-making with the support of process digital twin based on data quality* was identified. Figure 3.1 illustrates the research gap by showing the main literature and the overlap of each topic with the literature, where available.

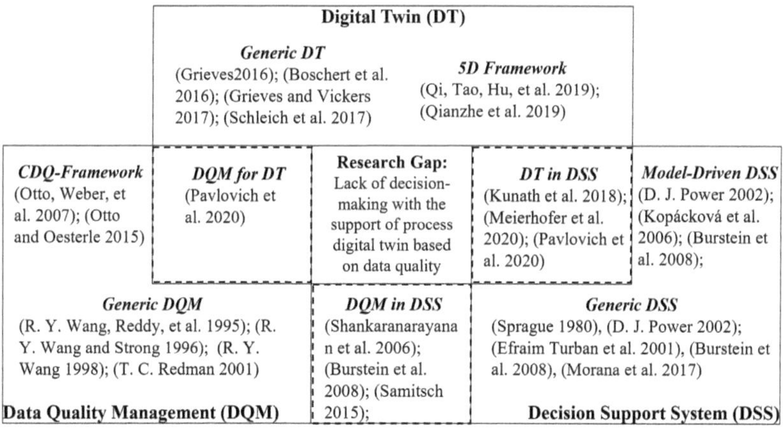

Figure 3.1 Research gap of the dissertation. (Source: Own Figure)

F. Blaschke, *Implementation and Benefits of Digital Twin on Decision Making and Data Quality Management*, https://doi.org/10.1007/978-3-658-44453-2_3

Here, the process digital twin is a possibility for end-to-end process digitization (Raj et al., 2020). This is a key objective of the digital transformation and thus of Industry 4.0, from which the end-to-end digitization of all physical assets and integration into a digital ecosystem is to be achieved (M.-X. Lee et al., 2017; Reis et al., 2018), making it a worthwhile subject for research. For this reason, the relevant literature, the current state of the art, the terminology, and the conceptual frameworks for possible integration into current industrial applications were reviewed. Emphasis was also placed on, but not limited to, the following **three objectives** from which the hypothesis was derived:

3.1 Strategic Positioning

1. *Analysis and determination of differences in data quality, digital twin and decision support in terms of industry, company size and management level for strategic positioning.*

Digital twin technology is becoming one of the most important research directions and promising technologies for the realization of Industry 4.0. It can be used for strategic positioning (decision-making), where managers do things differently by creating a unique value with the digital twin that is the key to competitive opportunity (Porter, 1996). Regarding market growth and thus the value of digital twin, Infiniti Research has estimated a market growth of 24.81 billion USD by 2025 (a compound annual growth rate (CAGR) of 39.48%) (Infiniti, 2021). MarketsandMarkets Research assume a growth from 3.1 billion in 2020 to 48.2 billion USD in 2026 (CAGR of 58%) (MarketsandMarkets, 2020). Prescient & Strategic Intelligence assume a growth from 3.6 billion in 2019 to 73.2 billion USD in 2030 (CAGR of 31.9%) (Prescient et al., 2020). Research and Markets assume a growth from 5.1 billion in 2020 to 115.1 billion USD in 2035 (CAGR of 23.2%) (Research et al., 2020). This proves the importance and value of digital twin technology and explains why it is important to increase efforts in the industry to generate a viable solution (Pires et al., 2019). For the implementation of a DTDDMM, it is therefore important for managers to know the status and progress of the data quality, the digital twin technology, and the decision support of competitors and how these vary depending on **(1) management levels**, **(2) company size** and **(3) industry**. Based on these differences, the manager can then decide whether a DTDDMM also offers a unique value for his own industry and company and whether it is the key to competitive opportunity. The manager can then use these differences to negotiate the importance of the topics with various hierarchical levels. Therefore, **hypothesis 1** is as follows: **There are differences in data quality, a digital twin and decision support in terms of management level, company size and industry**.

3.2 Digital Twin-Driven Decision-Making Model

2. *Elaboration of the theoretical DTDDMM for industries combining data quality, digital twin and decision-making.*

A theoretical DTDDMM consists of: (1) corporate data quality management, (2) process digital twin and (3) model-driven decision support systems shown in Figure 3.2.

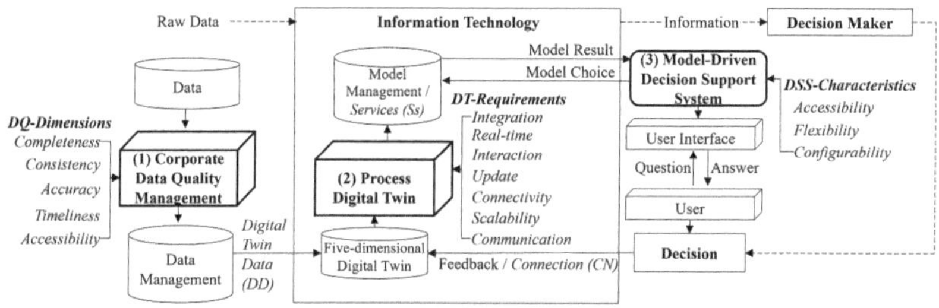

Figure 3.2 Basics of the digital twin-driven decision-making model

(1) **Corporate Data Quality Management: Data** are a collection of facts or information from various sources that are "dirty" and affect the quality of decision-making in an organization (Sulistyo et al., 2020). These are augmented by **BD**, which are high volume, high velocity, and/or highly varied information assets that require cost-effective, innovative forms of information processing and enable better insight, decision-making, and process automation (Mccarthy et al., 2019). **Data quality** provides data suitable for use by data consumers (Fürber, 2016). Therefore, **data quality management** is a management system for data that ensures high quality and defines, collects, stores, processes, or manipulates data (Glowalla, Balazy, et al., 2014) based on a coherent **corporate data quality management** (Otto, Weber,

et al., 2007). Lünendonk & Hossenfelder have shown that data quality in 155 companies has increased over the last five years.

However, 60% of companies still rate their data quality as only average (Zillmann, 2017), although they are aware that poor **data quality** affects efficiency and is an important success criterion. The Harvard Business Review surveyed 75 managers' records to determine data qual ity levels. On average, 47% of 100 newly created records had at least one critical error, and 3% were considered acceptable only at the loosest standard (Nagle et al., 2017). Digital twins are equipped with technologies like IoT, BD, cloud computing and AI (Pires et al., 2019) and are based on data. Thus, data quality directly determines the value of these technologies: the quality of a digital twin as well as the quality of the ensuing business decisions (Pavlovich et al., 2020).

Therefore, **hypothesis 2** is as follows: **Data quality management is a basic requirement for a digital twin.**

(2) **Process Digital Twin:** A **digital twin** is a digital representation of an entity that meets the needs of a range of use cases (Platenius-Mohr et al., 2020). It is a combination of data, analytics, and visualization of insights to support decision-making (Meierhofer et al., 2020). A **process digital twin** is an enterprise-level view to measure operational aspects across the enterprise-level view to measure operational aspects across the enterprise with end-to-end visibility to optimize throughput, quality, and process performance. It enables organizations to visualize and simulate alternative approaches to redesigning entire processes (Raj et al., 2020) based on a **five-dimensional digital twin** (Tao, M. Zhang, and Nee, 2019c). Since the digital twin can digitize processes end-to-end (Raj et al., 2020), which is a key objective of digital transformation and thus of Industry (M.-X. Lee et al., 2017; Reis et al., 2018), it is very important for strategic positioning and provides a competitive opportunity. So, **hypothesis 3** is as follows: **The implementation of a digital twin is a competitive opportunity.**

(3) **Model-Driven Decision Support System: Decisions** are defined as choices in a course of action, a strategy of action, or a goal achievement strategy (Rashidi, Ghodrat, et al., 2018). **Decision support systems** are interactive computer-based systems or subsystems designed to help decision makers use communication technologies, data, documents, knowledge, and/or models to identify and solve problems, complete decision-making tasks, and make decisions (Hosack et al., 2012; D. J. Power, 2003) which are **model-driven** (D. J. Power, 2002). A process digital twin can be used as a model,

supported by technologies such IoT, BD, cloud computing, and AI (Pires et al., 2019) to improve the decision-making process (Meierhofer et al., 2020). It is the **information technology** in the input-process-output model in Figure 2.12 (Raghunathan, 1999). Therefore, **hypothesis 4** is as follows: **Decision support systems are improved by digital twins.**

3.3 Operational Effectiveness

3. *Elaboration and analysis of the improvement in operational effectiveness using a digital twin for decision-making, focusing on data quality in a theoretical model.*

To achieve **operational effectiveness** (validation and execution), managers should adopt, acquire and extend best practices by doing things better and better (Porter, 1996). In this context, the **benefits** of a digital twin for decision-making based on data quality can be leveraged. In terms of a digital twin for decision-making, the end product of a manager's work are decisions that are made in business situations in three steps (Drucker, 1963):

1. **Analysis**: Managers need to analyse the facts, such as risks, options and programs, to achieve **certainty**. This can be supported by digital twins.
2. **Allocation**: Managers have to allocate opportunities and resources to achieve **efficiency**. This can be supported by digital twins.
3. **Decision-making**: Managers must base their decisions on the above analysis and allocations to achieve **quality**. This can be supported by digital twins.

Regarding decision-making, McKinsey & Company conducted a survey of 809 managers called *"Decision Making in the Age of Urgency"*. The results were as follows: 48% of the respondents believed their companies made decisions quickly, 57% of the respondents believed their companies consistently made high-quality decisions, with managers spending 37% of their time on decision-making of which 18.5% was **ineffective**[1] (Aminov, 2019). Therefore, the **benefits** generated by a DTDDMM are to increase decision certainty through transparency, new insights, and what-if analyses. A digital twin, through realistic process models, enables large amounts of data to be linked to rapid simulations, allowing early and efficient evaluation of the impact, performance and quality of decisions on processes (Tao, M. Zhang, and Nee, 2019b; Hao Zhang et al., 2017). This

[1] Fortune 500 companies: 53,001 days work time and ~ $250 labour costs per year lost

leads to reduced time-to-market, improved process monitoring, process diagnosis, time reduction, cost reduction, predictive maintenance and product improvement. The quality of decision-making is adversely affected by slow decisions made by the wrong people, in the wrong part of the organization, with the wrong information (Blenko et al., 2010). To sum up, distinguishing **alternatives** to gain **certainty** and allocating **resources** and **opportunities** effectively improves efficiency and thus operational effectiveness. Therefore, **hypothesis 5** is as follows: **A theoretical DTDDMM increases effectiveness by 10%.**

Materials and Methods of Dissertation 4

This chapter identifies the materials and methods that were used to analyse the quantitative data from the preliminary (The corresponding data can be viewed in Appendix Figure 3 in the electronic supplementary material) and main (The corresponding data can be viewed in Appendix Figure 4 in the electronic supplementary material) studies.

4.1 Research Design

This dissertation uses quantitative research (Williams, 2007) shown in Figure 4.1.

It includes numerical values and measurements that help researchers describe and determine some patterns by using mathematical methods, especially statistics (John W Creswell, 2002; Salehi, 2015) using a deductive approach. In this context, research methodology is concerned with quantifying and analysing variables to obtain results, using and analysing numerical data with specific statistical techniques to answer research questions (RQ) (Leedy et al., 2001). Furthermore, quantitative research begins with the formulation of a problem—the RQ—reviews the relevant literature, and quantitatively analyses the data using hypotheses (Williams, 2007). In addition, quantitative research involves investigative strategies such as surveys to collect data using predetermined instruments that provide statistical data (John W. Creswell, 2003). Although there are several types of quantitative research, this dissertation focuses on **survey research** (Apuke, 2017).

Supplementary Information The online version contains supplementary material available at https://doi.org/10.1007/978-3-658-44453-2_4.

F. Blaschke, *Implementation and Benefits of Digital Twin on Decision Making and Data Quality Management*, https://doi.org/10.1007/978-3-658-44453-2_4

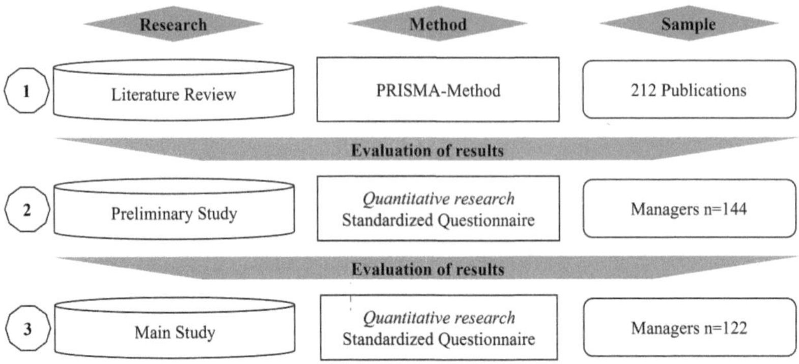

Figure 4.1 Research process of the dissertation. (Source: Own Figure)

Survey research uses a scientific sampling method with a designed survey to measure the characteristics of a specific population by applying statistical methods to obtain information from the population and then conducting an analysis to understand their behaviour and characteristics (Sukamolson, 2007). There are three basic principles of survey research: a survey is used to quantitatively describe some aspect of a particular population, which includes examining the relationship, collecting data from individuals, and drawing a sample from a portion of the population that is used to generalize the entire population (Krae mer, 1991).

4.2 Data Collection and Sample Description

The managers were divided into upper, middle, and lower management (Katz et al., 1978) and were recruited electronically via the LinkedIn business platform and email from university, personal, and professional environments. The **preliminary study** consisted of a 15-question industry-wide survey (The corresponding data can be viewed in Appendix Figure 3 in the electronic supplementary material), while the main study was a 50-question industry-wide survey (The corresponding data can be viewed in Appendix Figure 4 in the electronic supplementary material). It was requested that the link also be forwarded, so the actual number of link recipients is unknown. The **random sampling method** was used (Mitra et al., 1984).

4.2.1 Data Collection Procedure

To validate the preliminary and main studies, 10 managers were contacted personally by email and phone prior to publication and asked about the content of the survey and to suggest improvements, which were than incorporated into the surveys. There was consistently positive feedback concerning the relevance of the topic, the theoretical DTDDMM and the content of the surveys, which were assessed as precise and targeted.

4.2.1.1 Preliminary Study Procedure

The survey (The corresponding data can be viewed in Appendix Figure 3 in the electronic supplementary material) was devised in German and English on the SurveyMonkey platform, launched in 01 August 2021, and completed in 30 September 2021. A prologue on the introduction page outlined the research intentions, and anonymity was assured when responding to the survey. Participants were asked about their experiences with the digital twin, data quality management, and decision support systems in their companies. To ensure scientific quality, only managers were allowed to participate (**quality score 1**). The survey focus on the **awareness level**, if these answered with strongly disagree or disagree, the specific questions were skipped (**quality score 2**).

4.2.1.2 Main Study Procedure

The survey (The corresponding data can be viewed in Appendix Figure 4 in the electronic supplementary material) was devised in German and English on the SurveyMonkey platform, launched in 01 December 2021, and completed in 28 February 2022. A preface on the introduction page outlined the research intentions, and anonymity was assured when responding to the survey. Managers were asked about their experiences with digital twins, data quality management, and decision support systems in their respective companies. To ensure scientific quality, only managers were allowed to participate (**quality score 1**). It focused on the automotive, healthcare, retail, transport, construction, computer and food industries. Therefore, managers from other industries were disqualified (**quality score 2**). To ensure that the awareness derived from the preliminary study did not bias the results, managers who had no experience with digital twins, data quality management, and decision support systems were excluded (**quality score 3**).

4.2.2 Sample Description

The data collection procedure for the preliminary study consisted of 343 participants, resulting in a sample size of 144 managers. Therefore, 42% could be included in the survey, as 58% failed the quality assessment or didn't answer all the questions. For the main study, the data collection procedure consisted of 278 participants, resulting in a sample size of 122 managers. This meant that 44% could be included in the survey, as 56% failed the quality criteria or didn't answer all the questions. The speed of the average completion time (5 minutes for the preliminary study and 15 minutes for the main study) was due to the relevance of the topic and the simplicity of the surveys. The population of managers in Germany was set at a population of 3.16 million managerial positions (CRIF, 2018), with a margin of error for the preliminary study of 8% (confidence level of 95%) and for the main study of 9% (confidence level of 95%), which was acceptable. It should be noted, however, that both studies focused on managers from the automotive, healthcare, retail, transport, construction, computer, and food industries. The high number of managers from the automotive and retail industries was due to the fact that the author's direct network consisted mainly of managers from these industries.

4.2.2.1 Preliminary Study Sample

As shown in Figure 4.2, 19.4% of the respondents were lower-level managers, 58.3% were middlelevel managers, and 22.2% were upper-level managers.

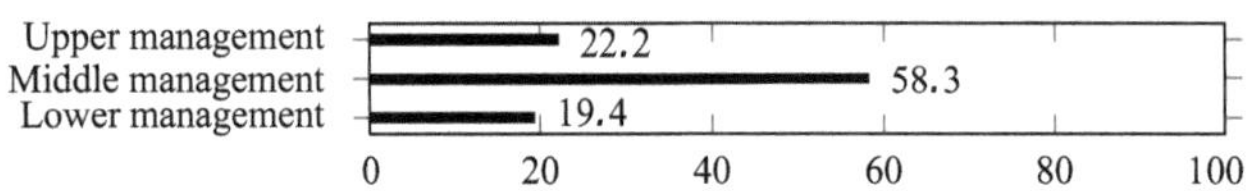

Figure 4.2 Preliminary study management levels in percent (N = 144). (Source: Own Figure)

Regarding age, 34.7% of the managers were between 18 and 30 years old, 30.6% were 31 to 40 years old and the remainder as follows: 41 to 50 years (18.8%) 51 to 60 years (11.8%) and 61 to 70 years (4.2%). Therefore, the majority of participants in the preliminary study were between 18 and 40 years old. Regarding gender, 66.7% were male and 33.3% were female. The average length of company affiliation in companies was 6 to 10 years, 34.7%; up to 5 years, 21.5%; 16 to 25 years, 20.8%; 11 to 15 years, 9%; 26 to 35 years, 9%; 36 to 40 years, 4.2%; and 41 to 50 years, 0.7%. This suggests that the length of company affiliation of the managers in this study was relatively short, although they may have worked in previous companies—company affiliation is calculated from the time of entry. The rather short length of company affiliation may be explained by the rather young age of the managers. Regarding **company size**, 41% worked in companies with 250 or more employees, 29.2% in companies with 50 to 249 employees, 16% in companies with 10 to 49 employees, and 13.9% in companies with up to 9 employees. So, most of the managers worked for large companies (Figure 4.3).

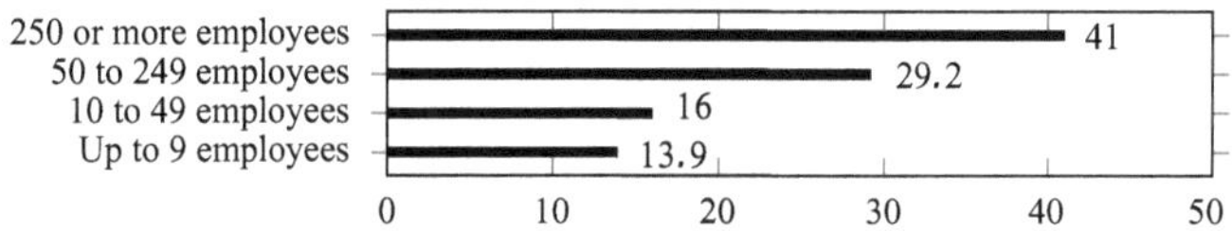

Figure 4.3 Preliminary study company size of the companies in percent (N = 144). (Source: Own Figure)

The **industry** distribution was as follows: automotive (23.6%), healthcare (16%), retail (11.8%), transport (11.1%), computer (10.4%), construction, and food (9%) (Figure 4.4).

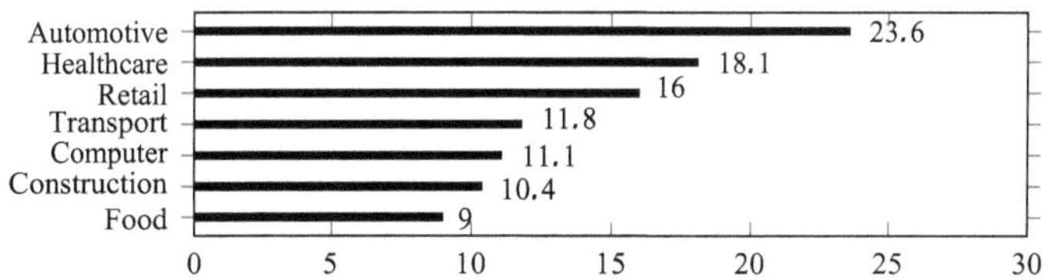

Figure 4.4 Preliminary study industry distribution of the companies in percent (N = 144). (Source: Own Figure)

In response to the statement *"digital twin technology is known in your company"*, 37.5% answered with, "I neither agree nor disagree", 22.2% agreed, 16% strongly disagreed, 12.5% strongly agreed, and 11.8% disagreed, which indicated that the concept was partly known. Apropos the statement *"data quality management is known in your company"*, 31.9% agreed, 27.1% neither agreed nor disagreed, 22.2% strongly agreed, 12.5% disagreed and 6.3% strongly disagreed, indicating that the concept was known. Concerning the statement, *"decision support systems are known in your company"*, 31.3% agreed, 25% neither agreed nor disagreed, 18.1% strongly agreed, 18.1% disagreed and 7.6% strongly disagreed, indicating that the concept was known. Regarding digital twin implementation plans, 36.5% planned to implement digital twin within the next 3 years, 22.1% within 1 year, 14.5% within 5 years, 13.5% reported that it was already available and 13.5% reported no plans for implementation existed. This indicated that the majority of companies plan digital twin implementation within the next 3 years. Regarding data quality management implementation plans (N = 117), 32.5% of the respondents reported plans within the next 3 years, 25.6% reported that it was already available, 23.9% reported implementation plans within 1 year, 12.8% within 5 years, and 5.1% reported that no implementation plans for data quality management existed. This suggests that for the majority, the concept had already been implemented or will be within the next 1 to 3 years. Regarding decision support system implementation plans (N = 107), 34.6% reported plans within the next 3 years, 27.1% reported that a decision support system was already available, 19.6% reported plans within 1 year, 10.3% reported no plans for implementation and 8.4% reported plans within 5 years. This indicated that the concept had already been implemented or will be within the next 1 to 3 years. Responding to the statement that digital twin is a competitive opportunity for your company (N = 104), 40.4% agreed, 28.8% neither agreed nor disagreed, 20.2% strongly agreed, 9.6% disagreed and 1% strongly disagreed. So, the majority believed that digital twin was a competitive opportunity. Regarding the statement that data quality management is a basic requirement for digital twins (N = 117), 33.3% agreed, 29.9% neither agreed nor disagreed, 28.2% strongly agreed, 6.8% disagreed and 1.7% strongly disagreed. This suggested a digital twin dependency on data quality management. Regarding the statement that decision support systems are improved by digital twins (N = 107), 37.4% agreed, 29% neither agreed nor disagreed, 22.4% strongly agreed, 5.6% disagreed and 5.6% strongly disagreed. This indicated that generally, decision support systems are improved by digital twin technology. Table 4.1 summarizes the findings with $\sum$ and frequencies of each group.

Table 4.1 Preliminary study sample description (N = 144)

No.	Characteristic	∑	I	II	III	IV	V	VI	VII	VIII	IX	X	XI	XII	XIII	XIV
1	Awareness Level Digital Twin															
	1 = Strongly disagree	23	11	9	3	8	3	7	5	4	7	8	0	2	2	0
	2 = Disagree	17	3	10	4	7	5	4	1	4	2	5	4	0	2	0
	3 = Neither agree nor disagree	54	6	33	15	20	19	8	7	13	9	7	7	6	4	8
	4 = Agree	32	6	23	3	14	12	3	3	5	6	2	5	7	4	3
	5 = Strongly agree	18	6	9	9	10	3	1	4	8	4	1	1	1	3	2
2	Implementation Level Digital Twin															
	1 = Already available	14	1	8	1	8	4	1	1	7	2	1	3	0	0	1
	2 = Within 1 year	23	4	16	4	6	10	3	4	7	2	2	2	4	3	3
	3 = Within 3 years	38	5	24	3	18	12	6	2	3	7	3	7	8	3	7
	4 = Within 5 years	15	4	10	4	6	4	1	4	5	4	5	0	1	2	1
	5 = Not planned	14	4	7	4	6	4	1	3	2	2	4	1	1	3	1
3	Digital Twin as competitive opportunity															
	1 = Strongly disagree	1	1	0	0	0	0	0	1	0	1	0	0	0	0	0
	2 = Disagree	10	4	4	2	2	5	1	2	0	1	3	1	2	2	1
	3 = Neither agree nor disagree	30	3	20	7	7	13	4	6	0	4	2	5	3	6	5
	4 = Agree	42	7	25	10	19	15	6	2	14	6	4	3	8	3	4
	5 = Strongly agree	21	3	16	2	16	1	1	3	7	5	1	4	1	0	3
4	Awareness Level Data Quality Management															
	1 = Strongly disagree	9	4	4	1	4	0	3	2	0	2	5	0	0	2	0

(continued)

Table 4.1 (continued)

No.	Characteristic	∑	I	II	III	IV	V	VI	VII	VIII	IX	X	XI	XII	XIII	XIV
	2 = Disagree	18	7	8	3	5	5	5	3	7	2	3	1	2	2	1
	3 = Neither agree nor disagree	39	4	26	9	16	11	6	6	7	9	6	5	5	3	4
	4 = Agree	46	7	32	7	17	18	8	3	11	8	3	8	5	6	5
	5 = Strongly agree	32	10	14	8	17	8	1	6	9	5	6	3	4	2	3
5	Implementation Level Data Quality Management															
	1 = Already available	30	5	17	8	18	8	1	3	9	7	5	4	2	2	1
	2 = Within 1 year	28	4	18	6	12	10	3	3	5	3	6	5	3	2	4
	3 = Within 3 years	38	6	24	8	13	13	8	4	7	7	3	5	5	6	5
	4 = Within 5 years	15	4	10	1	7	4	2	2	5	3	0	2	3	5	1
	5 = Not planned	6	2	3	1	0	2	1	3	1	2	1	0	1	0	1
6	Data Quality Management basic requirement Digital Twin															
	1 = Strongly disagree	2	0	1	1	1	0	1	0	0	0	1	0	0	1	0
	2 = Disagree	8	1	6	1	0	4	1	3	2	2	2	1	1	0	0
	3 = Neither agree nor disagree	35	4	22	9	13	12	6	4	6	5	6	4	5	4	5
	4 = Agree	39	13	19	7	14	16	4	5	9	8	2	5	7	5	3
	5 = Strongly agree	33	3	24	6	22	5	3	3	10	7	4	6	1	1	4
7	Awareness Level Decision Support System															
	1 = Strongly disagree	11	4	5	2	4	3	3	1	0	5	4	0	1	1	0
	2 = Disagree	26	6	18	2	14	5	2	5	6	2	4	4	3	4	3

(continued)

Table 4.1 (continued)

No.	Characteristic	∑	I	II	III	IV	V	VI	VII	VIII	IX	X	XI	XII	XIII	XIV
	3 = Neither agree nor disagree	36	7	21	8	13	11	6	6	9	5	5	6	4	5	2
	4 = Agree	45	7	26	12	14	18	9	4	11	8	8	4	6	3	5
	5 = Strongly agree	26	8	14	4	14	5	3	4	8	6	2	3	2	2	3
8	Implementation Level Decision Support System															
	1 = Already available	29	2	18	9	17	8	2	2	7	10	4	5	1	1	1
	2 = Within 1 year	21	6	13	2	9	5	4	3	5	2	3	4	3	2	2
	3 = Within 3 years	37	7	18	12	12	12	8	5	12	4	5	3	5	4	4
	4 = Within 5 years	9	5	4	0	3	2	2	2	1	1	1	0	3	2	5
	5 = Not planned	11	2	8	1	0	7	2	2	3	2	2	1	0	1	2
9	Improvement of Decision Support System by Digital Twin															
	1 = Strongly disagree	6	0	5	1	4	0	1	1	1	0	1	3	0	1	0
	2 = Disagree	6	1	3	2	1	2	2	1	3	2	1	0	0	0	0
	3 = Neither agree nor disagree	31	5	16	10	7	13	6	5	7	4	5	3	4	5	3
	4 = Agree	40	11	22	7	12	17	7	4	10	6	4	5	6	4	5
	5 = Strongly agree	24	5	15	4	17	2	2	3	1	7	4	2	2	0	2

Source: Own Table[1]

4.2.2.2 Main Study Sample

At the **management level**, 25.4% were lower management, 50.8% were middle management, and 23.8% were upper management (Figure 4.5).

[1] Legend: ∑ per group, I. Upper Management, II. Middle Management, III. Lower Management, IV. 250 or more employees, V. 50–249 employees, VI. 10–50 employees, VII. Up to 9 employees, VIII. Automotive, IX. Healthcare, X. Retail, XI. Transport, XII. Computer, XIII. Construction, XIV. Food

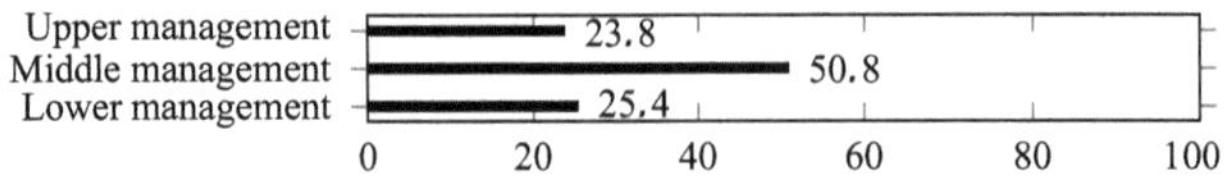

Figure 4.5 Main study management levels in percent (N = 122). (Source: Own Figure)

The average age was 37.40 years using a free text field rather than a corridor, but neither the procedure change nor the age had an effect on the dissertation. More men (59.8%) participated than women (40.2%). The average length of service in the companies was **8.40 years**, using a free text field and not a corridor. This rather short length of company affiliation could have been the result of the relatively young age of the managers, although they may have worked in previous companies—company affiliation is calculated from the time of entry. Regarding company size, as can be seen in Figure 4.6, most of the managers worked for large companies.

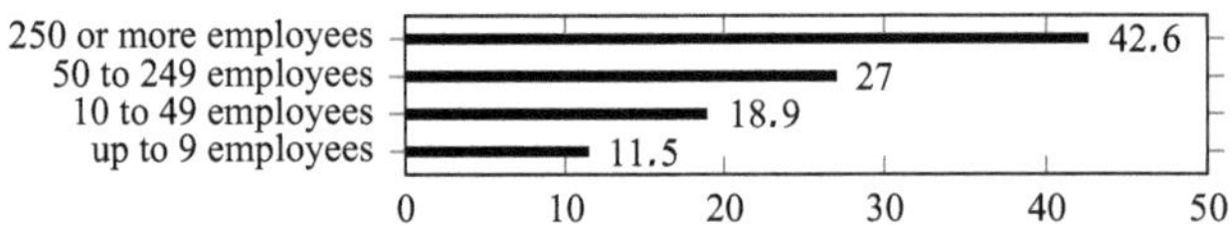

Figure 4.6 Main study company size of the companies in percent (N = 122). (Source: Own Figure)

The **industry** distribution was as follows: automotive (19.7%), retail (19.7%), computer (16.4%), healthcare (16.4%), construction (9.8%), transport (9.8%), and food (8.2%) (Figure 4.7).

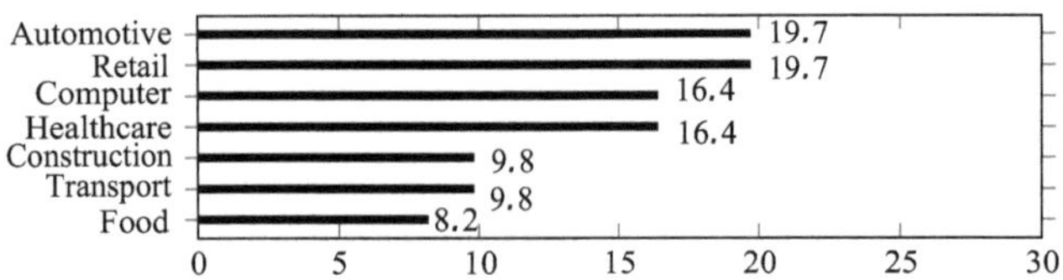

Figure 4.7 Main study industry distribution of the companies in percent (N = 122). (Source: Own Figure)

The majority of companies planned to implement digital twin within 5 years: 37.7% planned implementation within 1 year, 29.5% within 3 years, and 5.7% within 5 years. In 21.3% of the companies, a digital twin was already available, and in 5.7%, no implementation plans existed (N = 122). Data quality management had been either implemented or planned within the following 3 years: 37.7% stated that it was already available, 32.7% had plans to implement it within 1 year, 24.6% within 3 years, 4.1% within 5 years, and 1.6% had no implementation plans (N = 122). Regarding the implementation of a decision support system (N = 122), 35.2% stated that it was already available, 32.8% had plans to implement it within 1 year, 23% within 3 years, 5.7% within 5 years, and 3.3% had no implementation plans. So this concept had already been implemented or planned in most companies. In response to the statement that the implementation of a DTDDMM needs the full implementation of a digital twin, data quality management and a decision support system, 45.9% agreed, 23.8% neither agreed nor disagreed, 19.7% strongly agreed, 8.2% disagreed and 2.5% strongly disagreed, which shows the importance of full implementation. When asked whether digital twin provided a competitive opportunity, the majority agreed: 43.4% agreed, 33.6% neither agreed nor disagreed, 11.5% strongly agreed, 10.7% disagreed and 0.8% strongly disagreed. In response to the statement that data quality management is a basic requirement for the digital twin concept, 34.4% agreed, 33.6% strongly agreed, 20.5% neither agreed nor disagreed, 10.7% disagreed, and 0.8% strongly disagreed. So, the majority believed that there was a certain dependency. Similarly, regarding the statement that decision support systems are improved by digital twin, 43.4% agreed, 27% neither agreed nor disagreed, 23% strongly agreed, 5.7% disagreed and 0.8% strongly disagreed. In response to the statement that a DTDDMM is useful for their company, 37.7% agreed, 36.1% neither agreed nor disagreed, 16.4% strongly agreed, 8.2% disagreed, and 1.6% strongly disagreed.

So, the developed model would appear to be useful for the majority of managers. Asked how important it was to have a common understanding of the process of a digital twin as defined by (Raj et al., 2020): 45.9% agreed, 29.5% neither agreed nor disagreed, 16.4% strongly agreed, 7.4% disagreed and 0.8% strongly disagreed, which suggests that the concept of a process digital twin was largely understood. Regarding the data quality management of a DTDDMM, the average data quality was rated at 65%, suggesting that there is improvement potential here. In response to the statement that data quality management must be fully anchored at corporate level for successful implementation, 52.2% agreed, 18% strongly agreed, 14.8% neither agreed nor disagreed, 11.5% disagreed and 3.3% strongly disagreed. Regarding the statement that the process digital twin is dependent on the quality of the supplied data, 41.8% agreed, 32% strongly agreed, 15.6% neither agreed nor disagreed, 8.2% disagreed and 2.5% strongly disagreed, clearly showing that the process digital twin depends on data quality. Furthermore, when asked to comment on the statement that the success of a decision support system is dependent on the delivered data quality, 42.9% agreed, 27.9% strongly agreed, 18.9% neither agreed nor disagreed, 7.4% disagreed and 3.3% strongly disagreed, clearly showing that a decision support system is also dependent on data quality. Finally, the majority of managers believed that timeliness was the most important prerequisite and that process monitoring was the greatest benefit of a DTDDMM. Table 4.2 summarizes the findings with $\sum$ and frequencies of each group.

Table 4.2 Main study sample description (N = 122)

No.	Characteristic	$\sum$	I	II	III	IV	V	VI	VII	VIII	IX	X	XI	XII	XIII	XIV
1	Implementation Level Digital Twin															
	1 = Already available	26	6	13	7	16	4	1	5	7	4	3	4	2	3	3
	2 = Within 1 year	46	11	21	14	17	12	14	3	4	11	9	9	5	5	3
	3 = Within 3 years	36	9	21	6	13	11	8	4	11	7	3	5	3	3	4
	4 = Within 5 years	7	2	5	0	3	3	0	1	1	1	2	2	1	0	0
	5 = Not planned	7	1	2	4	3	3	0	1	1	1	3	0	1	1	0
2	Digital Twin as competitive opportunity															
	1 = Strongly disagree	1	1	0	0	0	0	0	1	0	1	0	0	0	0	0
	2 = Disagree	13	2	7	4	2	6	3	2	2	3	3	3	0	2	0
	3 = Neither agree nor disagree	41	7	24	10	14	12	10	5	9	7	4	6	6	6	3
	4 = Agree	53	15	22	16	26	13	9	5	11	9	11	9	5	3	5

(continued)

Table 4.2 (continued)

No.	Characteristic	∑	I	II	III	IV	V	VI	VII	VIII	IX	X	XI	XII	XIII	XIV
	5 = Strongly agree	14	4	9	1	10	2	1	1	2	4	2	2	1	1	2
3	Implementation Level Data Quality Management															
	1 = Already available	46	11	21	14	26	12	4	4	11	2	13	10	4	3	3
	2 = Within 1 year	39	12	20	7	12	9	13	5	3	13	3	5	6	5	4
	3 = Within 3 years	30	4	17	9	12	10	6	2	8	7	2	5	1	4	3
	4 = Within 5 years	5	1	3	1	2	1	0	2	2	1	1	0	1	0	0
	5 = Not planned	2	1	1	0	0	1	0	1	0	1	1	0	0	0	0
4	Data Quality Management basic requirement Digital Twin															
	1 = Strongly disagree	1	0	1	0	0	0	0	1	0	0	0	1	0	0	0
	2 = Disagree	13	3	7	3	3	4	5	1	3	2	2	2	2	1	1
	3 = Neither agree nor disagree	25	4	16	5	7	6	8	4	2	7	2	4	4	4	2
	4 = Agree	42	8	19	15	18	13	8	3	9	10	7	6	3	3	4
	5 = Strongly agree	41	14	19	8	24	10	2	5	10	5	9	7	3	4	3
5	Implementation Level Decision Support System															
	1 = Already available	43	15	19	9	23	8	6	6	12	4	7	8	4	5	3
	2 = Within 1 year	40	9	23	8	12	13	13	2	6	11	5	7	5	3	3
	3 = Within 3 years	28	2	16	10	12	10	3	3	6	6	3	4	2	4	3
	4 = Within 5 years	7	2	3	2	4	1	1	1	0	2	3	1	1	0	0
	5 = Not planned	4	1	1	2	1	1	0	2	0	1	2	0	0	0	1

(continued)

Table 4.2 (continued)

No.	Characteristic	∑	I	II	III	IV	V	VI	VII	VIII	IX	X	XI	XII	XIII	XIV
6	Improvement of Decision Support System by Digital Twin															
	1 = Strongly disagree	1	0	1	0	1	0	0	0	0	0	1	0	0	0	0
	2 = Disagree	7	2	4	1	2	3	1	1	2	2	0	2	0	1	0
	3 = Neither agree nor disagree	33	5	18	10	9	7	11	6	6	9	4	3	5	3	3
	4 = Agree	53	13	25	15	23	15	9	6	13	7	11	8	6	4	4
	5 = Strongly agree	28	9	14	5	17	8	2	1	3	6	4	7	1	4	3
7	Usefulness DTDDMM															
	1 = Strongly disagree	2	1	0	1	1	0	0	1	0	1	0	0	1	0	0
	2 = Disagree	10	1	6	3	2	4	2	2	1	1	3	3	1	1	0
	3 = Neither agree nor disagree	44	10	23	11	13	15	10	6	10	9	5	6	5	6	3
	4 = Agree	46	12	25	9	23	10	9	4	10	6	10	8	5	2	5
	5 = Strongly agree	20	5	8	7	13	4	2	1	3	7	2	3	0	3	2
8	Definition of Process Digital Twin															
	1 = Strongly disagree	1	0	0	1	1	0	0	0	0	0	1	0	0	0	0
	2 = Disagree	9	2	6	1	1	2	4	2	2	3	1	3	0	0	0
	3 = Neither agree nor disagree	36	9	19	8	11	10	10	5	6	5	5	4	6	5	5
	4 = Agree	56	11	28	17	30	15	6	5	15	9	9	11	5	4	3
	5 = Strongly agree	20	7	9	4	9	6	3	2	1	7	4	2	1	3	2
9	Corporate Data Quality Management for Model															
	1 = Strongly disagree	4	1	2	1	0	2	0	2	0	2	1	1	0	0	0

(continued)

Table 4.2 (continued)

No.	Characteristic	∑	I	II	III	IV	V	VI	VII	VIII	IX	X	XI	XII	XIII	XIV
	2 = Disagree	14	1	9	4	3	4	5	2	1	3	2	2	1	4	1
	3 = Neither agree nor disagree	18	6	8	4	3	6	6	3	4	7	0	3	3	0	1
	4 = Agree	64	16	32	16	33	15	9	7	15	7	12	13	7	4	6
	5 = Strongly agree	22	5	11	6	13	6	3	0	4	5	5	1	1	4	2
10	Process Digital Twin and Data Quality															
	1 = Strongly disagree	3	1	2	0	2	1	0	0	0	1	0	1	0	0	1
	2 = Disagree	10	3	6	1	0	5	2	3	3	1	2	1	1	1	1
	3 = Neither agree nor disagree	19	1	11	7	5	5	7	2	2	5	2	4	3	3	1
	4 = Agree	51	16	26	9	24	11	10	6	11	12	8	10	4	3	3
	5 = Strongly agree	39	8	17	14	21	11	4	3	8	6	8	4	4	5	4
11	Decision Support Systems and Data Quality															
	1 = Strongly disagree	4	2	2	0	1	1	0	2	1	1	0	1	0	1	0
	2 = Disagree	9	1	6	2	2	5	2	0	1	1	2	2	1	1	1
	3 = Neither agree nor disagree	23	4	14	5	3	8	9	3	3	9	3	3	2	1	2
	4 = Agree	52	11	28	13	28	11	8	5	7	8	10	11	7	5	4
	5 = Strongly agree	34	11	12	11	18	8	4	4	12	5	5	3	2	4	3
12	Full Implementation of three topics for Model															
	1 = Strongly disagree	3	0	3	0	1	0	1	1	0	0	1	2	0	0	0
	2 = Disagree	10	3	4	2	1	4	4	1	1	2	2	1	2	2	0
	3 = Neither agree nor disagree	29	4	17	8	11	8	6	4	3	3	3	8	4	4	4

(continued)

Table 4.2 (continued)

No.	Characteristic	$\sum$	I	II	III	IV	V	VI	VII	VIII	IX	X	XI	XII	XIII	XIV
	4 = Agree	56	13	28	15	26	15	10	5	13	14	9	7	5	3	5
	5 = Strongly agree	24	9	10	5	13	6	2	3	7	5	5	2	1	3	1

Source: Own Table[2]

4.3 Methods for Data Analysis

For the analysis of the data **IBM SPSS Statistics 28** was used focusing on two non-parametric tests in Table 4.3 to show **differences** (Hopkins et al., 2018; Mircioiu et al., 2017):

Table 4.3 Parametric and nonparametric analysis

Analysis	2 Independent Groups	2 Dependent Groups	>2 Independent Groups	>2 Dependent Groups
Parametric	Independent t test	Dependent t test	One-way ANOVA	Repeated-measures ANOVA
	N > 30	Sample sizes equal	No minimum N	No minimum N / Sample sizes equal
Nonparametric	Mann-Whitney	**Wilcoxon**	**Kruskal-Wallis**	Friedman's ANOVA
	N ≥ 8	N ≥ 5	No minimum N	No minimum N

Source: Own Table, derived from Hopkins et al., 2018

- Wilcoxon Signed-Ranks Test (Wilcoxon, 1945) to show differences within a group and
- Kruskal–Wallis test (Kruskal et al., 1952) to show differences across groups.

[2] Legend: $\sum$ per group, I. Upper Management, II. Middle Management, III. Lower Management, IV. 250 or more employees, V. 50–249 employees, VI. 10–50 employees, VII. Up to 9 employees, VIII. Automotive, IX. Retail, X. Computer XI. Healthcare, XII. Construction, XIII. Transport, XIV. Food

The tests are described in Sheskin, 2000: *Test 6. The Wilcoxon Signed-Ranks Test p. 143–156* and *Test 22. Kruskal–Wallis One-Way Analysis of Variance by Ranks p. 609–623.* To calculate the effect sizes, the Wilcoxon signed-rank test uses the Z-score to calculate the correlation coefficients in Equation 4.1[3] (Fritz et al., 2011):

$$r = \frac{Z}{\sqrt{n}};\ r^2\ or\ \eta^2 = \frac{Z^2}{n} \tag{4.1}$$

The Kruskal–Wallis one-way analysis of variance by ranks uses Equation 4.2 (B. H. Cohen, 2008) to calculate the effect sizes[4]:

$$\eta_H^2 = \frac{H - k + 1}{n - k} \tag{4.2}$$

Here, Cohen discusses the relationship between eta squared (η^2) and Cohen's f in Equation 4.3 (J. Cohen, 1988)[5].

$$\eta^2 = \frac{f^2}{1 + f^2};\ f^2 = \frac{\eta^2}{1 - \eta^2};\ f = \sqrt{\frac{\eta^2}{1 - \eta^2}} \tag{4.3}$$

If the model is a two-group ANOVA and the number of observations in each group is the same, then the standardized range of population means, Cohen's d with small (d = 0.2), medium (d = 0.5), and strong (d = 0.8) effects shown in Equation 4.4[6] (J. Cohen, 1988).

$$d = 2 * f \tag{4.4}$$

Besides the nonparametric analysis, **percentage points** show the arithmetic difference of two percentages (Rossouw, 2013). There are differences between a percentage change and a change in percentage points, where the difference between two percentages is expressed in Equation 4.5 (Rossouw, 2013; Walsh, 1959):[7]

---

[3] n: Total number of observations based on z

[4] H: Kruskal-Wallis test statistic; k: Number of groups; n: Total number of observations

[5] f^2: Square of the effect size; η^2: Partial eta-squared; f: Effect size

[6] f: Effect size

[7] x: Percentage Value; y: Percentages Point

$$x * \left(1 + \frac{y}{100}\right) \tag{4.5}$$

In order to make the results in this dissertation comparable, three assumptions were made:

- *Assumption 1*: The actual condition was 25%, and participants indicated an increase of 15%. Then these percentages were converted to 15 percentage points (3.75%), representing an in crease from 25% to 28.75%.
- *Assumption 2*: The actual condition was 25%, and participants indicated an increase of 75%. Then these percentages were converted to 50 percentage points (12.5%), representing an in crease from 25% to 37.5%.
- *Assumption 3*: If the increase in assumptions 1 and 2 was above 100%, these were not considered further in the evaluation of the results.

The results were compared using the mean value (all values were added and the sum was divided by the total number of values), here the actual state (%) was compared with the newly calculated state (%).

Results and Evaluation 5

5.1 Data Analysis—Preliminary Study

The objectives of the preliminary study were as follows:

1. To evaluate the **relevancy** and **need** of the dissertation and whether the topics were worth researching further in the **main study**.
2. To evaluate differences within and across **(1) management level**, **(2) company size** and **(3) industry** for H_1.
3. To evaluate the **results** for H_2, H_3, H_4 and the **implementation level**.

5.1.1 Strategic Positioning

5.1.1.1 Results Management Levels

The results are shown in Table 5.1, with descriptive statistics (The corresponding data can be viewed in Appendix Table 6 in the electronic supplementary material).

Supplementary Information The online version contains supplementary material available at https://doi.org/10.1007/978-3-658-44453-2_5.

F. Blaschke, *Implementation and Benefits of Digital Twin on Decision Making and Data Quality Management*, https://doi.org/10.1007/978-3-658-44453-2_5

Table 5.1 Hypothesis test summary within management levels 1

	No.	Null Hypothesis	Sig.[a,b]	Decision
Upper management level	6	Median of Data Quality Management basic requirement Digital Twin equals 3	<.001	Reject the null hypothesis
	9	Median of Improvement Decision Support Systems by Digital Twin equals 3	<.001	Reject the null hypothesis
Middle management level	3	Median of Digital Twin as competitive opportunity equals 3	<.001	Reject the null hypothesis
	4	Median of Awareness level of Data Quality Management equals 3	<.001	Reject the null hypothesis
	5	Median of Implementation level of Data Quality Management equals 3	<.001	Reject the null hypothesis
	6	Median of Data Quality Management basic requirement Digital Twin equals 3	<.001	Reject the null hypothesis
	7	Median of Awareness level of Decision Support Systems equals 3	.017	Reject the null hypothesis
	8	Median of Implementation level of Decision Support Systems equals 3	.016	Reject the null hypothesis
	9	Median of Improvement Decision Support Systems by Digital Twin equals 3	<.001	Reject the null hypothesis
Lower management level	3	Median of Digital Twin as competitive opportunity equals 3	.007	Reject the null hypothesis
	4	Median of Awareness level of Data Quality Management equals 3	.008	Reject the null hypothesis

(continued)

Table 5.1 (continued)

No.	Null Hypothesis	Sig.^{a,b}	Decision
5	Median of Implementation level of Data Quality Management equals 3	.006	Reject the null hypothesis
6	Median of Data Quality Management basic requirement Digital Twin equals 3	.011	Reject the null hypothesis
7	Median of Awareness level of Decision Support Systems equals 3	.032	Reject the null hypothesis
8	Median of Implementation level of Decision Support Systems equals 3	.008	Reject the null hypothesis
9	Median of Improvement Decision Support Systems by Digital Twin equals 3	.047	Reject the null hypothesis

a. The significance level is .05. b. Asymptotic significance is displayed.
Source: Own Table

The hypothesis test showed that the p-value was less than .05, and was thus assumed to be **significant** (The corresponding data can be viewed in Appendix Figure 5 in the electronic supplementary material):

- **Upper management:** Strong effects No.we6: d = 2.37 and No. 9: d = 2.20.
- **Middle management:** Strong effects No. 3: d = 1.79, No. 4: d = 0.97, No. 5: d = 0.90, No. 6: d = 1.55, No. 9: d = 1.01 and medium effects No. 7: d = 0.54, No. 8: d = 0.65.
- **Lower management:** Strong effects No. 3: d = 1.44, No. 4: d = 1.15, No. 5: d = 1.37, No. 6: d = 1.21, No. 7: d = 0.90, No. 8: d = 1.29 and No. 9: d = 0.90.

Across management levels: Table 5.2 showed **no rejected null hypotheses** with a p-value less than .05 and was therefore not assumed to be **significant**.

Table 5.2 Hypothesis test summary across management levels 1

	Null Hypothesis	Sig.^{a,b}	Decision
1	Distribution Company awareness of Digital Twin is the same across Management Level	.379	Retain the null hypothesis
2	Distribution Implementation level of Digital Twin is the same across Management Level	.273	Retain the null hypothesis
3	Distribution Digital Twin as competitive opportunity is the same across Management Level	.322	Retain the null hypothesis
4	Distribution Company awareness of Data Quality Management is the same across Management Level	.834	Retain the null hypothesis
5	Distribution Implementation level of Data Quality Management is the same across Management Level	.349	Retain the null hypothesis
6	Distribution Data Quality Management basic requirement Digital Twin is the same across Management Level	.798	Retain the null hypothesis
7	Distribution Company awareness of Decision Support Systems is the same across Management Level	.728	Retain the null hypothesis
8	Distribution Implementation level of Decision Support Systems is the same across Management Level	.147	Retain the null hypothesis
9	Distribution Improvement Decision Support Systems by Digital Twin is the same across Management Level	.314	Retain the null hypothesis

a. The significance level is .05. b. Asymptotic significance is displayed.
Source: Own Table

5.1.1.2 Evaluation Management Levels

Upper Management Level: Digital twins were both known and unknown at the upper management level, with Mdn = 3.00 [1.00, 5.00]. Here, at least 50% of managers said they had either implemented digital twins already or would within the next 3 years. 75% of the managers said they had either implemented digital twins already or would within the next 5 years. Digital twins were seen as a competitive opportunity (Mdn = 4.00 [2.00, 4.96]), and the concept of data quality management was known (*Mdn* = 4.00 [2.00, 5.00]). Here, at least 50% of managers said they had either implemented data quality management already or would within the next 3 years, and 75% of managers said they had either implemented data quality management already or would within the next 5 years. So, data quality management was seen as a significant and basic requirement for a digital twin (No. 6: $z = 3.50$, $p < .001$, $d = 2.37$) with *Mdn* = 4.00 [3.00, 4.48]. Decision support systems were neither known nor unknown in the upper management (*Mdn* = 3.00 [2.00, 5.00]). Here, at least 50% of managers said they had either implemented decision support systems already or would within the next 3 years, and 75% of managers said they had either implemented decision support systems already or would within the next 5 years. So, decision support systems improvement through a digital twin application was seen as significant (No. 9: $z = 3.47$, $p < .001$, $d = 2.20$) with *Mdn* = 4.00 [3.00, 5.00].

Middle Management: Digital twins were both known and unknown at middle management level (*Mdn* = 3.00 [2.00, 4.00]). Here, at least 50% of managers said they had either implemented digital twins already or would within the next 3 years, and 75% of managers said they had either implemented digital twins already or would within the next 5 years. Digital twins were seen as a significant competitive opportunity (No. 3: $z = 5.37$, $p < .001$, $D = 1.79$) with *Mdn* = 4.00 [3.00, 5.00]. For data quality management, there was a significantly high level of awareness (No. 4: $z = 3.99$, $p < .001$, $d = 0.97$) with *Mdn* = 4.00 [3.00, 5.00]. Here, at least 50% and 75% of managers said they had either implemented data quality management already or would within the next 3 years (No. 5: $z = -3.48$, $p < .001$, $d = 1.58$). So, data quality management was seen as significant and basic requirement for a digital twin concept (No. 6: $z = 5.20$, $p < .001$, $d = 1.55$) with *Mdn* = 4.00 [3.00, 5.00]. Regarding decision support systems, there was a significantly high level of awareness (No. 7: $z = 2.39$, $p = .017$, $d = 0.54$) with *Mdn* = 3.00 [2.00, 5.00]. Here, at least 50% of managers said they had either implemented decision support systems already or would within the next year, and 75% of managers said they had either implemented decision support systems already or would within the next 3 years (No. 8: $z = -2.41$, $p = .016$, $d = 0.65$). So, the improvement gained in decision support systems by the application of a digital twin was also seen as significant (No. 9: $z = 3.51$, $p < .001$, $d = 1.01$) with *Mdn* = 4.00 [3.00, 5.00].

Lower Management Level: Digital twin were both known and unknown at the lower management level, with *Mdn* = 3.00 [2.00, 4.00]. Here, at least 50% and 75% of managers said they had either implemented digital twins already or would do so within the next 3 years. A digital twin concept was seen as a significant competitive opportunity (No. 3: z = 2.68, p = .007, d = 1.44) with *Mdn* = 4.00 [3.00, 4.00]. For data quality management, there was a significantly high level of awareness (No. 4: z = 2.63, p = .008, d = 1.15) with *Mdn* = 4.00 [2.64, 5.00]. Here, at least 50% of managers said they had either implemented data quality management already or would do so within the next year and 75% of managers said they had either implemented data quality management already or would do so within the next 3 years (No. 5: z = −2.77, p = .006, d = 1.37). So, data quality management was seen as a significant and basic requirement for a digital twin concept (No. 6: z = 2.54, p = .011, d = 1.21) with *Mdn* = 4.00 [3.00, 5.00]. There was also a significantly high level of awareness of decision support systems (No. 7: z = 2.15, p = .032, d = 0.90) with *Mdn* = 4.00 [2.64, 4.36]. Here, at least 50% and 75% of managers said they had either implemented decision support systems already or would within the next 3 years (No. 8: z = −2.65, p = .008, d = 1.29). So, the improvement of decision support systems by digital twin was seen as significant (No. 9: z = 1.98, p = 0.47, d = 0.90) with *Mdn* = 5.00 [3.00, 5.00].

Across Management Levels: To sum up, there were no significant differences between the management levels, regarding whether digital twin were known about or unknown (*Mdn* = 3.00 [1.20, 4.00]). Furthermore, at least 50% of managers said they had either implemented digital twins already or would do so within the next 3 years and 75% of managers said they had either implemented digital twins already or would within the next 5 years. Overall, the digital twin was seen as a significant competitive opportunity (*Mdn* = 4.00 [3.00, 5.00]) and the concept of data quality management was understood (*Mdn* = 4.00 [2.00, 5.00]). At least 50% and 75% of managers said they had either implemented data quality management already or would within the next 3 years. Data quality management was also seen as a basic requirement for a digital twin (*Mdn* = 4.00 [2.00, 5.00]). Decision support systems were neither known nor unknown (*Mdn* = 3.00 [2.00, 5.00]). At least 50% and 75% of managers saying that they had either implemented decision support systems already or would within the next 3 years. The resulting improvement to decision support systems by the application of a digital twin was acknowledged (*Mdn* = 4.00 [3.00, 5.00]).

5.1.1.3 Results Company Size

The results are shown in Table 5.3 with descriptive statistics (The corresponding data can be viewed in Appendix Table 7 in the electronic supplementary material).

Table 5.3 Hypothesis test summary within company size 1

Industries	No.	Null Hypothesis	Sig.[a,b]	Decision
250 or more employees	3	Median of Digital Twin as competitive opportunity equals 3	<.001	Reject the null hypothesis
	4	Median of Awareness level of Data Quality Management equals 3	<.001	Reject the null hypothesis
	5	Median of Implementation level of Data Quality Management equals 3	<.001	Reject the null hypothesis
	6	Median of Data Quality Management basic requirement Digital Twin equals 3	<.001	Reject the null hypothesis
	7	Median of Awareness level of Decision Support Systems equals 3	.034	Reject the null hypothesis
	8	Median of Implementation level of Decision Support Systems equals 3	<.001	Reject the null hypothesis
	9	Median of Improvement Decision Support Systems by Digital Twin equals 3	.001	Reject the null hypothesis
50 to 249 employees	3	Median of Digital Twin as competitive opportunity equals 3	0,014	Reject the null hypothesis
	4	Median of Awareness level of Data Quality Management equals 3	<.001	Reject the null hypothesis
	5	Median of Implementation level of Data Quality Management equals 3	.017	Reject the null hypothesis
	6	Median of Data Quality Management basic requirement Digital Twin equals 3	.001	Reject the null hypothesis

(continued)

Table 5.3 (continued)

Industries	No.	Null Hypothesis	Sig.^{a,b}	Decision
	7	Median of Awareness level of Decision Support Systems equals 3	.029	Reject the null hypothesis
	9	Median of Improvement Decision Support Systems by Digital Twin equals 3	<.001	Reject the null hypothesis
10 to 49 employees	1	Median of Awareness level of Digital Twin equals 3	.033	Reject the null hypothesis
	3	Median of Digital Twin as competitive opportunity equals 3	.035	Reject the null hypothesis

a. The significance level is .05. b. Asymptotic significance is displayed.
Source: Own Table

The hypothesis test showed that the p-value was less than .05, and was thus assumed to be **significant** (The corresponding data can be viewed in Appendix Figure 6 in the electronic supplementary material):

- **250 or more employees**: Strong effects No. 3: d = 2.45, No. 4: d = 1.03, No. 5: d = 1.58, No. 6: d = 2.07, No. 8: d = 1.91, No. 9: d = 1.28 and medium effect No. 7: d = 0.60.
- **50 to 249 employees**: Strong effects No. 3: d = 0.93, No. 4: d = 1.50, No. 5: d = 0.86, No. 6: d = 1.38, No. 9: d = 1.60 and a medium effect No. 7: d = 0.71.
- **10 to 49 employees**: Strong effects No. 1: d = 0.99 and No. 3: d = 1.54.
- **Up to 9 employees**: No significant results.

Across Company Size: To compare the differences **across** the company size, Table 5.4 shows that **3**, **6** and **8** had to be examined further, with an asymptotic Sig. (2-sided test) of **<.001**, **.018** and **.012**.

The central tendencies of the groups had a strong effect d = 0.83 and medium effects d = 0.55 and d = 0.61. Table 5.5 shows which groups differed significantly

Table 5.4 Hypothesis test summary across company size 1

	Null Hypothesis	Sig.^{a,b}	Decision
1	Distribution Company awareness of Digital Twin is the same across Company Size	.081	Retain the null hypothesis
2	Distribution Implementation level of Digital Twin is the same across Company Size	.689	Retain the null hypothesis
3	Distribution Digital Twin as competitive opportunity is the same across Company Size	**<.001**	Reject the null hypothesis
4	Distribution Company awareness of Data Quality Management is the same across Company Size	.084	Retain the null hypothesis
5	Distribution Implementation level of Data Quality Management is the same across Company Size	.065	Retain the null hypothesis
6	Distribution Data Quality Management basic requirement Digital Twin is the same across Company Size	**.018**	Reject the null hypothesis
7	Distribution Company awareness of Decision Support Systems is the same across Company Size	.958	Retain the null hypothesis
8	Distribution Implementation level of Decision Support Systems is the same across Company Size	**.012**	Reject the null hypothesis
9	Distribution Improvement of Decision Support Systems by Digital Twin is the same across Company Size	.071	Retain the null hypothesis

a. The significance level is .05. b. Asymptotic significance is displayed.
Source: Own Table

The results indicate that for **3** that there was a significant difference with a medium effect between **No. 3** (50 to 249 employees and 250 or more employees d = 0.79), **No. 5** (up to 9 employees and 250 or more employees d = 0.65), and a small effect in **No. 6** (10 to 49 employees and 250 or more employees d = 0.42). The results indicate for **6** that there was a significant difference with a medium effect between **No. 3** (10 to 49 and 250 or more employees d = 0.50), **No. 5** (up to 9 and 250 or more employees d = 0.50), and **No. 6** (50 to 249 and 250 or more employees d = 0.54). The results indicate for **8** that there was a

Table 5.5 Pairwise comparisons of company size 1

	No.	Sample 1-Sample 2	Test Statistic	Std. Error	Std. Test Statistic	Sig.	Adj. Sig.[a]
3	1	50 to 249 employees-Up to 9 employees	−.002	9.093	.00	1.000	1.000
	2	50 to 249 employees-10 to 49 employees	7.032	9.615	.73	.465	1.000
	3	50 to 249 employees-250 or more employees	24.255	6.539	3.71	**<.001**	.001
	4	Up to 9 employees-10 to 49 employees	7.030	11.265	.624	.53	1.000
	5	Up to 9 employees-250 or more employees	24.253	8.787	2.76	**.006**	.035
	6	10 to 49 employees-250 or more employees	−17.223	9.326	−1.85	**.065**	.389
6	1	10 to 49 employees-Up to 9 employees	−1.34	11.838	−.115	.908	1.000
	2	10 to 49 employees-50 to 249 employees	−2.274	9.923	−.23	.819	1.000
	3	10 to 49 employees-250 or more employees	−20.683	9.544	−2.17	**.030**	.181
	4	Up to 9 employees-50 to 249 employees	.907	9.923	.09	.927	1.000
	5	Up to 9 employees-250 or more employees	19.317	9.544	2.02	**.043**	.258
	6	50 to 249 employees-250 or more employees	18.409	7.030	2.62	**.009**	.053

(continued)

Table 5.5 (continued)

	No.	Sample 1-Sample 2	Test Statistic	Std. Error	Std. Test Statistic	Sig.	Adj. Sig.[a]
8	1	250 or more employees-50 to 249 employees	−18.250	6.940	−2.63	**.009**	.051
	2	250 or more employees-10 to 49 employees	20.851	8.460	2.47	**.014**	.082
	3	250 or more employees-Up to 9 employees	−21.145	9.262	−2.28	**.022**	.135
	4	50 to 249 employees-10 to 49 employees	2.601	8.721	.29	.765	1.000
	5	50 to 249 employees-Up to 9 employees	−2.895	9.501	−.30	.761	1.000
	6	10 to 49 employees-Up to 9 employees	−.294	10.662	−.03	.978	1.000

Each row tests the null hypothesis that the Sample 1 and Sample 2 distributions are the same. Asymptotic significances (2-sided tests) are displayed. The significance level is .05.
a. Significance values have been adjusted by the Bonferroni correction for multiple tests.
Source: Own Table

significant difference, with a medium effect between **No. 1** (250 or more and 50 to 249 employees d = 0.54), **No. 2** (250 or more and 10 to 49 employees d = 0.57) and **No. 3** (250 or more and up to 9 employees d = 0.53).

5.1.1.4 Evaluation Company Size

250 or more employees: Digital twins were both known and unknown in companies with 250 or more employees (*Mdn* = 3.00 [2.00, 5.00]. Here, at least 50% and 75% of managers said they had either implemented digital twins already or would do so within the next 3 years. Digital twins were seen as a significant competitive opportunity (No. 3: $z = 5.14$, $p < .001$, $d = 2.45$) with *Mdn* = 4.00 [3.00, 5.00]. For data quality management, there was a significantly high level of awareness (No. 4: $z = 3.53$, $p < .001$, $d = 1.03$) with *Mdn* = 4.00 [2.60, 5.00]. Here, at least 50% of managers said they had either implemented data quality management already or would within the next year and 75% of managers said they had either implemented data quality management already or would do so within the next 3 years (No. 5: $z = -4.38$, $p < .001$, $d = 1.58$). Data quality management was seen as a significant and basic requirement for the digital twin (No. 6: $z = 5.09$, $p < .001$, $d = 2.07$) *Mdn* = 4.00 [3.00, 5.00]. Decision support systems were significantly neither known nor unknown (No. 7: $z = 2.12$, $p = .034$, $d = 0.60$) with *Mdn* = 3.00 [2.00, 5.00]. Here, at least 50% of managers said they had either implemented decision support systems already or would do so within the next year, and 75% of managers said they had either implemented decision support systems already or would do so within the next 3 years (No. 8: $z = -4.42$, $p < .001$, $d = 1.91$). The improvement of decision support systems through digital twin application was seen as significant (No. 9: $z = 3.45$, $p < .001$, $d = 1.28$) with *Mdn* = 4.00 [3.00, 5.00].

50 to 249 employees: Digital twins were both known and unknown in companies with 50 to 249 employees with *Mdn* = 3.00 [2.00, 4.00]. Here, at least 50% and 75% of managers said they had either implemented digital twin already or would within the next 3 years. Digital twin were seen as a significant competitive opportunity (No. 3: $z = 2.45$, $p = .014$, $d = 0.93$) with *Mdn* = 3.00 [2.60, 4.00]. For data quality management, there was a significantly high level of awareness (No. 4: $z = 3.89$, $p < .001$, $d = 1.50$) with *Mdn* = 4.00 [3.00, 4.00]. Here, at least 50% and 75% of managers said they had either implemented data quality management already or would do so within the next 3 years (No. 5: $z = -2.39$, $p = .017$, $d = 0.86$). Data quality management was seen as a significant basic requirement for the digital twin (No. 6: $z = 3.46$, $p < .001$, $d = 1.38$) with *Mdn* = 4.00 [3.00, 4.00]. Decision support systems were both known and unknown (No. 7: $z = 2.18$, $p = .029$, $d = 0.71$) with *Mdn* = 3.00 [3.00, 4.00]. Here, at least 50% of managers said they had either implemented decision support systems already or would do so within the next 3 years and 75% of managers said they had either implemented decision support systems already or would do so within the next 5 years. The improvement of decision support systems through digital twin application was seen as significant (No. 9: $z = 3.65$, $p < .001$, $d = 1.60$) with *Mdn* = 4.00 [3.00, 4.00].

10 to 49 employees: Digital twin had a significant low awareness level in companies with 10 to 49 employees (No. 1: $z = -2.13$, $p = .033$, $d = 0.99$) with *Mdn* = 3.00 [1.00, 4.00]. Here, at least 50% and 75% of managers said they had either implemented digital twin already or would do so within the next 3 years. The digital twin was seen as a significant competitive opportunity (No. 3: $z = 2.11$, $p = .035$, $d = 1.54$) with *Mdn* = 4.00 [3.00, 4.00]. Data Quality Management was both known about and unknown in companies with 10 to 49 employees with *Mdn* = 3.00 [1.84, 4.00]. Here, at least 50% and 75% of managers said they had either implemented data quality management already or would do so within the next 3 years. Data quality management was seen as a basic requirement for digital twins with *Mdn* = 3.00 [2.56, 5.00]. Decision support systems were known about in companies with 10 to 49 employees, with *Mdn* = 4.00 [1.84, 4.16]. Here, at least 50% and 75% of managers said they had either implemented decision support systems already or would do so within the next 3 years. The improvement to decision support systems through digital twin application was acknowledged (*Mdn* = 3.50 [2.04, 4.00]).

Up to 9 employees: The digital twin was both known about and unknown in companies with up to 9 employees (*Mdn* = 3.00 [1.00, 5.00]). Here, at least 50% of managers said they had either implemented digital twin already or would do so within the next 3 years, and 75% of managers said they had either implemented digital twin already or would do so within the next 5 years. Digital twins were seen as a competitive opportunity (*Mdn* = 3.00 [2.00, 5.00]). Data quality management was both known and unknown in companies with up to 9 employees (*Mdn* = 3.00 [2.00, 5.00]). Here, at least 50% of managers said they had either implemented data quality management already or would do so within the next 3 years, and 75% of managers said they had either implemented data quality management already or would do so within the next 5 years. Data quality management was seen as a basic requirement for digital twin application (*Mdn* = 4.00 [2.00, 5.00]). Decision support systems were both known about and unknown in companies with up to 9 employees (*Mdn* = 3.00 [2.00, 5.00]). Here, at least 50% of managers said they had either implemented decision support systems already or would do so within the next 3 years, and 75% of managers said they had either implemented decision support systems already or would do so within the next 5 years. Where The improvement of decision support systems through digital twin application was acknowledged (*Mdn* = 3.50 [2.40, 5.00]).

Across Company Size: Based on Tables 5.4 and 5.5, it can be concluded that there were significant differences depending on company size in **(3)**, **(6)** and **(8)**. However, digital twins were both known about and unknown (*Mdn* = 3.00 [1.20, 4.00]). Furthermore, at least 50% and 75% of managers said they had either implemented digital twins already or would do so within the next 5 years. Data quality management was known, with *Mdn* = 4.00 [2.00, 5.00], and at least 50% and 75% of managers said they had either implemented data quality management already or would do so within the next 3 years. Decision support systems were both known about and unknown (*Mdn* = 3.00 [2.00, 5.00]). Here, at least 50% and 75% of managers said they had either implemented decision support systems already or would do so within the next 3 years.

3. There were significant differences concerning the perception of the extent to which digital twins provided competitive opportunity **$H(3) = 16.74$, $p < .001$, $d = 0.83$** between 50 to 249 and 250 or more employees, up to 9 and 250 or more employees, and 10 to 49 and 250 or more employees.

Here, differences were found between the 250+ group and all other groups. By contrast, no statistically significant differences were found between the groups with fewer than 250 employees. The mean for the 250+ group was *Mdn* = 4.00 [3.00, 5.00], for 50–249 *Mdn* = 3.00 [2.60, 4.00], for 10–49 *Mdn* = 4.00 [3.00, 4.00], and up to 9 *Mdn* = 3.00 [2.00, 5.00]. The statistical significance of the difference between group 250+ and groups 50–249 and 1–9, can be attributed to the higher mean value in group 250+. However, regarding the statistically significant difference between the 250+ and 10–49 groups, this was more likely a result of the spread of values around the mean, as the mean was the same in both groups. Here, the spread between the 16th and 84th percentiles in the 250+ group indicated that 68% of the responses fell within the value range of 3 to 5, whereas in the 10–49 group they fell between 3 and 4. As a result, agreement in the group 10–49 was less positive than in the group 250+.

6. There were significant differences regarding data quality management being a basic requirement for a digital twin application: **$H(3) = 10.01$, $p = .018$, $d = 0.55$** between 10 to 49 and 250 or more employees, up to 9 and 250 or more employees, and 50 to 249 and 250 or more employees.

Differences concerning this were found between the 250+ group and all other groups. By contrast, no statistically significant differences were found between the groups with fewer than 250 employees. The mean for the 250+ group was

Mdn = 4.00 [3.00, 5.00], for 50–249 *Mdn* = 4.00 [3.00, 4.00], for 10–49 *Mdn* = 3.00 [2.56, 5.00] and for up to 9 *Mdn* = 4.00 [2.00, 5.00]. The statistical significance of the differences between the 250+ group and the other groups, can be attributed to the spread of values around the mean, as the mean was the same in 3 out of 4 groups. The scatter between the 16th and 84th percentiles of group 250+ indicates that 68% of the responses here were in the 3–5 value range. The spread in the 50–249 group here indicates a lower level of agreement and even disapproval. For the groups 10–49 and 1–9, on the other hand, there were only negative attitudes.

8. There were significant differences regarding the implementation level of decision support systems: **H(3) = 10.96, p = .012, d = 0.61** between 250 or more and 50 to 249 employees, 250 or more and 10 to 49 employees, and 250 or more -and up to 9 employees.

Differences here were found between the 250+ group and all other groups. In contrast, no statistically significant differences were found between the groups with fewer than 250 employees. The mean for the 250+ group was *Mdn* = 2.00 [1.00, 3.00], for 50–249 *Mdn* = 3.00 [1.00, 5.00], for 10–49 it *Mdn* = 3.00 [2.00, 4.00], and for up to 9 *Mdn* = 3.00 [1.40, 4.60]. The statistical significance of the differences between the 250+ group and the other groups, can be attributed to the lower median value, as the median was the same in 3 out of 4 groups and was lower only in the 250+ group. The spread between the 16th and 84th percentiles of group 250+ indicates that 68% of the responses were in the 1–3 value range. The dispersion in the other groups indicates a lower number of disapproving and a higher number of approving attitudes due to the partly higher 16th and 84th percentile values.

5.1.1.5 Results Industries

The results are shown in Table 5.6 with descriptive statistics (The corresponding data can be viewed in Appendix Table 8 in the electronic supplementary material).

Table 5.6 Hypothesis test summary within industries 1

	No.	Null Hypothesis	Sig.[a,b]	Decision
Automotive	3	Median of Digital Twin as competitive opportunity equals 3	<.001	Reject the null hypothesis
	4	Median of Awareness level of Data Quality Management equals 3	.002	Reject the null hypothesis
	5	Median of Implementation level of Data Quality Management equals 3	.017	Reject the null hypothesis
	6	Median of Data Quality Management basic requirement Digital Twin equals 3	<.001	Reject the null hypothesis
	7	Median of Awareness level of Decision Support Systems equals 3	.002	Reject the null hypothesis
	9	Median of Improvement Decision Support Systems by Digital Twin equals 3	.006	Reject the null hypothesis
Healthcare	3	Median of Digital Twin as competitive opportunity equals 3	.026	Reject the null hypothesis
	6	Median of Data Quality Management basic requirement Digital Twin equals 3	.001	Reject the null hypothesis
	8	Median of Implementation level of Decision Support Systems equals 3	.018	Reject the null hypothesis
	9	Median of Improvement Decision Support Systems by Digital Twin equals 3	.003	Reject the null hypothesis
Retail	1	Median of Awareness level of Digital Twin equals 3	.011	Reject the null hypothesis
	5	Median of Implementation level of Data Quality Management equals 3	.017	Reject the null hypothesis

(continued)

Table 5.6 (continued)

	No.	Null Hypothesis	Sig.^{a,b}	Decision
Transport	3	Median of Digital Twin as competitive opportunity equals 3	.026	Reject the null hypothesis
	4	Median of Awareness level of Data Quality Management equals 3	.005	Reject the null hypothesis
	5	Median of Implementation level of Data Quality Management equals 3	.022	Reject the null hypothesis
	6	Median of Data Quality Management basic requirement Digital Twin equals 3	.004	Reject the null hypothesis
	8	Median of Implementation level of Decision Support Systems equals 3	.036	Reject the null hypothesis
Computer	3	Median of Digital Twin as competitive opportunity equals 3	.033	Reject the null hypothesis
	4	Median of Awareness level of Data Quality Management equals 3	.022	Reject the null hypothesis
	6	Median of Data Quality Management basic requirement Digital Twin equals 3	.021	Reject the null hypothesis
	9	Median of Improvement Decision Support Systems by Digital Twin equals 3	.008	Reject the null hypothesis
Food	1	Median of Awareness level of Digital Twin equals 3	.038	Reject the null hypothesis
	3	Median of Digital Twin as competitive opportunity equals 3	.030	Reject the null hypothesis
	4	Median of Awareness level of Data Quality Management equals 3	.020	Reject the null hypothesis

(continued)

Table 5.6 (continued)

	No.	Null Hypothesis	Sig.^{a,b}	Decision
	6	Median of Data Quality Management basic requirement Digital Twin equals 3	.015	Reject the null hypothesis
	9	Median of Improvement Decision Support Systems by Digital Twin equals 3	.014	Reject the null hypothesis

a. The significance level is .05. b. Asymptotic significance is displayed.
Source: Own Table

The hypothesis test showed that the p-value was less than .05 and was thus assumed to be **significant** (The corresponding data can be viewed in Appendix Figure 7 in the electronic supplementary material):

1. **Automotive Industry:** Strong effects No. 3: d = 2.86, No. 4: d = 1.24, No. 5: d = 1.03, No. 6: d = 2.04, No. 7: d = 1.23 and No. 9: d = 1.23.
2. **Healthcare Industry:** Strong effects No. 3: d = 1.29, No. 6: d = 1.87, No. 8: d = 1.29 and No. 9: d = 1.87.
3. **Retail Industry:** Strong effects No. 1: d = 1.26 and No. 5: d = 1.76.
4. **Transport:** Strong effects No. 3: d = 1.57, No. 4: d = 1.85, No. 5: d = 1.41, No. 6: d = 2.05 and No. 8: d = 1.43.
5. **Computer Industry:** Strong effects No. 3: d = 1.38, No. 4: d = 1.41, No. 6: d = 1.57 and No. 9: d = 2.35.
6. **Construction Industry:** No significant results.
7. **Food Industry:** Strong effects No. 1: d = 1.40, No. 3: d = 1.51, No. 4: d = 1.70, No. 6: d = 1.97 and No. 9: d = 2.48.

Across Industries: To compare the differences **across** industries Table 5.7 shows that **1** must be examined further, with an asymptotic Sig. (2-sided test) of **.022**.

Table 5.7 Hypothesis test summary across industries 1

	Null Hypothesis	Sig.[a,b]	Decision
1	Distribution Awareness level of Digital Twin same across Industries	**.022**	Reject the null hypothesis
2	Distribution Implementation Level of Digital Twin same across Industries	.187	Retain the null hypothesis
3	Distribution Digital Twin as competitive opportunity same across Industries	.074	Retain the null hypothesis
4	Distribution Awareness level of Data Quality Management same across Industries	.685	Retain the null hypothesis
5	Distribution Implementation Level of Data Quality Management same across Industries	.540	Retain the null hypothesis
6	Distribution Data Quality Management basic requirement Digital Twin same across Industries	.414	Retain the null hypothesis
7	Distribution Company awareness of Decision Support System same across Industries	.588	Retain the null hypothesis
8	Distribution Implementation level of Decision Support System same across Industries	.146	Retain the null hypothesis
9	Distribution Improvement of Decision Support System by Digital Twin same across Industries	.533	Retain the null hypothesis

a. The significance level is .05. b. Asymptotic significance is displayed.
Source: Own Table

The central tendencies of the groups had a medium effect with d = 0.55. Table 5.8 shows which groups differed significantly.

The results indicate that there was a significant difference between the retail and transport industries with a medium effect of d = 0.75 **(No. 2)**, the retail and automotive industries d = 0.85 **(No. 3)**, with strong effects between the retail and construction industries d = 0.88 **(No. 4)**, the retail and computer industries d = 0.99 **(No. 5)** and the retail and food industries d = 1.11 **(No. 6)**.

Table 5.8 Pairwise comparisons of industries 1

No.	Sample 1-Sample 2	Test Statistic	Std. Error	Std. Test Statistic	Sig.	Adj. Sig.[a]
1	Retail industry-Healthcare industry	17.80	11.50	1.54	.122	1.000
2	Retail industry-Transport industry	−28.62	12.85	−2.22	**.026**	.546
3	Retail industry-Automotive industry	31.94	10.85	2.94	**.003**	.068
4	Retail industry-Construction industry	−33.25	13.34	−2.49	**.013**	.266
5	Retail industry-Computer industry	−36.45	13.08	−2.78	**.005**	.112
6	Retail industry-Food industry	−40.71	13.94	−2.91	**.004**	.074
7	Healthcare industry-Transport industry	−10.81	12.53	−.86	.388	1.000
8	Healthcare industry-Automotive industry	14.13	10.47	1.35	.177	1.000
9	Healthcare industry-Construction industry	−15.45	13.03	−1.18	.236	1.000
10	Healthcare industry-Computer industry	−18.64	12.77	−1.46	.144	1.000
11	Healthcare industry-Food industry	−22.90	13.65	−1.67	.093	1.000
12	Transport industry-Automotive industry	3.32	11.94	.27	.781	1.000

(continued)

Table 5.8 (continued)

No.	Sample 1-Sample 2	Test Statistic	Std. Error	Std. Test Statistic	Sig.	Adj. Sig.[a]
13	Transport industry-Construction industry	−4.63	14.24	−.32	.745	1.000
14	Transport industry-Computer industry	−7.83	14.00	−.55	.576	1.000
15	Transport industry-Food industry	−12.09	14.81	−.81	.414	1.000
16	Automotive industry-Construction industry	−1.31	12.46	−.10	.916	1.000
17	Automotive industry-Computer industry	−4.50	12.18	−.37	.711	1.000
18	Automotive industry-Food industry	−8.76	13.10	−.66	.504	1.000
19	Construction industry-Computer industry	−3.19	14.44	−.22	.825	1.000
20	Construction industry-Food industry	−7.45	15.23	−.48	.625	1.000
21	Computer industry-Food industry	−4.26	15.01	−.28	.777	1.000

Each row tests the null hypothesis that the Sample 1 and Sample 2 distributions are the same. Asymptotic significances (2-sided tests) are displayed. The significance level is .05.
a. Significance values have been adjusted by the Bonferroni correction for multiple tests.
Source: Own Table

5.1.1.6 Evaluation Industries

Automotive Industry: The digital twin was both known and unknown in the automotive industry with *Mdn* = 3.00 [2.00, 5.00]. Here, at least 50% of managers said they had either implemented digital twin already or would do so within the next 3 years, and 75% of managers said they had either implemented digital twin already or would do so within the next 5 years. Digital twins were seen as a significant competitive opportunity (No. 3: $z = 4.18$, $p < .001$, $d = 2.86$) with *Mdn* = 4.00 [3.00, 5.00]. For data quality management, there was a significantly high level of awareness (No. 4: $z = 3.07$, $p = .002$, $d = 1.24$) with *Mdn* = 4.00 [2.00, 5.00]. Here, at least 50% of managers said they had either implemented data quality management already or would do so within the next year, and 75% of managers said they had either implemented data quality management already or would do so within the next 3 years (No. 5: $z = -2.38$, $p = .017$, $d = 1.03$). Data quality management was seen as a significant and basic requirement for digital twins (No. 6: $z = 3.71$, $p < .001$, $d = 2.04$), with *Mdn* = 4.00 [3.00, 5.00]. Decision support systems had a significantly high level of awareness (No. 7: $z = 3.05$, $p = .002$, $d = 1.23$), with *Mdn* = 4.00 [2.00, 5.00]. Here, at least 50% and 75% of managers said they had either implemented decision support systems already or would do so within the next 3 years. The improvement to decision support systems through digital twin application was acknowledged (No. 9: $z = 2.77$, $p = .006$, $d = 1.23$) with *Mdn* = 4.00 [2.64, 5.00].

Healthcare Industry: The digital twin had a low awareness level in the healthcare industry with *Mdn* = 3.00 [1.00, 4.00]. Here, at least 50% of managers said they had either implemented digital twin already or would do so within the next 3 years, and 75% of managers said they had either implemented digital twin already or would do so within the next 5 years. Digital twins were seen as a significant competitive opportunity (No. 3: $z = 2.23$, $p = .026$, $d = 1.29$), with *Mdn* = 4.00 [2.88, 5.00]. Data quality management was known about in the healthcare industry with *Mdn* = 3.50 [2.32, 5.00]. Here, at least 50% and 75% of managers said they had either implemented data quality management already or would do so within the next 3 years. Data quality management was seen as a significant and basic requirement for digital twin technology (No. 6: $z = 3.20$, $p = .001$, $d = 1.87$), with *Mdn* = 4.00 [3.00, 5.00]. Decision support systems had a significantly high level of awareness, with *Mdn* = 4.00 [1.00, 5.00]. Here, at least 50% of managers said they had implemented decision support systems already, and 75% of managers said they had either implemented decision support systems already or would do so within the next 3 years (No. 8: $z = -2.36$, $p = .018$, $d = 1.29$). The improvement of decision support systems through digital twin application was acknowledged. (No. 9: $z = 2.98$, $p = .003$, $d = 1.87$) with *Mdn* = 4.00 [3.00, 5.00].

Retail Industry: The digital twin had the lowest awareness level in the retail industry (No. 1: $z = -2.56$, $p = .011$, $d = 1.26$), with *Mdn* = 2.00 [1.00, 3.16]. Here, at least 50% of managers said they had either implemented digital twin already or would do so within the next 5 years. Digital twins were seen as a competitive opportunity, with *Mdn* = 3.50 [2.00, 4.24]. Data quality management was both known and unknown in the retail industry, with *Mdn* = 3.00 [1.00,

5.00]. Here, at least 50% of managers said they had either implemented data quality management already or would do so within the next year, and 75% of managers said they had either implemented data quality management already or would do so within the next 3 years (No. 5: z = −2.38, p = .017, d = 1.76). Data quality management was seen as a basic requirement for digital twin application, with *Mdn* = 3.00 [2.00, 5.00]. Decision support systems were both known and unknown in the retail industry, with *Mdn* = 3.00 [1.00, 4.00]. Here, at least 50% and 75% of managers said they had either implemented decision support systems already or would do so within the next 3 years. The improvement of decision support systems through digital twin application was acknowledged, with *Mdn* = 4.00 [2.56, 5.00].

Transport Industry: Digital twins were both known and unknown in the transport industry with *Mdn* = 3.00 [2.00, 4.00]. Here, at least 50% and 75% of managers said they had either implemented digital twins already or would do so within the next 3 years. Digital twins were seen as a significant competitive opportunity (No. 3: z = 2.23, p = .026, d = 1.57), with *Mdn* = 4.00 [3.00, 5.00]. For data quality management, there was a significantly high level of awareness (No. 4: z = 2.80, p = .005, d = 1.85), with *Mdn* = 4.00 [3.00, 5.00]. At least 50% of managers said they had either implemented data quality management already or would do so within the next year, and 75% of managers said they had either implemented data quality management already or would do so within the next 3 years (No. 5: z = −2.30, p = .022, d = 1.41). Data quality management was seen as a significant basic requirement for digital twin application (No. 6: z = 2.86, p = .004, d = 2.05), with *Mdn* = 4.00 [3.00, 5.00]. Decision support systems were both known about and unknown in the transport industry with *Mdn* = 3.00 [2.00, 5.00]. Here, at least 50% of managers said they had either implemented decision support systems already or would do so within the next year, and 75% of managers said they had either implemented decision support systems already or would do so within the next 3 years (No. 8: z = −2.10, p = .036, d = 1.43). The improvement of decision support systems through digital twin application was acknowledged with *Mdn* = 4.00 [1.00, 4.76].

Computer Industry: Digital twins was known in the computer industry with *Mdn* = 3.50 [2.44, 4.00]. Here, at least 50% and 75% of managers said they had either implemented digital twin already or would do so within the next 3 years. Digital twins were seen as a significant competitive opportunity (No. 3: z = 2.12, p = .033, d = 1.38) with *Mdn* = 4.00 [2.40, 4.00]. For data quality management, there was a significantly high level of awareness (No. 4: z = 2.30, p = .022, d = 1.41) with *Mdn* = 4.00 [2.72, 5.00]. At least 50% of managers said they had either implemented data quality management already or would do so within the next 3 years, and 75% of managers said they had either implemented data quality management already or would do so within the next 5 years. Data quality management was seen as a significant basic requirement for digital twin applications (No. 6: z = 2.31, p = .021, d = 1.57) with *Mdn* = 4.00 [3.00, 4.00]. Decision support systems were known in the computer industry, with *Mdn* = 3.50 [2.00, 4.28]. At least 50% of managers said they had either implemented decision support systems already or would do so within the next 3 years, and 75% of managers said they had either implemented decision support systems already or would do so within the next 5 years. The improvement of decision support systems through digital twin application was acknowledged as significant (No. 9: z = 2.64, p = .008, d = 2.35) with *Mdn* = 4.00 [3.00, 4.92].

Construction Industry: Digital twins were both known and unknown in the construction industry, with *Mdn* = 3.00 [1.56, 5.00]. At least 50% of managers said they had either implemented digital twin already or would do so within the next 3 years. Digital twins were seen as competitive opportunity, with *Mdn* = 3.00 [2.00, 4.00]. For data quality management, there was a high level of awareness, with *Mdn* = 4.00 [1.56, 4.44]. At least 50% and 75% of managers said they had either implemented data quality management already or would do so within the next 3 years. Data quality management was seen as a basic requirement for the digital twin application, with *Mdn* = 4.00 [2.84, 4.08]. Decision support systems were both known and unknown in the construction industry, with *Mdn* = 3.00 [2.00, 4.44]. At least 50% of managers said they had either implemented decision support systems already or would do so within the next 3 years, and 75% of managers said they had either implemented decision support systems already or would do so within the next 5 years. The improvement of decision support systems through digital twin was acknowledged, with *Mdn* = 3.00 [2.52, 4.00].

Food Industry: Digital twins were known in the food industry (No. 1: z = 2.07, p = .038, d = 1.40) with *Mdn* = 3.00 [3.00, 4.76]. At least 50% and 75% of managers said they had either implemented digital twin already or would do so within the next 3 years. Digital twins were seen as a significant competitive opportunity (No. 3: z = 2.17, p = .030, d = 1.51) with *Mdn* = 4.00 [3.00, 5.00]. There was a significantly high level of awareness of data quality management (No. 4: z = 2.33, p = .020, d = 1.70) with *Mdn* = 4.00 [3.00, 5.00]. At least 50% and 75% of managers said they had either implemented data quality management already or would do so within the next 3 years, and data quality management was seen as a significant basic requirement for the digital twin (No. 6: z = 2.43, p = .015, d = 1.97) with *Mdn* = 4.00 [3.00, 5.00]. Decision support systems had a significantly high level of awareness, with *Mdn* = 4.00 [2.00, 5.00]. At least 50% of managers said they had either implemented decision support systems already or would do so within the next 3 years, and 75% of managers said they had either implemented decision support systems already or would do so within the next 5 years. The improvement of decision support systems through digital twin applications was significantly acknowledged (No. 9: z = 2.46, p = .014, d = 2.48) with *Mdn* = 4.00 [3.00, 5.00].

Across Industries: Based Table 5.7 and the Table 5.8 it can be concluded that there were significant differences between the industries in **(1)**. However, the digital twin was both known and unknown, with *Mdn* = 3.00 [1.20, 4.00]. Furthermore, at least 50% of managers said they had either implemented digital twin already or would do so within the next 3 years, and 75% of managers said they had either implemented digital twin already or would do so within the next 5 years. Data quality management was known with *Mdn* = 4.00 [2.00, 5.00]. Here, at least 50% and 75% of managers said they had either implemented data quality management already or would do so within the next 5 years. Decision support systems were both known and unknown, with *Mdn* = 3.00 [2.00, 5.00], and at least 50% and 75% of managers said they had either implemented decision support systems already or would do so within the next 3 years.

1. There were significant differences in the level of digital twin awareness between the retail industry and all the other industries with the exception of the healthcare industry: **H(6) = 14.79, p = .022, d = 0.55**

By contrast, no statistically significant difference was found between the other industry combinations. The mean values were, *Mdn* = 2.00 [1.00, 3.16] for the retail industry, *Mdn* = 3.00 [2.00, 5.00] for the automative industry, *Mdn* = 3.00 [2.00, 4.00] for the transport industry, *Mdn* = 3.50 [2.44, 4.00] for the computer industry, *Mdn* = 3.00 [1.56, 5.00] for the construction industry, *Mdn* = 3.00 [3.00, 4.76] for the food industry, and *Mdn* = 3.00 [1.00, 4.00] for the healthcare industry. The statistical significance of the differences between the industries can be attributed to the lower median value of the retail industry, since the median was 3 in all the other industries. The dispersion between the 16th and 84th percentiles of the retail industry indicates that 68% of the responses here fell within the value range of 1.00 to 3.16 and thus within the range of low agreement. The scatter in the other industries indicates a tendency towards higher agreement and lower disagreement due to the partly higher percentile values.

5.1.2 The Digital Twin-Driven Decision-Making Model

The **implementation level** in Figure 5.1 is the most important part for a DTD-DMM, showing that at least 50% of managers said they had either implemented digital twins (N = 104) already or would do so within the next 3 years, and 75% of managers said they had either implemented digital twins already or would do so within the next 5 years. At least 50% and 75% of managers said they had either implemented data quality management (N = 117) and decision support systems (N = 107) or would do so within the next 3 years. Making it worthwhile to investigate further in the **main study**.

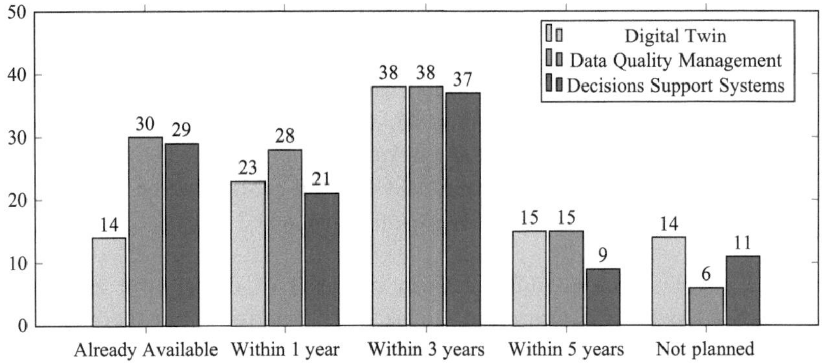

Figure 5.1 Preliminary study implementation level. (Source: Own Figure)

5.1.2.1 Results for the Model

Table 5.9 shows that the p-value was less than .05 and was thus assumed to be significant with strong effects No. 1: d = 1.54, No. 2: d = 1.45 and No. 3: d = 1.14, as shown in Figure 5.2.

1. H_2: *Data quality management is a basic requirement for a digital twin*—Data quality management basic requirement digital twin: $z = 6.59$, $p < .001$, $d = 1.54$
2. H_3: *The implementation of the digital twin is a competitive opportunity for a company*—Digital twin as competitive opportunity: $z = 5.98$, $p < .001$, $d = 1.45$
3. H_4: *Decision support systems are improved by digital twins*—Improvement of decision support systems by digital twin: $z = 5.11$, $p < .001$, $d = 1.14$

Table 5.9 Preliminary study hypothesis test for H_2, H_3, H_4

	Null Hypothesis	Sig.[a,b]	N	Std. Test Statistic	Decision
1	Median of Data Quality Management basic requirement Digital Twin equals 3.	<.001	117	6.59	Reject the null hypothesis.
2	Median of Digital Twin as competitive opportunity equals 3.	<.001	104	5.98	Reject the null hypothesis.
3	Median of Improvement of Decision Support System by Digital Twin equals 3.	<.001	107	5.11	Reject the null hypothesis.

a. The significance level is .05. b. Asymptotic significance is displayed.
Source: Own Table

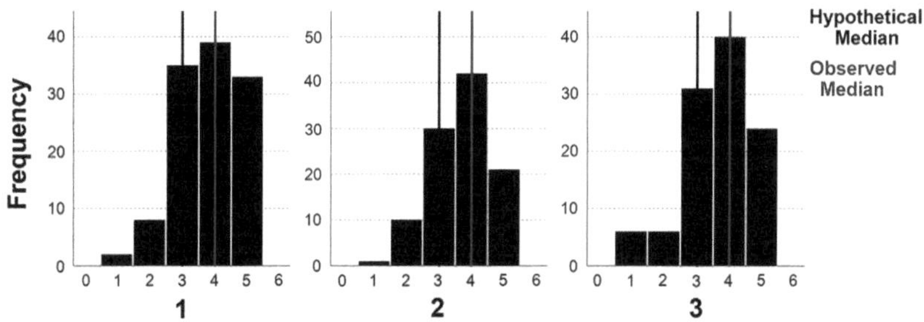

Figure 5.2 Preliminary study wilcoxon signed rank test for H_2, H_3, H_4. (Source: Own Figure, modified and derived from IBM SPSS Statistics 28)

5.1.2.2 Evaluation for the Model

For the DTDDMM, this meant that data quality management was a basic requirement for the digital twin (H_2) with *Mdn* = 4.00 [3.00, 5.00], that digital twins were a competitive opportunity (H_3) with *Mdn* = 4.00 [3.00, 5.00], and that decision support systems were improved through digital twin application (H_4) with *Mdn* = 4.00 [3.00, 5.00]. Table 5.10 summarizes all *Mdn*s, which made further investigation in the **main study** worthwhile.

Table 5.10 Preliminary study summary of medians (N = 144)

No.	∑	I	II	III	IV	V	VI	VII	VIII	IX	X	XI	XII	XIII	XIV
1	**3.00**	3.00	3.00	3.00	3.00	3.00	3.00	3.00	3.00	3.00	2.00	3.00	3.50	3.00	3.00
2	**3.00**	3.00	3.00	3.00	3.00	3.00	3.00	3.50	2.00	3.00	4.00	3.00	3.00	3.00	3.00
3	**4.00**	4.00	4.00	4.00	4.00	3.00	4.00	3.00	4.00	4.00	3.50	4.00	4.00	3.00	4.00
4	**4.00**	4.00	4.00	4.00	4.00	4.00	3.00	3.00	4.00	3.50	3.00	4.00	4.00	4.00	4.00
5	**3.00**	3.00	3.00	2.00	2.00	3.00	3.00	3.00	2.00	3.00	2.00	2.00	3.00	3.00	3.00
6	**4.00**	4.00	4.00	4.00	4.00	4.00	3.00	4.00	4.00	4.00	3.00	4.00	4.00	4.00	4.00
7	**3.00**	3.00	3.00	4.00	3.00	4.00	4.00	3.00	4.00	4.00	3.00	3.00	3.50	3.00	4.00
8	**3.00**	3.00	2.00	3.00	2.00	3.00	3.00	3.00	3.00	1.00	3.00	2.00	3.00	3.00	3.00
9	**4.00**	4.00	4.00	4.00	4.00	4.00	3.50	3.50	4.00	4.00	4.00	4.00	4.00	3.00	4.00

Source: Own Table[1]

[1] Legend: ∑ per group, I. Upper Management, II. Middle Management, III. Lower Management, IV. 250 or more employees, V. 50-249 employees, VI. 10-50 employees, VII. Up to 9 employees, VIII. Automotive, IX. Healthcare, X. Retail, XI. Transport, XII. Computer, XIII. Construction, XIV. Food

5.2 Data Analysis—Main Study

The objectives of the main study were as follows:

1. To evaluate differences within and across **(1) management level**, **(2) company size** and **(3) industry** for H_1.
2. To evaluate the **results** for H_2, H_3, H_4 and the **implementation level**.
3. To evaluate **requirements** and **benefits** of the DTDDMM.
4. To evaluate the **improvement** of decision **certainty**, **efficiency** and **quality** for H_5.
5. To evaluate the theoretical **DTDDMM** based on H_1, H_2, H_3, H_4, H_5 for strategic positioning and operational effectiveness.

5.2.1 Strategic Positioning

5.2.1.1 Results Management Levels

The results are shown in Table 5.11 with descriptive statistics (The corresponding data can be viewed in Appendix Table 9 in the electronic supplementary material).

The hypothesis test shows that the p-value was less than 05, and was thus assumed to be **significant** (The corresponding data can be viewed in Appendix Figure 8 in the electronic supplementary material):

- **Upper management:** Strong effects No. 1: d = 1.26, No. 2: d = 1.37, No. 3: d = 1.96, No. 4: d = 2.23, No. 5: d = 2.11, No. 6: d = 2.18, No. 7: d = 1.34, No. 8: d = 1.74, No. 9: d = 1.70, No. 10: d = 1.75, No. 11: d = 1.53, No. 12: d = 2.02.
- **Middle management:** Strong effects No. 1: d = 1.17, No. 2: d = 1.21, No. 3: d = 1.77, No. 4: d = 1.45, No. 5: d = 1.77, No. 6: d = 1.56, No. 7: d = 1.34, No. 8: d = 1.51, No. 9: d = 1.25, No. 10: d = 1.47, No. 11: d = 1.31, No. 12: d = 1.16.
- **Lower management:** Strong effects No. 1: d = 0.90, No. 2: d = 1.20, No. 3: d = 2.20, No. 4: d = 1.96, No. 5: d = 1.10, No. 6: d = 1.99, No. 7: d = 1.10, No. 8: d = 1.60, No. 9: d = 1.35, No. 10: d = 2.39, No. 11: d = 2.29, No. 12: d = 1.65.

Table 5.11 Hypothesis test summary within management levels 2

	No.	Null Hypothesis	Sig.[a,b]	Decision
Upper management level	1	Median of Implementation Level Digital Twin equals 3	.004	Reject the null hypothesis
	2	Median of Digital Twin as competitive opportunity equals 3	.002	Reject the null hypothesis
	3	Median of Implementation Level Data Quality Management equals 3	<.001	Reject the null hypothesis
	4	Median of Data Quality Management basic requirement Digital Twin equals 3	<.001	Reject the null hypothesis
	5	Median of Implementation Level Decision Support Systems equals 3	<.001	Reject the null hypothesis
	6	Median of Improvement Decision Support Systems by Digital Twin equals 3	<.001	Reject the null hypothesis
	7	Median of Usefulness DTDDMM equals 3	.003	Reject the null hypothesis
	8	Median of Definition of Process Digital Twin equals 3	<.001	Reject the null hypothesis
	9	Median of Corporate Data Quality Management for Model equals 3	<.001	Reject the null hypothesis
	10	Median of Process Digital Twin and Data Quality equals 3	<.001	Reject the null hypothesis
	11	Median of Decision Support Systems and Data Quality equals 3	.001	Reject the null hypothesis
	12	Median of Full Implementation of three topics for Model equals 3	<.001	Reject the null hypothesis
Middle management level	1	Median of Implementation Level Digital Twin equals 3	<.001	Reject the null hypothesis
	2	Median of Digital Twin as competitive opportunity equals 3	<.001	Reject the null hypothesis
	3	Median of Implementation Level Data Quality Management equals 3	<.001	Reject the null hypothesis
	4	Median of Data Quality Management basic requirement Digital Twin equals 3	<.001	Reject the null hypothesis
	5	Median of Implementation Level Decision Support Systems equals 3	<.001	Reject the null hypothesis

(continued)

Table 5.11 (continued)

	No.	Null Hypothesis	Sig.^{a,b}	Decision
	6	Median of Improvement Decision Support Systems by Digital Twin equals 3	<.001	Reject the null hypothesis
	7	Median of Usefulness DTDDMM equals 3	<.001	Reject the null hypothesis
	8	Median of Definition of Process Digital Twin equals 3	<.001	Reject the null hypothesis
	9	Median of Corporate Data Quality Management for Model equals 3	<.001	Reject the null hypothesis
	10	Median of Process Digital Twin and Data Quality equals 3	<.001	Reject the null hypothesis
	11	Median of Decision Support Systems and Data Quality equals 3	<.001	Reject the null hypothesis
	12	Median of Full Implementation of three topics for Model equals 3	<.001	Reject the null hypothesis
Lower management level	1	Median of Implementation Level Digital Twin equals 3	.022	Reject the null hypothesis
	2	Median of Digital Twin as competitive opportunity equals 3	.004	Reject the null hypothesis
	3	Median of Implementation Level Data Quality Management equals 3	<.001	Reject the null hypothesis
	4	Median of Data Quality Management basic requirement Digital Twin equals 3	<.001	Reject the null hypothesis
	5	Median of Implementation Level Decision Support Systems equals 3	.009	Reject the null hypothesis
	6	Median of Improvement Decision Support Systems by Digital Twin equals 3	<.001	Reject the null hypothesis
	7	Median of Usefulness DTDDMM equals 3	.008	Reject the null hypothesis
	8	Median of Definition of Process Digital Twin equals 3	<.001	Reject the null hypothesis
	9	Median of Corporate Data Quality Management for Model equals 3	.002	Reject the null hypothesis
	10	Median of Process Digital Twin and Data Quality equals 3	<.001	Reject the null hypothesis

(continued)

Table 5.11 (continued)

	No.	Null Hypothesis	Sig.^{a,b}	Decision
	11	Median of Decision Support Systems and Data Quality equals 3	<.001	Reject the null hypothesis
	12	Median of Full Implementation of three topics for Model equals 3	<.001	Reject the null hypothesis

a. The significance level is .05. b. Asymptotic significance is displayed.
Source: Own Table

Across management levels: Table 5.12 shows that **no rejected null hypotheses** with p- value less than .05 were assumed to be **significant**.

Table 5.12 Hypothesis test summary across management levels 2

	Null Hypothesis	Sig.^{a,b}	Decision
1	Distribution Implementation Level Digital Twin is the same across Management Level	.808	Retain the null hypothesis
2	Distribution Digital Twin as competitive opportunity is the same across Management Level	.530	Retain the null hypothesis
3	Distribution Implementation Level Data Quality Management is the same across Management Level	.608	Retain the null hypothesis
4	Distribution Data Quality Management basic requirement Digital Twin is the same across Management Level	.239	Retain the null hypothesis
5	Distribution Implementation Level Decision Support Systems is the same across Management Level	.072	Retain the null hypothesis
6	Distribution Improvement Decision Support Systems by Digital Twin is the same across Management Level	.397	Retain the null hypothesis
7	Distribution Usefulness DTDDMM is the same across Management Level	.843	Retain the null hypothesis
8	Distribution Definition of Process Digital Twin is the same across Management Level	.739	Retain the null hypothesis

(continued)

Table 5.12 (continued)

	Null Hypothesis	Sig.[a,b]	Decision
9	Distribution Corporate Data Quality Management for Model is the same across Management Level	.926	Retain the null hypothesis
10	Distribution Process Digital Twin and Data Quality is the same across Management Level	.304	Retain the null hypothesis
11	Distribution Decision Support Systems and Data Quality is the same across Management Level	.110	Retain the null hypothesis
12	Distribution Full Implementation of three topics for Model is the same across Management Level	.228	Retain the null hypothesis

a. The significance level is .05. b. Asymptotic significance is displayed.
Source: Own Table

5.2.1.2 Evaluation Management Levels

Upper Management Level: At least 50% of managers said they had either implemented digital twins already or would do so within the next year, and 75% of managers said they had either implemented digital twins already or would do so within the next 3 years (No. 1 $z = -2.87$, $p = .004$, $d = 1.26$). Digital twins were seen as a significant competitive opportunity (No. 2 $z = 3.05$, $p = .002$, $d = 1.37$) with *Mdn* = 4.00 [3.00, 4.20]. At least 50% and 75% of managers said they had either implemented data quality management already or would do so within the next year (No. 3 $z = -3.77$, $p < .001$, $d = 1.96$), and data quality management was seen as a significant basic requirement for digital twin application (No. 4 $z = 4.01$, $p < .001$, $d = 2.23$) with *Mdn* = 5.00 [3.00, 5.00]. At least 50% of managers said they had implemented decision support systems already, and 75% of managers said they had either implemented decision support systems already or would do so within the next year (No. 5 $z = -3.91$, $p < .001$, $d = 2.11$). The improvement of decision support systems through digital twin application was significantly acknowledged (No. 6 $z = 3.97$, $p < .001$, $d = 2.18$) with *Mdn* = 4.00 [3.00, 5.00]. Regarding the DTDDMM, its usefulness was significantly acknowledged (No. 7 $z = 3.00$, $p = .003$, $d = 1.34$) with *Mdn* = 4.00 [3.00, 5.00], and the definition of a process digital twin was significantly understood (No. 8 $z = 3.53$, $p < .001$, $d = 1.74$) with *Mdn* = 4.00 [3.00, 5.00]. Regarding data quality for the model, the managers believed that corporate data quality management must be fully implemented (No. 9 $z = 3.48$, $p < .001$, $d = 1.70$) with *Mdn* = 4.00 [3.00, 5.00], and that there was a significant relationship between process digital twin and data quality (No. 10 $z = 3.54$, $p < .001$, $d = 1.75$) with *Mdn* = 4.00 [2.80, 5.00], and decision support systems and data quality (No. 11 $z = 3.27$, $p = .001$, $d = 1.53$) with *Mdn* = 4.00 [2.80, 5.00]. The full implementation of digital twin, data quality management and decision support systems was seen as a significant and basic requirement for the model (No. 12 $z = 3.83$, $p < .001$, $d = 2.02$) with *Mdn* = 4.00 [2.80, 5.00].

Middle Management: At least 50% of managers said they had either implemented digital twins already or would do so within the next year, and 75% of managers said they had either implemented digital twins already or would do so within the next 3 years (No. 1 $z = -3.97$, $p < .001$, $d = 1.17$). Digital twins were seen as significant competitive opportunity (No. 2 $z = 4.08$, $p < .001$, $d = 1.21$) with *Mdn* = 3.50 [3.00, 4.00]. Here, at least 50% of managers said they had either implemented data quality management already or would do so within the next year, and 75% of managers said they had either implemented data quality management already or would do so within the next 3 years (No. 3 $z = -5.21$, $p < .001$, $d = 1.77$), and data quality management was seen as a significant and basic requirement for the digital twin (No. 4 $z = 4.62$, $p < .001$, $d = 1.45$) with *Mdn* = 4.00 [3.00, 5.00]. At least 50% of managers said they had implemented decision support systems already or would do so within the next year, and 75% of managers said they had either implemented decision support systems already or would do so within the next 3 years (No. 5 $z = -5.22$, $p < .001$, $d = 1.77$). The improvement of decision support systems through the application of digital twins was significantly acknowledged (No. 6 $z = 4.84$, $p < .001$, $d = 1.56$) with *Mdn* = 4.00 [3.00, 5.00]. With regard to the DTDDMM, its usefulness was significantly acknowledged (No. 7 $z = 4.38$, $p < .001$, $d = 1.34$) with *Mdn* = 4.00 [3.00, 4.00], and the definition of a process digital twin was significantly understood (No. 8 $z = 4.74$, $p < .001$, $d = 1.51$) with *Mdn* = 4.00 [3.00, 4.00]. Regarding data quality for the model, the managers believed that corporate data quality management must be significantly implemented (No. 9 $z = 4.18$, $p < .001$, $d = 1.25$) with *Mdn* = 4.00 [2.00, 5.00], and that there was a significant relationship between process digital twin and data quality (No. 10 $z = 4.67$, $p < .001$, $d = 1.47$) with *Mdn* = 4.00 [3.00, 5.00] and decision support systems and data quality (No. 11 $z = 4.31$, $p < .001$, $d = 1.31$) with *Mdn* = 4.00 [3.00, 5.00]. The full implementation of digital twin, data quality management and decision support systems was seen as a basic requirement for the model (No. 12 $z = 3.96$, $p < .001$, $d = 1.16$) with *Mdn* = 4.00 [3.00, 4.92].

Lower Management Level: At least 50% of managers said they had either implemented digital twins already or would do so within the next year, and 75% of managers said they had either implemented digital twins already or would do so within the next 3 years (No. 1 $z = -2.29$, $p = .022$, $d = 0.90$). Digital twins were seen as a significant competitive opportunity (No. 2 $z = 2.86$, $p = .004$, $d = 1.20$) with *Mdn* = 4.00 [3.00, 4.00]. At least 50% of managers said they had either implemented data quality management already or would do so within the next year, and 75% of managers said they had either implemented data quality management already or would do so within the next 3 years (No. 3 $z = -4.11$, $p < .001$, $d = 2.20$), and data quality management was seen as a significant and basic requirement for digital twins (No. 4 $z = 3.90$, $p < .001$, $d = 1.96$) with *Mdn* = 4.00 [3.00, 5.00]. At least 50% of managers said they had implemented decision support systems already or would do so within the next year, and 75% of managers said they had either implemented decision support systems already or would do so within the next 3 years (No. 5 $z = -2.60$, $p = .009$, $d = 1.10$). The improvement of decision support systems through digital twin application was acknowledged as significant (No. 6 $z = 3.93$, $p < .001$, $d = 1.99$) with *Mdn* = 4.00 [3.00, 4.88]. With regard to the DTDDMM, its usefulness was significantly acknowledged (No. 7 $z = 2.66$, $p = .008$, $d = 1.10$) with Mdn = 4.00 [3.00, 5.00], and the definition of process digital twin was significantly understood (No. 8 $z = 3.47$, $p < .001$, $d = 1.60$) with *Mdn* = 4.00 [3.00, 4.00]. Regarding data quality for the model, the managers believed that corporate data quality management had to be significantly implemented (No. 9 $z = 3.12$, $p = .002$, $d = 1.35$) with *Mdn* = 4.00 [2.12, 5.00], and that there was a significant relationship between process digital twin and data quality (No. 10 $z = 4.27$, $p < .001$, $d = 2.39$) with *Mdn* = 4.00 [3.00, 5.00], decision support systems and data quality (No. 11 $z = 4.19$, $p < .001$, $d = 2.29$) with *Mdn* = 4.00 [3.00, 5.00]. The full implementation of digital twin, data quality management and decision support systems was seen as a significant and basic requirement for the model (No. 12 $z = 3.54$, $p < .001$, $d = 1.65$) with *Mdn* = 4.00 [3.00, 4.88].

Across Management Levels: Thus, it can be concluded that there were no significant differences. At least 50% of managers said they had either implemented digital twins already or would do so within the next year, and 75% of managers said they had either implemented digital twins already or would do so within the next 3 years. Digital twins were seen as a competitive opportunity with *Mdn* = 4.00 [3.00, 4.00]. At least 50% of managers said they had either implemented data quality management already or would do so within the next year, and 75% of managers said they had either implemented data quality management already or would do so within the next 3 years, and data quality management was seen as a basic requirement for digital twins *Mdn* = 4.00 [3.00, 5.00]. At least 50% of managers said they had implemented decision support systems already or would do so within the next year, and 75% of managers said they had either implemented decision support systems already or would do so within the next 3 years. The improvement of decision support systems through digital twins was acknowledged with *Mdn* = 4.00 [3.00, 5.00]. With regard to the DTDDMM, its usefulness was also acknowledged with *Mdn* = 4.00 [3.00, 5.00] and the definition of process digital twin was understood with *Mdn* = 4.00 [3.00, 5.00]. Regarding data quality for the model, the managers believed that corporate data quality management had to be implemented with *Mdn* = 4.00 [3.00, 5.00], and that there was a relationship between process digital twin and data quality with *Mdn* = 4.00 [3.00, 5.00], and decision support systems and data quality with *Mdn* = 4.00 [3.00, 5.00]. The full implementation of digital twin, data quality management and decision support systems was seen as a basic requirement for the model with *Mdn* = 4.00 [3.00, 5.00].

5.2.1.3 Results Company Size

The results are shown in Table 5.13 with descriptive statistics (The corresponding data can be viewed in Appendix Table 10 in the electronic supplementary material).

The hypothesis test shows that the p-value was less than .05 and was thus assumed to be **significant** (The corresponding data can be viewed in Appendix Figure 9 in the electronic supplementary material):

- **250 or more employees**: Strong effects No. 1: d = 1.27, No. 2: d = 2.10, No. 3: d = 2.38, No. 4: d = 2.51, No. 5: d = 1.81, No. 6: d = 2.04, No. 7: d = 1.79, No. 8: d = 2.07, No. 9: d = 2.76, No. 10: d = 2.23, No. 11: d = 2.44, No. 12: d = 2.05.
- **50 to 249 employees**: Strong effects No. 3: d = 1.63, No. 4: d = 1.77, No. 5: d = 1.54, No. 6: d = 1.85, No. 7: d = 0.99, No. 8: d = 1.80, No. 9: d = 1.00, No. 10: d = 1.37, No. 11: d = 1.10, No. 12: d = 1.53 and medium effect No. 2: d = 0.79.
- **10 to 49 employees**: Strong effects No. 1: d = 2.54, No. 2: d = 0.92, No. 3: d = 2.65, No. 5: d = 2.62, No. 6: d = 1.45, No. 7: d = 1.24, No. 9: d = 0.91, No. 10: d = 1.60, No. 11: d = 1.38.
- **Up to 9 employees**: Strong effects No. 6: d = 1.37 and No. 10: d = 1.25.

Table 5.13 Hypothesis test Summary within company size 2

	No.	Null Hypothesis	Sig.[a,b]	Decision
250 or more employees	1	Median of Implementation Level Digital Twin equals 3	<.001	Reject the null hypothesis
	2	Median of Digital Twin as competitive opportunity equals 3	<.001	Reject the null hypothesis
	3	Median of Implementation Level Data Quality Management equals 3	<.001	Reject the null hypothesis
	4	Median of Data Quality Management basic requirement Digital Twin equals 3	<.001	Reject the null hypothesis
	5	Median of Implementation Level Decision Support Systems equals 3	<.001	Reject the null hypothesis
	6	Median of Improvement Decision Support Systems by Digital Twin equals 3	<.001	Reject the null hypothesis
	7	Median of Usefulness DTDDMM equals 3	<.001	Reject the null hypothesis
	8	Median of Definition of Process Digital Twin equals 3	<.001	Reject the null hypothesis
	9	Median of Corporate Data Quality Management for Model equals 3	<.001	Reject the null hypothesis
	10	Median of Process Digital Twin and Data Quality equals 3	<.001	Reject the null hypothesis
	11	Median of Decision Support Systems and Data Quality equals 3	<.001	Reject the null hypothesis

(continued)

Table 5.13 (continued)

	No.	Null Hypothesis	Sig.[a,b]	Decision
	12	Median of Full Implementation of three topics for Model equals 3	<.001	Reject the null hypothesis
50 to 249 employees	2	Median of Digital Twin as competitive opportunity equals 3	0.034	Reject the null hypothesis
	3	Median of Implementation Level Data Quality Management equals 3	<.001	Reject the null hypothesis
	4	Median of Data Quality Management basic requirement Digital Twin equals 3	<.001	Reject the null hypothesis
	5	Median of Implementation Level Decision Support Systems equals 3	<.001	Reject the null hypothesis
	6	Median of Improvement Decision Support Systems by Digital Twin equals 3	<.001	Reject the null hypothesis
	7	Median of Usefulness DTDDMM equals 3	0.010	Reject the null hypothesis
	8	Median of Definition of Process Digital Twin equals 3	<.001	Reject the null hypothesis
	9	Median of Corporate Data Quality Management for Model equals 3	0.010	Reject the null hypothesis
	10	Median of Process Digital Twin and Data Quality equals 3	0.001	Reject the null hypothesis
	11	Median of Decision Support Systems and Data Quality equals 3	0.006	Reject the null hypothesis

(continued)

Table 5.13 (continued)

	No.	Null Hypothesis	Sig.^{a,b}	Decision
	12	Median of Full Implementation of three topics for Model equals 3	<.001	Reject the null hypothesis
10 to 49 employees	1	Median of Implementation Level Digital Twin equals 3	<.001	Reject the null hypothesis
	2	Median of Digital Twin as competitive opportunity equals 3	0.046	Reject the null hypothesis
	3	Median of Implementation Level Data Quality Management equals 3	<.001	Reject the null hypothesis
	5	Median of Implementation Level Decision Support Systems equals 3	<.001	Reject the null hypothesis
	6	Median of Improvement Decision Support Systems by Digital Twin equals 3	0.005	Reject the null hypothesis
	7	Median of Usefulness DTDDMM equals 3	0.012	Reject the null hypothesis
	9	Median of Corporate Data Quality Management for Model equals 3	0.048	Reject the null hypothesis
	10	Median of Process Digital Twin and Data Quality equals 3	0.003	Reject the null hypothesis
	11	Median of Decision Support Systems and Data Quality equals 3	0.006	Reject the null hypothesis

(continued)

Table 5.13 (continued)

	No.	Null Hypothesis	Sig.^{a,b}	Decision
Up to 9 employees	6	Median of Improvement Decision Support Systems by Digital Twin equals 3	0.035	Reject the null hypothesis
	10	Median of Process Digital Twin and Data Quality equals 3	0.048	Reject the null hypothesis

a. The significance level is .05. b. Asymptotic significance is displayed.
Source: Own Table

Across Company Size: To compare the differences across the company size, Table 5.14 shows that **2**, **4**, **6**, **7**, **9** and **11** had to be examined further, with an asymptotic Sig. (2-sided test) of **.012**, **.003**, **.023**, **.018**, **.002** and **.024**.

The central tendencies of the groups had medium effects with d = 0.57, d = 0.66, d = 0.51, d = 0.54, d = 0.70 and d = 0.52. Table 5.15 shows which groups significantly differed.

The results indicate that in **2** there was a significant difference with a medium effect between **No. 3** (up to 9 and 250 or more employees of d = 0.56), **No. 5** (10 to 49 and 250 or more employees d = 0.57) and **No. 6** (50 to 249 and 250 or more employees d = 0.60). The results indicate that in **4** there was a significant difference with a medium effect in **No. 2** (10 to 49 and 50 to 249 employees d = 0.60) and a strong effect in **No. 3** (10 to 49 and 250 or more employees d = 0.94). The results indicate that in **6** there was a significant difference with a medium effect between **No. 3** (up to 9 and 250 or more employees d = 0.57) and **No. 5** (10 to 49 and 250 or more employees d = 0.64). The results indicate in **7** there was a significant difference with a medium effect between **No. 3** (up to 9 and 250 or more employees d = 0.66) and **No. 5** (50 to 249 and 250 or more employees d = 0.54). The results indicate that in **9** there was a significant difference with a strong effect in **No. 3** (up to 9 and 250 or more employees d = 0.86), a medium effect in **No. 5** (10 to 49 and 250 or more employees d = 0.68) and a small effect in **No. 6** (50 to 249 and 250 or more employees d = 0.48). The results indicate that in **11** there was a significant difference with a medium effect between **No. 3** (10 to 49 and 250 or more employees d = 0.62) and **No. 5** (50 to 249 and 250 or more employees d = 0.55).

Table 5.14 Hypothesis test summary across company size 2

	Null Hypothesis	Sig.^{a,b}	Decision
1	Distribution Implementation Level Digital Twin is the same across Company Size	.269	Retain the null hypothesis
2	Distribution Digital Twin as competitive opportunity is the same across Company Size	**.012**	Reject the null hypothesis
3	Distribution Implementation Level Data Quality Management is the same across Company Size	.255	Retain the null hypothesis
4	Distribution Data Quality Management basic requirement Digital Twin is the same across Company Size	**.003**	Reject the null hypothesis
5	Distribution Implementation Level Decision Support Systems is the same across Company Size	.645	Retain the null hypothesis
6	Distribution Improvement Decision Support Systems by Digital Twin is the same across Company Size	**.023**	Reject the null hypothesis
7	Distribution Usefulness DTDDMM is the same across Company Size	**.018**	Reject the null hypothesis
8	Distribution Definition of Process Digital Twin is the same across Company Size	.060	Retain the null hypothesis
9	Distribution Corporate Data Quality Management for Model is the same across Company Size	**.002**	Reject the null hypothesis
10	Distribution Process Digital Twin and Data Quality is the same across Company Size	.054	Retain the null hypothesis
11	Distribution Decision Support Systems and Data Quality is the same across Company Size	**.024**	Reject the null hypothesis
12	Distribution Full Implementation of three topics for Model is the same across Company Size	.106	Retain the null hypothesis

a. The significance level is .05. b. Asymptotic significance is displayed.
Source: Own Table

Table 5.15 Pairwise comparisons of company size 2

	No.	Sample 1–Sample 2	Test Statistic	Std. Error	Std. Test Statistic	Sig.	Adj. Sig.[a]
2	1	Up to 9 employees-10 to 49 employees	2.120	11.228	.189	.850	1.000
	2	Up to 9 employees-50 to 249 employees	2.235	10.565	.212	.832	1.000
	3	Up to 9 employees-250 or more employees	21.692	9.973	2.175	**.030**	.178
	4	10 to 49 employees-50 to 249 employees	−.115	8.997	−.013	.990	1.000
	5	10 to 49 employees-250 or more employees	−19.573	8.295	−2.360	**.018**	.110
	6	50 to 249 employees-250 or more employees	19.457	7.372	2.639	**.008**	.050
4	1	10 to 49 employees-Up to 9 employees	−16.707	11.444	−1.460	.144	.866
	2	10 to 49 employees-50 to 249 employees	−19.578	9.170	−2.135	**.033**	.197
	3	10 to 49 employees-250 or more employees	−31.072	8.454	−3.675	**<.001**	.001
	4	Up to 9 employees-50 to 249 employees	2.871	10.768	.267	.790	1.000
	5	Up to 9 employees-250 or more employees	14.365	10.165	1.413	.158	.946
	6	50 to 249 employees-250 or more employees	11.494	7.514	1.530	.126	.757

(continued)

Table 5.15 (continued)

	No.	Sample 1–Sample 2	Test Statistic	Std. Error	Std. Test Statistic	Sig.	Adj. Sig.[a]
6	1	Up to 9 employees-10 to 49 employees	.253	11.283	.022	.982	1.000
	2	Up to 9 employees-50 to 249 employees	15.005	10.617	1.413	.158	.945
	3	Up to 9 employees-250 or more employees	22.122	10.022	2.207	**.027**	.164
	4	10 to 49 employees-50 to 249 employees	−14.752	9.041	−1.632	.103	.617
	5	10 to 49 employees-250 or more employees	−21.869	8.335	−2.624	**.009**	.052
	6	50 to 249 employees-250 or more employees	7.117	7.408	.961	.337	1.000
7	1	Up to 9 employees-50 to 249 employees	7.604	10.668	.713	.476	1.000
	2	Up to 9 employees-10 to 49 employees	9.829	11.338	.867	.386	1.000
	3	Up to 9 employees-250 or more employees	25.516	10.071	2.534	**.011**	.068
	4	50 to 249 employees-10 to 49 employees	2.225	9.085	.245	.807	1.000
	5	50 to 249 employees-250 or more employees	17.913	7.444	2.406	**.016**	.097
	6	10 to 49 employees-250 or more employees	−15.687	8.376	−1.873	.061	.366

(continued)

Table 5.15 (continued)

	No.	Sample 1–Sample 2	Test Statistic	Std. Error	Std. Test Statistic	Sig.	Adj. Sig.[a]
9	1	Up to 9 employees-10 to 49 employees	8.879	11.019	.806	.420	1.000
	2	Up to 9 employees-50 to 249 employees	15.812	10.369	1.525	.127	.764
	3	Up to 9 employees-250 or more employees	31.453	9.788	3.213	**.001**	.008
	4	10 to 49 employees-50 to 249 employees	−6.933	8.830	−.785	.432	1.000
	5	10 to 49 employees-250 or more employees	−22.574	8.141	−2.773	**.006**	.033
	6	50 to 249 employees-250 or more employees	15.642	7.235	2.162	**.031**	.184
11	1	10 to 49 employees-50 to 249 employees	−3.257	9.081	−.359	.720	1.000
	2	10 to 49 employees-Up to 9 employees	−7.526	11.333	−.664	.507	1.000
	3	10 to 49 employees-250 or more employees	−21.357	8.372	−2.551	**.011**	.064
	4	50 to 249 employees-Up to 9 employees	−4.269	10.664	−.400	.689	1.000
	5	50 to 249 employees-250 or more employees	18.101	7.441	2.433	**.015**	.090
	6	Up to 9 employees-250 or more employees	13.831	10.067	1.374	.169	1.000

Each row tests the null hypothesis that the Sample 1 and Sample 2 distributions are the same. Asymptotic significances (2-sided tests) are displayed. The significance level is .05.
a. Significance values have been adjusted by the Bonferroni correction for multiple tests.
Source: Own Table

5.2.1.4 Evaluation Company Size

250 or more employees: At least 50% of managers said they had either implemented digital twins already or would do so within the next year, and 75% of managers said they had either implemented digital twins already or would do so within the next 3 years (No. 1 $z = -3.86$, $p < .001$, $d = 1.27$). Digital twins were seen as a significant competitive opportunity (No. 2 $z = 5.22$, $p < .001$, $d = 2.10$) with *Mdn* = 4.00 [3.00, 5.00]. At least 50% of managers said they had either implemented data quality management already or would do so within the next year, and 75% of managers said they had either implemented data quality management already or would do so within the next 3 years (No. 3 $z = -5.52$, $p < .001$, $d = 2.38$), and data quality management was seen as a significant and basic requirement for digital twins (No. 4 $z = 5.64$, $p < .001$, $d = 2.51$) with *Mdn* = 4.00 [3.00, 5.00]. At least 50% of managers said they had implemented decision support systems already or would do so within the next year, and 75% of managers said they had either implemented decision support systems already or would do so within the next 3 years (No. 5 $z = -4.84$, $p < .001$, $d = 1.81$). The improvement of decision support systems through digital twins was seen as significant (No. 6 $z = 5.15$, $p < .001$, $d = 2.04$) with *Mdn* = 4.00 [3.00, 5.00]. With regard to the DTDDMM, its usefulness was acknowledged as significant (No. 7 $z = 4.81$, $p < .001$, $d = 1.79$) with *Mdn* = 4.00 [3.00, 5.00] and the definition of a process digital twin was significantly understood (No. 8 $z = 5.19$, $p < .001$, $d = 2.07$) with *Mdn* = 4.00 [3.00, 5.00]. Regarding data quality for the model, the managers believed that corporate data quality management had to be significantly implemented (No. 9 $z = 5.84$, $p < .001$, $d = 2.76$) with *Mdn* = 4.00 [4.00, 5.00], and that there was a significant relationship between process digital twin and data quality (No. 10 $z = 5.37$, $p < .001$, $d = 2.23$) with *Mdn* = 4.00 [4.00, 5.00], and decision support systems and data quality (No. 11 $z = 5.58$, $p < .001$, $d = 2.44$) with *Mdn* = 4.00 [4.00, 5.00]. The full implementation of digital twin, data quality management and decision support systems was seen as a significant and basic requirement for the model (No. 12 $z = 5.16$, $p < .001$, $d = 2.05$) with *Mdn* = 4.00 [3.00, 5.00].

50 to 249 employees: Here, At least 50% and 75% of managers said they had either implemented digital twins already or would do so within the next 3 years. Digital twins were seen as a significant competitive opportunity (No. 2 $z = 2.12$, $p = .034$, $d = 0.79$) with *Mdn* = 3.00 [2.00, 4.00]. At least 50% of managers said they had either implemented data quality management already or would do so within the next year, and 75% of managers said they had either implemented data quality management already or would do so within the next 3 years (No. 3 $z = -3.63$, $p < .001$, $d = 1.63$), and data quality management was seen as a significant and basic requirement for digital twins (No. 4 z = 3.81, p < .001, d = 1.77) with *Mdn* = 4.00 [3.00, 5.00]. At least 50% of managers said they had implemented decision support systems already or would do so within the next year, and 75% of managers said they had either implemented decision support systems already or would do so within the next 3 years (No. 5 z = −3.51, p < .001, d = 1.54). The improvement of decision support systems through digital twins was acknowledged as significant (No. 6 z = 3.90, p < .001, d = 1.85) with *Mdn* = 4.00 [3.00, 5.00]. With regard to a DTDDMM, its usefulness was seen as significant (No. 7 z = 2.56, p = .010, d = 0.99) with *Mdn* = 3.00 [3.00, 4.00] and the definition of a process digital twin was significantly understood (No. 8 z = 3.84, p < .001, d = 1.80) with *Mdn* = 4.00 [3.00, 5.00]. Regarding data quality for the model, the managers believed that corporate data quality management had to be significantly implemented (No. 9 z = 2.57, p = .010, d = 1.00) with *Mdn* = 4.00 [2.00, 5.00], and that there was a significant relationship between a process digital twin and data quality (No. 10 z = 3.25, p = .001, d = 1.37) with *Mdn* = 4.00 [2.00, 5.00], and decision support systems and data quality (No. 11 z = 2.77, p = .006, d = 1.10) with Mdn = 4.00 [2.00, 5.00]. The full implementation of digital twin, data quality management and decision support systems was seen as a significant and basic requirement for the model (No. 12 z = 3.49, p < .001, d = 1.53) with *Mdn* = 4.00 [3.00, 5.00].

10 to 49 employees: At least 50% of managers said they had either implemented digital twins already or would do so within the next year, and 75% of managers said they had either implemented digital twins already or would do so within the next 3 years (No. 1 z = −3.77, p < .001, d = 2.54). Digital twins were seen as a significant competitive opportunity (No. 2 z = 2.00, p = .046, d = 0.92) with *Mdn* = 3.00 [2.84, 4.00]. Here, at least 50% of managers said they had either implemented data quality management already or would do so within the next year, and 75% of managers said they had either implemented data quality management already or would do so within the next 3 years (No. 3 z = −3.83, p < .001, d = 2.65), and data quality management was seen as a basic requirement for digital twins with *Mdn* = 3.00 [2.00, 4.00]. At least 50% and 75% of managers said they had either implemented decision support systems already (No. 5 z = −3.81, p < .001, d = 2.62). The improvement to decision support systems through digital twins was seen as significant (No. 6 z = 2.81, p = .005, d = 1.45) with *Mdn* = 3.00 [3.00, 4.00]. With regard to the DTDDMM, its usefulness was seen as significant (No. 7 z = 2.52, p = .012, d = 1.24) with *Mdn* = 3.00 [3.00, 4.00], and the definition of a process digital twin was understood with *Mdn* = 3.00 [2.00, 4.16]. Regarding data quality for the model, the managers believed that corporate data quality management had to be significantly implemented (No. 9 $z = 1.98$, $p = .048$, $d = 0.91$) with *Mdn* = 4.00 [2.00, 4.16], and that there was a significant relationship between a process digital twin and data quality (No. 10 $z = 2.99$, $p = .003$, $d = 1.60$) with *Mdn* = 4.00 [3.00, 5.00], and decision support systems and data quality (No. 11 $z = 2.73$, $p = .006$, $d = 1.38$) with *Mdn* = 4.00 [3.00, 5.00]. The full implementation of digital twin, data quality management and decision support systems was seen as a basic requirement for the model with *Mdn* = 4.00 [2.00, 4.00].

Up to 9 employees: Here, at least 50% of managers said they had either implemented digital twins already or would do so within the next year, 75% of managers said they had either implemented digital twins already or would do so within the next 3 years. Digital twins were seen as competitive opportunity, with *Mdn* = 3.00 [2.00, 4.00]. At least 50% of managers said they had either implemented data quality management already or would do so within the next year, and 75% of managers said they had either implemented data quality management already or would do so within the next 3 years. Data quality management was seen as a basic requirement for a digital twin, with *Mdn* = 4.00 [2.40, 5.00]. At least 50% of managers said they had implemented decision support systems already or would do so within the next year, and 75% of managers said they had either implemented decision support systems already or would do within the next 3 years. The improvement of decision support systems through digital twin implementation was seen as significant (No. 6 $z = 2.11$, $p = .035$, $d = 1.37$) with *Mdn* = 3.50 [3.00, 4.00]. With regard to a DTDDMM, its usefulness was acknowledged with *Mdn* = 3.00 [2.00, 4.00], and the definition of process digital twin was understood with *Mdn* = 3.50 [2.40, 4.60]. Regarding data quality for the model, most managers believed that corporate data quality management should be implemented, with *Mdn* = 3.00 [1.40, 4.60], and that there was a significant relationship between process digital twin and data quality (No. 10 $z = 1.98$, $p = .048$, $d = 1.25$) with *Mdn* = 4.00 [2.00, 5.00], and decision support systems and data quality with *Mdn* = 4.00 [1.80, 5.00]. The full implementation of digital twin, data quality management and decision support systems was seen as a basic requirement for the model, with *Mdn* = 4.00 [2.40, 5.00].

Across Company Size: Based on Table 5.14 and Table 5.15 it can be concluded that there were significant differences depending on company size with **(2)**, **(4)**, **(6)**, **(7)**, **(9)** and **(11)**. However, at least 50% of managers said they had either implemented digital twin already or would do so within the next year, and 75% of managers said they had either implemented digital twin already or would do so within the next 3 years. At least 50% of managers said they had either implemented data quality management already or would do so within the next year, and 75% of managers said they had either implemented data quality management already or would do so within the next 3 years. Furthermore, at least 50% of managers said they had implemented decision support systems already or would do so within the next year, and 75% of managers said they had either implemented decision support systems already or would do so within the next 3 years. With regard to the DTDDMM, the definition of process digital twin was understood, with *Mdn* = 4.00 [3.00, 5.00]. Regarding data quality for the model, the relationship between process digital twin and data quality with *Mdn* = 4.00 [3.00, 5.00] was acknowledged. The full implementation of digital twin, data quality management and decision support systems was seen as a significant and basic requirement for the model, with *Mdn* = 4.00 [3.00, 5.00].

2. There were significant differences regarding the extent to which managers viewed digital twin technology as a competitive opportunity: **H(3) = 10.86, p = .012, d = 0.57** between up to 9 and 250 or more employees, 10 to 49 and 250 or more employees, and 50 to 249 and 250 or more employees.

Differences here were found between the 250+ group and all other groups. By contrast, no statistically significant differences were found between the groups with fewer than 250 employees. The mean value for the group 250+ was *Mdn* = 4.00 [3.00, 5.00], for 50–249 *Mdn* = 3.00 [2.00, 4.00], for 10–49 *Mdn* = 3.00 [2.84, 4.00], and for up to 9 *Mdn* = 3.00 [2.00, 4.00]. The statistical significance of the differences between the 250+ group and the groups with a lower number of employees could be attributed to the higher mean value in the 250+ group. The spread between the 16th and 84th percentiles of the 250+ group indicated that 68% of the responses here laid in the value range of 3 to 5.

4. There were also differences regarding the importance of data quality management being a basic requirement for digital twins: **H(3) = 13.78, p = .003, d = 0.66** between 10 to 49 and 50 to 249 employees, and 10 to 49 and 250 or more employees.

These differences were found between the 250+ group and all other groups. By contrast, no statistically significant differences were found between the groups with fewer than 250 employees. The mean value for the group 250+ was *Mdn* = 4.00 [3.00, 5.00], for 50–249 *Mdn* = 3.00 [2.00, 4.00], for 10–49 *Mdn* = 3.00 [2.84, 4.00], and for up to 9 *Mdn* = 3.00 [2.00, 4.00]. The statistical significance of the differences between the 10–49 group and the 50–249, and 250+ groups can be attributed to the lower mean score of the 10–49 group. The spread between the 16th and 84th percentiles of group 10–49 indicates that 68% of the responses here, were in the 2–4 value range. The scatter in the other groups, due to the higher percentile values, indicates a higher approval, or a lower number of disapproving attitudes.

6. There were significant differences regarding the extent to which digital twins improved decision support systems: **H(3) = 9.50, p = .023, d = 0.52** between up to 9 and 250 or more employees, and 10 to 49 and 250 or more employees.

Here, differences were found between the group 250+ and both groups up to 9 and 10–49. The mean value for the group 250+ was *Mdn* = 4.00 [3.00, 5.00], for 50–249 *Mdn* = 4.00 [3.00, 5.00], for 10–49 *Mdn* = 3.00 [3.00, 4.00], and for up to 9 *Mdn* = 3.50 [3.00, 4.00]. The statistical significance of the differences between the group 250+ and both groups 1–9 and 10–49, can be attributed to the lower mean. The scatter between the 16th and 84th percentiles of group 250+ indicates that 68% of the responses here were in the value range of 3–5. The spread in the 1–9 and 10–49 groups indicates a smaller number of high agreements due to the lower 84th percentile values.

7. There was a significant difference in opinion regarding the usefulness of a DTDDMM: **H(3) = 10.12, p = .018, d = 0.54** between up to 9 and 250 or more employees and 50–249 and 250 or more employees.

These differences were found between group 250+ and both groups 50–249 and up to 9. The mean for group 250+ was *Mdn* = 4.00 [3.00, 5.00], for 50–249 *Mdn* = 3.00 [3.00, 4.00], for up to 9 *Mdn* = 3.00 [2.00, 4.00], and for 10–49 *Mdn* = 3.00 [3.00, 4.00]. The statistical significance of the differences between the 250+ group and both the 50–249 and 1–9 groups, can be attributed to the lower mean. Although the difference between the 250+ group and the 10–49 group was not statistically significant, it can still be assumed on the basis of the descriptive statistics that there was also a difference with this group. This assumption is derived from the fact that the 16th, 25th, 50th, 75th, and 84th percentile values for group 10–49 were identical to those for group 50–249, to which again a statistically significant difference was found. However, the two groups differed in group size, which was 33 respondents for group 50–249 and only 23 respondents for group 10–49. The p-value for the difference between group 250+ and 10–49 also confirms this assumption due to its proximity to the significance level, p = .061. The spread between the 16th and 84th percentiles of group 250+ indicates that 68% of the responses here were in the 3–5 value range. The spread in the

1–9, 10–49, and 50–249 groups indicates a smaller number of high agreements due to the lower 84th percentile values.

9. There were significant differences regarding the importance of implementing corporate data quality management for the model: **H(3) = 14.95, p = .002, d = 0.70** between up to 9 and 250 or more employees, 10 to 49 and 250 or more employees, and 50 to 249 and 250 or more employees.

These differences were found between the 250+ group to all other groups respectively. By contrast, no statistically significant differences were found between the groups with fewer than 250 employees. The mean for the 250+ group was *Mdn* = 4.00 [4.00, 5.00], for 50–249 *Mdn* = 4.00 [2.00, 5.00], for 10–49 *Mdn* = 4.00 [2.00, 4.16], and for up to 9 *Mdn* = 3.50 [1.40, 4.00].

The statistical significance of the differences between the 250+ group and the groups with a lower number of employees can be attributed to a higher number of negative attitudes and a partly decreasing number of positive attitudes in the groups with a lower number of employees. The spread between the 16th and 84th percentiles of the 250+ group indicates that 68% of the answers here laid in the value range from 4–5. This shows a particularly homogeneous picture in the responses, which is significantly more heterogeneous in the groups with a lower number of employees.

11. There were significant differences of opinion regarding the extent of the dependency of decision support systems on data quality: **H(3) = 9.40, p = .24, d = 0.52** between 10 to 49 and 250 or more employees, and 50 to 249 and 250 or more employees.

These differences were found between group 250+ and both groups 10–49 and 50–249. The mean for group 250+ was *Mdn* = 4.00 [4.00, 5.00], for 50–249 *Mdn* = 4.00 [2.00, 5.00], for 10–49 *Mdn* = 4.00 [3.00, 5.00], and for up to 9 Mdn = 4.00 [1.80, 5.00]. The statistical significance of the differences between the 250+ group and both the 10–49 and 50–249 groups, can be attributed to the increase in negative attitudes. The scatter between the 16th and 84th percentiles of the 250+ group indicates that 68% of the responses here were in the 4–5 value range. The spread in the 10–49 and 50–249 groups indicates a higher number of negative attitudes due to the lower 16th percentile values. This trend was also found in group 1–9. The fact that the difference with this group was not statistically significant, despite a fairly similar distribution, can also be attributed to a significantly lower group population. This was 33 respondents in group 50–249, 23 respondents in group 10–49 and only 14 respondents in group 1–9.

5.2.1.5 Results Industries

The results are shown in Table 5.16 with descriptive statistics (The corresponding data can be viewed in Appendix Table 11 in the electronic supplementary material).

The Hypothesis Test shows that the p-value is less than .05 and was thus assumed to be **significant** (The corresponding data can be viewed in Appendix Figure 10 in the electronic supplementary material):

1. **Automotive Industry:** Strong effects No. 1: d = 1.11, No. 2: d = 1.42, No. 3: d = 1.86, No. 4: d = 2.14, No. 5: d = 2.58, No. 6: d = 2.10, No. 7: d = 1.63, No. 8: d = 1.79, No. 9: d = 2.53, No. 10: d = 2.04, No. 11: d = 1.99, No. 12: d = 2.65.
2. **Retail Industry:** Strong effects No. 1: d = 1.34, No. 2: d = 0.95, No. 3: d = 1.31, No. 4: d = 1.67, No. 5: d = 1.21, No. 6: d = 1.49, No. 7: d = 1.25, No. 8: d = 1.68, No. 10: d = 1.67, No. 11: d = 1.18, No. 12: d = 2.19.
3. **Computer Industry:** Strong effects No. 2: d = 1.40, No. 3: d = 2.19, No. 4: d = 2.32, No. 6: d = 1.71, No. 7: d = 1.27, No. 8: d = 1.31, No. 9: d = 1.64, No. 10: d = 2.26, No. 11: d = 1.97, No. 12: d = 1.32.
4. **Healthcare Industry:** Strong effects No. 1: d = 1.66, No. 2: d = 1.16, No. 3: d = 2.59, No. 4: d = 1.33, No. 5: d = 2.31, No. 6: d = 2.04, No. 7: d = 1.20, No. 8: d = 1.40, No. 9: d = 1.20, No. 10: d = 1.43, No. 11: d = 1.24.
5. **Construction Industry:** Strong effects No. 2: d = 1.82, No. 3: d = 2.42, No. 5: d = 2.12, No. 6: d = 2.14, No. 8: d = 1.82, No. 9: d = 1.79, No. 10: d = 1.88, No. 11: d = 2.05.
6. **Transport Industry:** Strong effects No. 3: d = 2.27, No. 4: d = 1.68, No. 5: d = 2.27, No. 6: d = 1.88, No. 8: d = 1.97, No. 10: d = 1.97.
7. **Food Industry:** Strong effects No. 1: d = 2.02, No. 2: d = 2.48, No. 3: d = 2.40, No. 4: d = 1.87, No. 6: d = 2.40, No. 7: d = 2.48, No. 8: d = 1.73, No. 9: d = 2.14, No. 11: d = 1.89, No. 12: d = 2.18.

Table 5.16 Hypothesis test summary within industries 2

	No.	Null Hypothesis	Sig.^{a,b}	Decision
Automotive	1	Median of Implementation level Digital Twin equals 3	0.017	Reject the null hypothesis
	2	Median of Digital Twin as competitive opportunity 3	0.005	Reject the null hypothesis
	3	Median of Implementation level of Data Quality Management equals 3	<.001	Reject the null hypothesis
	4	Median of Data Quality Management basic requirement Digital Twin equals 3	<.001	Reject the null hypothesis
	5	Median of Implementation level of Decision Support Systems equals 3	<.001	Reject the null hypothesis
	6	Median of Improvement Decision Support Systems by Digital Twin equals 3	<.001	Reject the null hypothesis
	7	Median of Usefulness DTDDMM equals 3	0.002	Reject the null hypothesis
	8	Median of Definition Process Digital Twin equals 3	<.001	Reject the null hypothesis
	9	Median of Corporate Data Quality Management and Model equals 3	<.001	Reject the null hypothesis
	10	Median of Process Digital Twin and Data Quality equals 3	<.001	Reject the null hypothesis
	11	Median of Decision Support Systems and Data Quality equals 3	<.001	Reject the null hypothesis
	12	Median of Full Implementation of three topics for Model equals 3	<.001	Reject the null hypothesis
Retail	1	Median of Implementation level Digital Twin equals 3	0.006	Reject the null hypothesis

(continued)

Table 5.16 (continued)

	No.	Null Hypothesis	Sig.[a,b]	Decision
	2	Median of Digital Twin as competitive opportunity 3	0.038	Reject the null hypothesis
	3	Median of Implementation level of Data Quality Management equals 3	0.007	Reject the null hypothesis
	4	Median of Data Quality Management basic requirement Digital Twin equals 3	0.002	Reject the null hypothesis
	5	Median of Implementation level of Decision Support Systems equals 3	0.011	Reject the null hypothesis
	6	Median of Improvement Decision Support Systems by Digital Twin equals 3	0.003	Reject the null hypothesis
	7	Median of Usefulness DTDDMM equals 3	0.009	Reject the null hypothesis
	8	Median of Definition Process Digital Twin equals 3	0.002	Reject the null hypothesis
	10	Median of Process Digital Twin and Data Quality equals 3	0.002	Reject the null hypothesis
	11	Median of Decision Support Systems and Data Quality equals 3	0.013	Reject the null hypothesis
	12	Median of Full Implementation of three topics for Model equals 3	<.001	Reject the null hypothesis
Computer	2	Median of Digital Twin as competitive opportunity 3	0.011	Reject the null hypothesis
	3	Median of Implementation level of Data Quality Management equals 3	<.001	Reject the null hypothesis

(continued)

Table 5.16 (continued)

	No.	Null Hypothesis	Sig.^{a,b}	Decision
	4	Median of Data Quality Management basic requirement Digital Twin equals 3	<.001	Reject the null hypothesis
	6	Median of Improvement Decision Support Systems by Digital Twin equals 3	0.004	Reject the null hypothesis
	7	Median of Usefulness DTDDMM equals 3	0.016	Reject the null hypothesis
	8	Median of Definition Process Digital Twin equals 3	0.014	Reject the null hypothesis
	9	Median of Corporate Data Quality Management and Model equals 3	0.005	Reject the null hypothesis
	10	Median of Process Digital Twin and Data Quality equals 3	<.001	Reject the null hypothesis
	11	Median of Decision Support Systems and Data Quality equals 3	0.002	Reject the null hypothesis
	12	Median of Full Implementation of three topics for Model equals 3	0.014	Reject the null hypothesis
Healthcare	1	Median of Implementation level Digital Twin equals 3	0.004	Reject the null hypothesis
	2	Median of Digital Twin as competitive opportunity 3	0.025	Reject the null hypothesis
	3	Median of Implementation level of Data Quality Management equals 3	<.001	Reject the null hypothesis
	4	Median of Data Quality Management basic requirement Digital Twin equals 3	0.013	Reject the null hypothesis

(continued)

Table 5.16 (continued)

	No.	Null Hypothesis	Sig.^{a,b}	Decision
	5	Median of Implementation level of Decision Support Systems equals 3	<.001	Reject the null hypothesis
	6	Median of Improvement Decision Support Systems by Digital Twin equals 3	<.001	Reject the null hypothesis
	7	Median of Usefulness DTDDMM equals 3	0.022	Reject the null hypothesis
	8	Median of Definition Process Digital Twin equals 3	0.011	Reject the null hypothesis
	9	Median of Corporate Data Quality Management and Model equals 3	0.023	Reject the null hypothesis
	10	Median of Process Digital Twin and Data Quality equals 3	0.010	Reject the null hypothesis
	11	Median of Decision Support Systems and Data Quality equals 3	0.019	Reject the null hypothesis
Construction	2	Median of Digital Twin as competitive opportunity 3	0.020	Reject the null hypothesis
	3	Median of Implementation level of Data Quality Management equals 3	0.008	Reject the null hypothesis
	5	Median of Implementation level of Decision Support Systems equals 3	0.012	Reject the null hypothesis
	6	Median of Improvement Decision Support Systems by Digital Twin equals 3	0.011	Reject the null hypothesis
	8	Median of Definition Process Digital Twin equals 3	0.020	Reject the null hypothesis

(continued)

Table 5.16 (continued)

	No.	Null Hypothesis	Sig.^{a,b}	Decision
	9	Median of Corporate Data Quality Management and Model equals 3	0.021	Reject the null hypothesis
	10	Median of Process Digital Twin and Data Quality equals 3	0.018	Reject the null hypothesis
	11	Median of Decision Support Systems and Data Quality equals 3	0.013	Reject the null hypothesis
Transport	3	Median of Implementation level of Data Quality Management equals 3	0.009	Reject the null hypothesis
	4	Median of Data Quality Management basic requirement Digital Twin equals 3	0.026	Reject the null hypothesis
	5	Median of Implementation level of Decision Support Systems equals 3	0.009	Reject the null hypothesis
	6	Median of Improvement Decision Support Systems by Digital Twin equals 3	0.018	Reject the null hypothesis
	8	Median of Definition Process Digital Twin equals 3	0.015	Reject the null hypothesis
	10	Median of Process Digital Twin and Data Quality equals 3	0.015	Reject the null hypothesis
Food	1	Median of Implementation level Digital Twin equals 3	0.024	Reject the null hypothesis
	2	Median of Digital Twin as competitive opportunity 3	0.014	Reject the null hypothesis
	3	Median of Implementation level of Data Quality Management equals 3	0.015	Reject the null hypothesis

(continued)

Table 5.16 (continued)

	No.	Null Hypothesis	Sig.^{a,b}	Decision
	4	Median of Data Quality Management basic requirement Digital Twin equals 3	0.030	Reject the null hypothesis
	6	Median of Improvement Decision Support Systems by Digital Twin equals 3	0.015	Reject the null hypothesis
	7	Median of Usefulness DTDDMM equals 3	0.014	Reject the null hypothesis
	8	Median of Definition Process Digital Twin equals 3	0.038	Reject the null hypothesis
	9	Median of Corporate Data Quality Management and Model equals 3	0.021	Reject the null hypothesis
	11	Median of Decision Support Systems and Data Quality equals 3	0.030	Reject the null hypothesis
	12	Median of Full Implementation of three topics for Model equals 3	0.020	Reject the null hypothesis

a. The significance level is .05. b. Asymptotic significance is displayed.
Source: Own Table

Across Industries: Table 5.17 shows **no rejected null hypotheses** with no p-value less than .05 and was therefore not assumed to be **significant**.

Table 5.17 Hypothesis test summary across industries 2

	Null Hypothesis	Sig.^{a,b}	Decision
1	Distribution Implementation level Digital Twin same across Industries	.963	Retain the null hypothesis.
2	Distribution Digital Twin as competitive opportunity same across Industries	.740	Retain the null hypothesis.
3	Distribution Implementation level of Data Quality Management same across Industries	.110	Retain the null hypothesis.
4	Distribution Data Quality Management basic requirement Digital Twin same across Industries	.592	Retain the null hypothesis.
5	Distribution Implementation level of Decision Support Systems same across Industries	.421	Retain the null hypothesis.
6	Distribution Improvement Decision Support Systems by Digital Twin same across Industries	.764	Retain the null hypothesis.
7	Distribution Usefulness DTDDMM same across Industries	.741	Retain the null hypothesis.
8	Distribution Definition Process Digital Twin same across Industries	.936	Retain the null hypothesis.
9	Distribution Corporate Data Quality Management and Model same across Industries	.546	Retain the null hypothesis.
10	Distribution Process Digital Twin and Data Quality same across Industries	.935	Retain the null hypothesis.
11	Distribution Decision Support Systems and Data Quality same across Industries	.392	Retain the null hypothesis.
12	Distribution Full Implementation of three topics for Model same across Industries	.111	Retain the null hypothesis.

a. The significance level is .05. b. Asymptotic significance is displayed.
Source: Own Table

5.2.1.6 Evaluation Industries

Automotive Industry: At least 50% and 75% of managers said they had either implemented digital twins already or would do so within the next 3 years (No. 1 $z = -2.38$, $p = .017$, $d = 1.11$). Digital twins were seen as a significant competitive opportunity (No. 2 $z = 2.83$, $p = .005$, $d = 1.42$) with $Mdn = 4.00$ [3.00,

4.00]. At least 50% of managers said they had either implemented data quality management already or would do so within the next year and 75% of managers said they had either implemented data quality management already or would do so within the next 3 years (No. 3 $z = -3.34$, $p < .001$, $d = 1.86$), and data quality management was seen as a significant and basic requirement for the digital twin (No. 4 $z = 3.58$, $p < .001$, $d = 2.14$) with *Mdn* = 4.00 [3.00, 5.00]. At least 50% of managers said they had implemented decision support systems already or would do so within the next year and 75% of managers said they had either implemented decision support systems already or would do so within the next 3 years (No. 5 $z = -3.87$, $p < .001$, $d = 2.58$). The improvement of decision support systems improvement through digital twin implementation was also significantly acknowledged (No. 6 $z = 3.52$, $p = .001$, $d = 2.10$) with *Mdn* = 4.00 [3.00, 4.00]. With regard to a DTDDMM, its usefulness was also significantly acknowledged (No. 7 $z = 3.10$, $p = .002$, $d = 1.63$) with *Mdn* = 4.00 [3.00, 4.00] and the definition of process digital twin was generally understood (No. 8 $z = 3.27$, $p = .001$, $d = 1.79$) with *Mdn* = 4.00 [3.00, 4.00]. Regarding the importance of data quality for the model, most managers believed that corporate data quality management must be significantly implemented (No. 9 $z = 3.84$, $p < .001$, $d = 2.53$) with *Mdn* = 4.00 [3.00, 5.00], and that there was a significant relationship between both a process digital twin and data quality (No. 10 $z = 3.50$, $p < .001$, $d = 2.04$) with *Mdn* = 4.00 [3.00, 5.00], and decision support systems and data quality (No. 11 $z = 3.46$, $p < .001$, $d = 1.99$) with *Mdn* = 4.50 [3.00, 5.00]. The full implementation of digital twin, data quality management and decision support systems was seen as a significant and basic requirement for the model (No. 12 $z = 3.91$, $p < .001$, $d = 2.65$) with *Mdn* = 4.00 [3.00, 5.00].

Retail Industry: At least 50% of managers said they had either implemented digital twin already or would do so within the next year, and 75% of managers said they had either implemented digital twin already or would do so within the next 3 years (No. 1 $z = -2.72$, $p = .006$, $d = 1.34$). Digital twins were seen as a significant competitive opportunity (No. 2 $z = 2.10$, $p = .038$, $d = 0.95$) with *Mdn* = 4.00 [2.00, 5.00]. At least 50% of managers said they had either implemented data quality management already or would do so within the next year, and 75% of managers said they had either implemented data quality management already or would do so within the next 3 years (No. 3 $z = -2.69$, $p = .007$, $d = 1.31$). Data quality management was seen as a significant and basic requirement for digital twins (No. 4 $z = 3.14$, $p = .002$, $d = 1.67$) with *Mdn* = 4.00 [3.00, 5.00]. At least 50% of managers said they had implemented decision support systems already or would do so within the next year, and 75% of managers said they had either implemented decision support systems already or would do so within the next 3 years (No. 5 $z = -2.54$, $p = .011$, $d = 1.21$). The improvement of decision support systems through digital twin implementation was significantly acknowledged (No. 6 $z = 2.93$, $p = .003$, $d = 1.49$) with *Mdn* = 4.00 [3.00, 5.00]. With regard to a DTDDMM, its usefulness was also significantly acknowledged (No. 7 $z = 2.60$, $p = .009$, $d = 1.25$) with *Mdn* = 4.00 [3.00, 5.00] and the definition of process digital twin was significantly understood (No. 8 $z = 3.15$, $p = .002$, $d = 1.68$) with *Mdn* = 4.00 [3.00, 5.00]. Regarding data quality for the model, most managers believed that corporate data quality management must be implemented with Mdn = 3.50 [2.00, 5.00], and that there was a significant relationship between process digital twin and data quality (No. 10 $z = 3.14$, $p = .002$, $d = 1.67$) with *Mdn* = 4.00 [3.00, 5.00] as well as decision support systems and data quality (No. 11 $z = 2.49$, $p = .013$, $d = 1.18$) with *Mdn* = 4.00 [3.00, 5.00]. The full implementation of digital twin, data quality management and decision support systems was seen as a significant and basic requirement for the model (No. 12 $z = 3.62$, $p < .001$, $d = 2.19$) with *Mdn* = 4.00 [3.00, 5.00].

Computer Industry: At least 50% of managers said they had either implemented digital twins already or would do so within the next year, and 75% of managers said they had either implemented digital twins already or would do so within the next 3 years. Digital twins were seen as a significantly competitive opportunity (No. 2 $z = 2.56$, $p = .011$, $d = 1.40$) with *Mdn* = 4.00 [2.36, 4.00]. At least 50% of managers said they had implemented data quality management already, and 75% of managers said they had either implemented data quality management already or would do so within the next year (No. 3 $z = -3.30$, $p < .001$, $d = 2.19$). Data quality management was seen as a significant and basic requirement for digital twins (No. 4 $z = 3.39$, $p < .001$, $d = 2.32$) with *Mdn* = 4.00 [3.00, 5.00]. At least 50% of managers said they had implemented decision support systems already or would do so within the next year, and 75% of managers said they had either implemented decision support systems already or would do so within the next 3 years. The improvement of decision support systems improvement through digital twin implementation was acknowledged (No. 6 $z = 2.91$, $p = .004$, $d = 1.71$) with *Mdn* = 4.00 [3.00, 5.00]. Regarding a DTDDMM, its usefulness was also significantly acknowledged (No. 7 $z = 2.40$, $p = .016$, $d = 1.27$) with *Mdn* = 4.00 [2.36, 4.00] and the definition of process digital twin was significantly understood (No. 8 $z = 2.45$, $p = .014$, $d = 1.31$) with *Mdn* = 4.00 [3.00, 5.00]. Regarding data quality for the model, most managers believed that corporate data quality management must be significantly implemented (No. 9 $z = 2.83$, $p = .005$, $d = 1.64$) with *Mdn* = 4.00 [2.72, 5.00], and that there was a significant relationship between both process digital twins and data quality (No. 10 $z = 3.35$, $p < .001$, $d = 2.26$) with *Mdn* = 4.00 [3.00, 5.00] and decision support systems and data quality (No. 11 $z = 3.14$, $p = .002$, $d = 1.97$) with *Mdn* = 4.00 [3.00, 5.00]. The full implementation of digital twin, data quality management and decision support systems was seen as a significant and basic requirement for the model (No. 12 $z = 2.46$, $p = .014$, $d = 1.32$) with *Mdn* = 4.00 [2.36, 5.00].

Healthcare Industry: At least 50% of managers said they had either implemented digital twins already or would do so within the next year, and 75% of managers said they had either implemented digital twins already or would do so within the next 3 years (No. 1 $z = -2.86$, $p = .004$, $d = 1.66$). Digital twins were perceived as providing a significant competitive opportunity (No. 2 $z = 2.24$, $p = .025$, $d = 1.16$) with *Mdn* = 4.00 [2.36, 4.00]. At least 50% of managers said they had either implemented data quality management already or would do so within the next year, and 75% would do so within the next 3 years (No. 3 $z = -3.54$, $p < .001$, $d = 2.59$). Data quality management was seen as a significant and basic requirement for digital twin implementation (No. 4 $z = 2.47$, $p = .013$, $d = 1.33$) with *Mdn* = 4.00 [2.36, 5.00]. At least 50% of managers said they had implemented decision support systems already or would do so within the next year, and 75% of managers said they had either implemented decision support systems already or would do so within the next 3 (No. 5 $z = -3.38$, $p < .001$, $d = 2.31$). The improvement of decision support systems as a result of digital twin implementation was significantly acknowledged (No. 6 $z = 3.20$, $p = .001$, $d = 2.04$) with *Mdn* = 4.00 [3.00, 5.00]. Regarding the DTDDMM, its usefulness was also significantly acknowledged (No. 7 $z = 2.30$, $p = .022$, $d = 1.20$) with *Mdn* = 4.00 [2.36, 4.64] and the definition of a process digital twin was significantly understood (No. 8 $z = 2.56$, $p = .011$, $d = 1.40$) with Mdn = 4.00 [2.36, 4.00]. Regarding data quality for the model, most managers believed that data quality management had to be implemented at corporate level (No. 9 $z = 2.30$, $p = .023$, $d = 1.20$) with *Mdn* = 4.00 [2.36, 4.00], and that there was a significant relationship between both a process digital twin and data quality (No. 10 $z = 2.60$, $p = .010$, $d = 1.43$) with *Mdn* = 4.00 [3.00, 5.00] and decision support systems and data quality (No. 11 $z = 2.35$, $p = .019$, $d = 1.24$) with *Mdn* = 4.00 [2.36, 4.64]. The full implementation of digital twin, data quality management and decision support systems was seen as a basic requirement for the model with *Mdn* = 3.00 [2.36, 4.00].

Construction Industry: At least 50% of managers said they had either implemented digital twins already or would do so within the next year, and 75% of managers said they would do so within the next 3 years. Digital twins were perceived as providing a significant competitive opportunity (No. 2 $z = 2.33$, $p =$

.020, d = 1.82) with *Mdn* = 3.50 [2.36, 4.00]. At least 50% and 75% of managers said they had either implemented data quality management already or would do so within the next year (No. 3 z = −2.67, p = .008, d = 2.42). Data quality management was seen as a basic requirement for digital twin implementation, with *Mdn* = 3.50 [2.08, 5.00]. At least 50% of managers said they had implemented decision support systems already or would do so within the next year and 75% of managers said they had either implemented decision support systems already or would do so within the next 3 years (No. 5 z = −2.52, p = .012, d = 2.12). The improvement of decision support systems through digital twin implementation was significantly acknowledged (No. 6 z = 2.53, p = .011, d = 2.14) with *Mdn* = 4.00 [3.00, 4.00]. Regarding the DTDDMM, its usefulness was also acknowledged with *Mdn* = 3.00 [2.08, 4.00], and the definition of a process digital twin was significantly understood (No. 8 z = 2.33, p = .020, d = 1.82) with *Mdn* = 3.50 [3.00, 4.00]. Regarding data quality for the model, most managers believed that data quality management had to be implemented at corporate level (No. 9 z = 2.31, p = .021, d = 1.79) with *Mdn* = 4.00 [3.00, 4.00], and that there was a significant relationship between both a process digital twin and data quality (No. 10 z = 2.37, p = .018, d = 1.88) with *Mdn* = 4.00 [3.00, 5.00], and decision support systems and data quality (No. 11 z = 2.48, p = .013, d = 2.05) with *Mdn* = 4.00 [3.00, 4.92]. The full implementation of digital twin, data quality management and decision support systems was seen as a basic requirement for the model with *Mdn* = 3.50 [2.08, 4.00].

Transport Industry: At least 50% of managers said they had either implemented digital twins already or would do so within the next year, and 75% of managers said they had either implemented digital twins already or would do so within the next 3 years. Digital twins were perceived as providing a competitive opportunity with *Mdn* = 3.50 [2.08, 4.00]. At least 50% of managers said they had either implemented data quality management already or would do so within the next year, and 75% of managers said they had either implemented data quality management already or would do so within the next 3 years (No. 3 z = −2.60, p = .009, d = 2.27). Data quality management was seen as a significant and basic requirement for digital twins (No. 4 z = 2.23, p = .026, d = 1.68) with *Mdn* = 4.00 [3.00, 5.00]. At least 50% of managers said they had implemented decision support systems already or would do so within the next year, and 75% of managers said they had either implemented decision support systems already or would do so within the next 3 years (No. 5 z = −2.60, p = .009, d = 2.27). The improvement of decision support systems improvement through digital twin implementation was significantly acknowledged (No. 6 z = 2.37, p = .018, d = 1.88) with *Mdn* = 4.00 [3.00, 5.00]. Regarding a DTDDMM, its usefulness was also acknowledged, with *Mdn* = 3.00 [3.00, 5.00], and the definition of a process digital twin was significantly understood (No. 8 $z = 2.43$, $p = .015$, $d = 1.97$) with *Mdn* = 4.00 [3.00, 5.00]. Regarding data quality for the model, most managers believed that data quality management had to be implemented at corporate level, with *Mdn* = 4.00 [2.00, 5.00], and that there was a significant relationship between both a process digital twin and data quality (No. 10 $z = 2.43$, $p = .015$, $d = 1.97$) with *Mdn* = 4.00 [3.00, 5.00], and decision support systems and data quality with *Mdn* = 4.00 [2.08, 5.00]. The full implementation of digital twin, data quality management and decision support systems was seen as a basic requirement for the model with *Mdn* = 3.50 [2.08, 5.00].

Food Industry: At least 50% of managers said they had either implemented digital twins already or would do so within the next year, and 75% of managers said they had either implemented digital twins already or would do so within the next 3 years (No. 1 $z = -2.25$, $p = .024$, $d = 2.02$). Digital twins were perceived to provide a significant competitive opportunity (No. 2 $z = 2.46$, $p = .014$, $d = 2.48$) with *Mdn* = 4.00 [3.00, 5.00]. At least 50% of managers said they had either implemented data quality management already or would do so within the next year, and 75% of managers said they had either implemented data quality management already or would do so within the next 3 years (No. 3 $z = -2.43$, $p = .015$, $d = 2.40$). Data quality management was seen as a significant and basic requirement for digital twins (No. 4 $z = 2.16$, $p = .030$, $d = 1.87$) with *Mdn* = 4.00 [2.76, 5.00]. At least 50% of managers said they had implemented decision support systems already or would do so within the next year, and 75% of managers said they had either implemented decision support systems already or would within the next 3 years. The improvement of decision support systems improvement as a result of digital twin implementation was significantly acknowledged (No. 6 $z = 2.43$, $p = .015$, $d = 2.40$) with *Mdn* = 4.00 [3.00, 5.00]. Regarding a DTDDMM, its usefulness was also significantly acknowledged (No. 7 $z = 2.46$, $p = .014$, $d = 2.48$) with *Mdn* = 4.00 [3.00, 5.00], and the definition of a process digital twin was significantly understood (No. 8 $z = 2.07$, $p = .038$, $d = 1.73$) with *Mdn* = 3.50 [3.00, 5.00]. Regarding data quality for the model, most managers believed that data quality management had to be implemented at corporate level (No. 9 $z = 2.31$, $p = .021$, $d = 2.14$) with *Mdn* = 4.00 [2.76, 5.00], and that there was relationship between a process digital twin and data quality with *Mdn* = 4.00 [1.76, 5.00] as well as a significant relationship between decision support systems and data quality (No. 11 $z = 2.17$, $p = .030$, $d = 1.89$) with *Mdn* = 4.00 [2.76, 5.00]. The full implementation of digital twin, data quality management and decision support systems was seen as a significant and basic requirement for the model (No. 12 $z = 2.33$, $p = .020$, $d = 2.18$) with Mdn = 4.00 [3.00, 4.24].

Across Industries: Thus, it can be concluded that there were no significant differences. At least 50% of managers said they had either implemented digital twins already or would do so within the next year, and 75% of managers said they had either implemented digital twins already or would do so within the next 3 years. Digital twins were perceived as providing a considerable competitive opportunity with *Mdn* = 4.00 [3.00, 4.00]. At least 50% of managers said they had either implemented data quality management already or would do so within the next year, and 75% of managers said they had either implemented data quality management already or would do so within the next 3 years. Data quality management was seen as a basic requirement for digital twins with *Mdn* = 4.00 [3.00, 5.00]. At least 50% of managers said they had implemented decision support systems already or would do so within the next year, and 75% of managers said they had either implemented decision support systems already or would do so within the next 3 years. Where the improvement of decision support systems as a result of digital twin implementation was acknowledged, with *Mdn* = 4.00 [3.00, 5.00]. Regarding a DTDDMM, its usefulness was also acknowledged, with *Mdn* = 4.00 [3.00, 5.00], and the definition of a process digital twin was understood, with *Mdn* = 4.00 [3.00, 5.00]. Regarding data quality for the model, most managers believed that data quality management had to be implemented at corporate level, with *Mdn* = 4.00 [3.00, 5.00], and that there was a relationship between a process digital twin and data quality with *Mdn* = 4.00 [3.00, 5.00] as well as between decision support systems and data quality with *Mdn* = 4.00 [3.00, 5.00]. The full implementation of digital twin, data quality management and decision support systems was seen as a basic requirement for the model, with *Mdn* = 4.00 [3.00, 5.00].

5.2.2 The Digital Twin-Driven Decision-Making Model

The **implementation level** in Figure 5.3 is the most important part for a DTD-DMM, showing that at least 84% of managers *(N = 122)* said they had either implemented digital twin, data quality management and decision support systems already or would within the next 3 years.

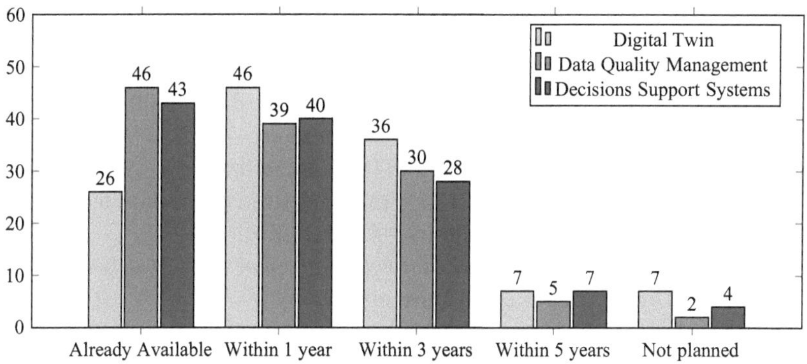

Figure 5.3 Main study implementation level. (Source: Own Figure)

5.2.2.1 Results for Model

Table 5.18 shows that the p-value was less than .05 and was thus assumed to be significant, with strong effects in No. 1: d = 1.71, No. 2: d = 1.23 and No. 3: d = 1.76, as seen in Figure 5.4.

Table 5.18 Main study hypothesis test for H_2, H_3, H_4

	Null Hypothesis	Sig.^{a,b}	Std. Test Statistic	Decision
1	Median of Data Quality Management basic requirement Digital Twin equals 3	<,001	7.20	Reject the null hypothesis.
2	Median of Digital Twin as competitive opportunity equals 3	<,001	5.82	Reject the null hypothesis.
3	Median of Improvement of Decision Support System by Digital Twin equals 3	<,001	7.32	Reject the null hypothesis.

a. The significance level is .05. b. Asymptotic significance is displayed.
Source: Own Table

1. *H_2: Data quality management is a basic requirement for a digital twin*—Data quality management basic requirement digital twin: z = 7.20, p < .001, d = 1.71

   However, there were industry differences in the **data quality score**: (1) Food industry—71.20% *(N = 10)*, (2) retail industry—68.58% *(N = 24)*, (3) computer industry—66.85% *(N = 20)*, (4) healthcare industry—64.30% *(N = 20)*, (5) automotive industry—63.33% *(N = 24)*, (6) construction industry—62.33 *(N = 12)*, (7) transport industry—55.50% *(N = 12)*.
2. *H_3: The implementation of the digital twin is a competitive opportunity for a company*—Digital twin as competitive opportunity: z = 5.82, p < .001, d = 1.23
3. *H_4: Decision support systems are improved by digital twins*—Improvement of decision support systems by digital twin: z = 7.32, p < .001, d = 1.76

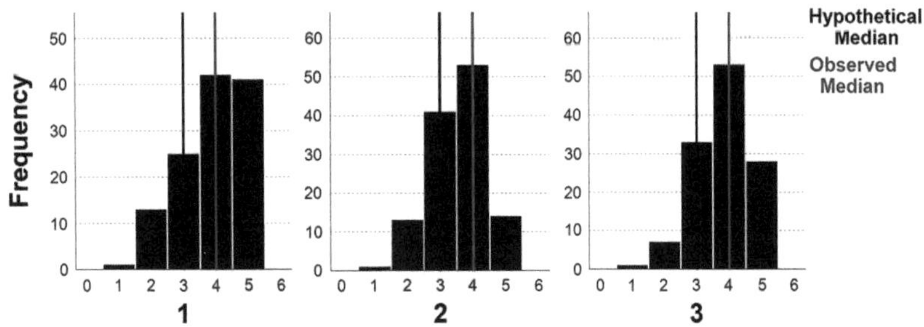

Figure 5.4 Main study wilcoxon signed rank test for H_2, H_3, H_4. (Source: Own Figure, modified and derived from IBM SPSS Statistics 28)

Table 5.19 shows no significant differences and the ranking of the **requirements**. Table 5.20 shows no significant differences and the ranking of the **benefits**.

Table 5.19 Hypothesis test summary and ranking of requirements

Ranking	Null Hypothesis	Sig.[a,b]	Decision	Sum	Mean	Std. Deviation
1	Distribution Timeliness same across Industries	.343	Retain the null hypothesis	482	3.95	0.995
2	Distribution Consistency same across Industries	.313	Retain the null hypothesis	481	3.94	0.903
3	Distribution Accuracy same across Industries	.317	Retain the null hypothesis	480	3.93	0.960
4	Distribution Integration same across Industries	.156	Retain the null hypothesis	475	3.89	0.898
5	Distribution Update same across Industries	.744	Retain the null hypothesis	471	3.86	1.007
6	Distribution Completeness same across Industries	.888	Retain the null hypothesis	471	3.86	0.956
7	Distribution Real-time same across Industries	.614	Retain the null hypothesis	466	3.82	0.936
8	Distribution Configurablility same across Industries	.665	Retain the null hypothesis	461	3.78	0.940
9	Distribution Communication same across Industries	.636	Retain the null hypothesis	460	3.77	0.925
10	Distribution Connectivity same across Industries	.892	Retain the null hypothesis	458	3.75	0.930
11	Distribution Accessibility same across Industries	.258	Retain the null hypothesis	453	3.71	0.904
12	Distribution Flexibility same across Industries	.946	Retain the null hypothesis	452	3.70	0.897
13	Distribution Scalability same across Industries	.806	Retain the null hypothesis	450	3.69	0.919
14	Distribution Interaction same across Industries	.695	Retain the null hypothesis	447	3.66	1.017

a. The significance level is .05. b. Asymptotic significance is displayed.
Source: Own Table

Table 5.20 Hypothesis test summary and ranking of benefits

Ranking	Null Hypothesis	Sig.[a,b]	Decision	Sum	Mean	Std. Deviation
1	Distribution Process monitoring same across Industries	.921	Retain the null hypothesis	483	3.96	0.866
2	Distribution Time reduction same across Industries	.948	Retain the null hypothesis	476	3.90	0.974
3	Distribution Process diagnosis same across Industries	.066	Retain the null hypothesis	470	3.85	0.951
4	Distribution New insights same across Industries	.432	Retain the null hypothesis	469	3.84	0.918
5	Distribution Transparency same across Industries	.615	Retain the null hypothesis	466	3.82	0.863
6	Distribution What-if-analyses same across Industries	.135	Retain the null hypothesis	465	3.81	0.846
7	Distribution Product improvement same across Industries	.420	Retain the null hypothesis	464	3.80	0.924
8	Distribution Predictive maintenance same across Industries	.330	Retain the null hypothesis	459	3.76	0.882
9	Distribution Reduced time-to-market same across Industries	.948	Retain the null hypothesis	449	3.68	1.023
10	Distribution Cost reduction same across Industries	.733	Retain the null hypothesis	443	3.63	1.014

a. The significance level is .05. b. Asymptotic significance is displayed.
Source: Own Table

5.2.2.2 Evaluation for Model

For a DTDDMM this means that data quality management is a basic requirement for digital twin implementation (H_2) with *Mdn* = 4.00 [3.00, 5.00]. However, there were industry differences in the **data quality score** where the average data quality score was rated with **64.88%** as shown in Equation 5.1, meaning that there is potential for significant improvement potential across the industries.

$$DataQualityScore = \frac{7915}{122} = 64.88\% \tag{5.1}$$

Furthermore, it was acknowledged that digital twins provide a competitive opportunity (H_3) with *Mdn* = 4.00 [3.00, 4.00] and decision support systems are improved by digital twins (H_4) with *Mdn* = 4.00 [3.00, 5.00], with Table 5.21 summarizing all *Mdn*s.

There were no differences across industries regarding **requirements** and **benefits**. There were three requirements of data quality management among the top five requirements: timeliness, with *Mdn* = 4.00 [3.00, 5.00]; consistency, with *Mdn* = 4.00 [3.00, 5.00]; and accuracy, with *Mdn* = 4.00 [3.00, 5.00]; as well as integration, with *Mdn* = 4.00 [3.00, 5.00] and update, with *Mdn* = 4.00 [3.00, 5.00]. This proves the importance of data quality management for a DTDDMM. The ranking can be seen as requirement priorities, corresponding to the descriptions from the literature review. As two of the top five benefits related to process improvement: process monitoring, with *Mdn* = 4.00 [3.00, 5.00]; and diagnosis, with *Mdn* = 4.00 [3.00, 5.00]. The others were time reduction with *Mdn* = 4.00 [3.00, 5.00], new insights with *Mdn* = 4.00 [3.00, 5.00] and transparency with *Mdn* = 4.00 [3.00, 5.00]. This all proves the importance of the process digital twin for DTDDMM—and *rank 1*, process monitoring and *rank 3*, process diagnosis—further show that the intention of a DTDDMM was understood by the managers. The benefits correspond to the descriptions from the literature review, although the rapidly changing digitization may create more benefits.

Table 5.21 Main study summary of medians (N = 122)

No.	$\sum$	I	II	III	IV	V	VI	VII	VIII	IX	X	XI	XII	XIII	XIV
1	**2.00**	2.00	2.00	2.00	2.00	3.00	2.00	2.00	3.00	2.00	2.00	2.00	2.00	2.00	2.00
2	**4.00**	4.00	3.50	4.00	4.00	3.00	3.00	3.00	4.00	4.00	4.00	4.00	3.50	3.00	4.00
3	**2.00**	2.00	2.00	2.00	1.50	2.00	2.00	2.00	2.00	2.00	1.00	1.50	2.00	2.00	2.00
4	**4.00**	4.00	4.00	4.00	4.00	4.00	3.00	4.00	4.00	4.00	4.00	4.00	3.50	4.00	4.00
5	**2.00**	2.00	1.00	2.00	2.00	2.00	2.00	2.00	1.50	2.00	2.00	2.00	2.00	2.00	2.00
6	**4.00**	4.00	4.00	4.00	4.00	4.00	3.00	3.50	4.00	4.00	4.00	4.00	4.00	4.00	4.00
7	**4.00**	4.00	4.00	4.00	4.00	3.00	3.00	3.00	4.00	4.00	4.00	4.00	3.00	3.00	4.00
8	**4.00**	4.00	4.00	4.00	4.00	4.00	3.00	3.50	4.00	4.00	4.00	4.00	3.50	4.00	3.50
9	**4.00**	4.00	4.00	4.00	4.00	4.00	4.00	3.50	4.00	3.50	4.00	4.00	4.00	4.00	4.00
10	**4.00**	4.00	4.00	4.00	4.00	4.00	4.00	4.00	4.00	4.00	4.00	4.00	4.00	4.00	4.00
11	**4.00**	4.00	4.00	4.00	4.00	4.00	4.00	4.00	4.50	4.00	4.00	4.00	4.00	4.00	4.00
12	**4.00**	4.00	4.00	4.00	4.00	4.00	4.00	4.00	4.00	4.00	4.00	3.00	3.50	3.50	4.00

Source: Own Table[2]

[2] Legend: $\sum$ per group, I. Upper Management, II. Middle Management, III. Lower Management, IV. 250 or more employees, V. 50–249 employees, VI. 10–50 employees, VII. Up to 9 employees, VIII. Automotive, IX. Retail, X. Computer, XI. Healthcare, XII. Construction, XIII. Transport, XIV. Food

5.2.3 Operational Effectiveness

The main study demonstrated the effectiveness of the digital twin-driven decision-making model (H_5) (The corresponding data can be viewed in Appendix Table 12 in the electronic supplementary material). These were achieved through the benefits of digital twins regarding (1) decision certainty—through transparency, new insights and what-if analyses—and (2) decision efficiency—through reduced time-to-market, process monitoring, process diagnostics, time reduction, cost reduction, predictive maintenance and product improvement. Decision certainty and efficiency led to an improvement of **11.13%** in decision quality (Figure 5.5), and a corresponding improvement in operational effectiveness.

5.2.3.1 Results Certainty

The results are shown in Equation 5.2, where the percentages of unstructured decisions (high uncertainty) in each company were queried (*Is-StateUnstructuredDecisions*) as well as the increases of **certainty** of unstructured decisions, where both the new state (*New-StateStructured Decisions*) and the improvement (*Improvement Certainty*) were determined.

$$
\begin{aligned}
Is{-}StateUnstructuredDecisions &= \frac{4527}{93} = 48.68\% \\
New{-}StateStructuredDecisions &= \frac{5583.46}{93} = 60.4\% \\
ImprovementCertainty &= 60.4\%{-}48.16\% = 11.36\%
\end{aligned}
\qquad (5.2)
$$

5.2.3.2 Evaluation Certainty

Here, the manager needed to analyse certainty—the facts such as risks, options and programs, which can be supported by digital twins. The important factor in the context of uncertainty, is the improvement of certainty, so that unstructured decisions become structured decisions through transparency, new insights and what-if analyses. The DTDDMM reduced the proportion of unstructured decisions in the company from 48.68% to 37.32%, which means that unstructured decision decreased by 11.36%.

5.2.3.3 Results Efficiency

The results are shown in Equation 5.3, where the percentages of **efficiency** in decision-making in each company were queried (*Is-StateEfficiencyDecisions*) as well as the increases of efficiency in decision-making, were both the new state

(*New-StateEfficiencyDecisions*) and the improvement (*ImprovementEfficiency*) were determined.

$$Is\text{-}StateEfficiencyDecisions = \frac{5430}{94} = 57.77\%$$
$$New\text{-}StateEfficiencyDecisions = \frac{6541.67}{94} = 69.59\%$$
$$ImprovementEfficiency = 69.59\% - 57.77\% = 11.83\% \tag{5.3}$$

5.2.3.4 Evaluation Efficiency

Here, the managers had to allocate opportunities and resources, which can be supported by digital twins. The DTDDMM improved the efficiency of decisions through reduced time-to-market, process monitoring, process diagnostics, time reduction, cost reduction, predictive maintenance and product improvement in the company from 57.77% to 69.59%, which means that decision-making efficiency increased by 11.83%.

5.2.3.5 Results Quality

The results are shown in Equation 5.4, where the percentages of quality in decision-making in each company were queried (Is-StateQualityDecisions) as well as the increases of quality in decision-making, where both the new state (New-StateQualityDecisions) and the improvement (ImprovementQuality) were determined.

$$Is\text{-}StateQualityDecisions = \frac{5474}{94} = 57.77\%$$
$$New\text{-}StateQualityDecisions = \frac{6520.63}{94} = 69.37\%$$
$$ImprovementQuality = 69.37\% - 58.23\% = 11.13\% \tag{5.4}$$

5.2.3.6 Evaluation Quality

Here, the manager had to evaluate quality based on analysis (**certainty**) and the allocation of resources (**efficiency**), that could be supported by digital twins. The DTDDMM improved the quality of decisions in the company from 58.23% to 69.37%, which meant that decision quality and thus operational effectiveness increased by **11.13%** (Figure 5.5).

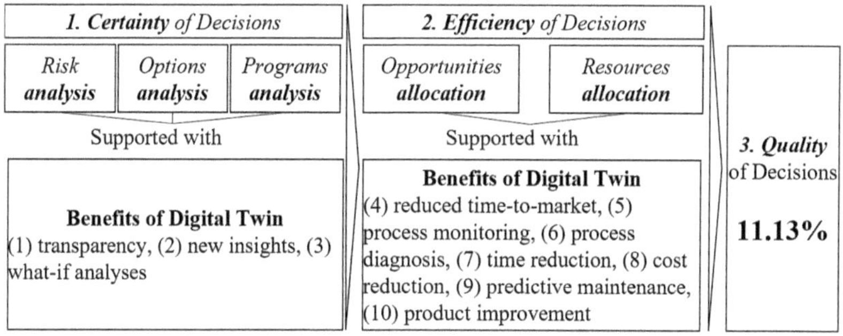

Figure 5.5 Result of quality decision-making process with digital twin. (Source: Own Figure, modified and derived from Negulescu et al., 2014)

6 Conclusions and Recommendations

> **"By 2021, half of large industrial companies will use digital twins, resulting in those organizations gaining a 10% improvement in effectiveness."** (Gartner, 2017b)

As only 30% of the large companies (250 employees or more) focused on in this study had implemented a digital twin by 2021, Gartner's prediction was only partly accurate. However, operational effectiveness, as shown in Equation 5.4, can be increased by more than 10% (11.13%) through the theoretical application of a DTDDMM.

6.1 Conclusion of Hypotheses

RQ 1 Are there differences in data quality, digital twins and decision support in terms of management level, company size and industry for strategic positioning?

For H_1, it can be noted that there were differences **across company sizes** in both the preliminary and main studies and **across industries** in the preliminary study, which were mainly due to company size. The differences in digital twin awareness level **across industries (H(6) = 14.79, p = .022, d = 0.55)** showed that awareness tended to be lower in the **retail industry** than in the other industries. The transport, automotive, construction, computer and food industries, on the other hand, were not statistically significantly different from one another in

---

Supplementary Information The online version contains supplementary material available at https://doi.org/10.1007/978-3-658-44453-2_6.

F. Blaschke, *Implementation and Benefits of Digital Twin on Decision Making and Data Quality Management*, https://doi.org/10.1007/978-3-658-44453-2_6

this respect, and the difference in the healthcare industry was relatively minor. Regarding the awareness level, therefore, it is recommended that digital twins be anchored in the Industry 4.0 strategy of every company. Next, the difference **across company sizes** will be focused on, with the differences discovered in the preliminary study being addressed first. Here, a significant differences for digital twin as competitive opportunity emerged in both the preliminary study, **$H(3) = 16.74, p < .001, d = 0.83$**, and main study, **$H(3) = 10.86, p = .012, d = 0.57$**, where agreement in the group 250 + tended to be higher than in the groups with fewer employees. The groups with a lower number of employees, on the other hand, did not differ statistically significantly from one another, although it was striking that the number of negative attitudes increased with a decrease in the number of employees. Based on these findings, it can be concluded that the digital twin was seen by 250+ companies as a competitive opportunity. Similarly, regarding data quality management being a basic requirement for digital twins, differences were discovered in both the preliminary study, **$H(3) = 10.01, p = .018, d = 0.55$**, and main study, **$H(3) = 13.78, p = .003, d = 0.66$**. Again, the trend was seen in the 250+ companies. However, in the preliminary study, it was noted that agreement tended to be higher in the 250+ group than in the groups with a smaller number of employees, which were not statistically significantly different from each other, although descriptive statistics indicated that the number of negative attitudes increased as the number of employees decreased. By contrast, in the main study, it was noted that agreement in the group 10–49 tended to be lower than in the other groups, although this difference was not statistically significant with respect to the group 1–9, it differed with respect to the smaller companies. It can be concluded, however, that data quality management was seen as a basic requirement for digital twins in companies with 250+ employees. Now the differences that occurred only in the preliminary or main study will be examined. A difference emerged in the preliminary study regarding the implementation level of decision support systems, **$H(3) = 10.96, p = .012, d = 0.61$**, where agreement tended to be lower in the 250+ group than in the groups with fewer employees.

On the other hand, there was no statistically significant difference between the groups with a low number of employees. From this, it can be concluded that decision support systems are more relevant in smaller companies. Subsequently, there were three differences that occurred only in the main study. The first concerned the usefulness of a DTDDMM, **$H(3) = 10.12, p = .018, d = 0.54$**, where the level of agreement in the 250+ group tended to be higher than in the other groups. So, even the difference with the 10–49 group was not shown to be statistically significant in this case. From this, it can be concluded that a DTDDMM is useful for companies with 250+ employees. The second concerned the implementation of corporate data quality management, where differences occurred for the model **H(3) = 14.95, p = .002, d = 0.70**, and where agreement in the 250+ group tended to be higher than in the groups with fewer employees. The groups with a lower number of employees, on the other hand, did not differ from each other in a statistically significant way, although the number of negative attitudes increased with a decrease in the number of employees. It can therefore be concluded that corporate data quality management must be implemented for the model in companies with more than 250 employees, which is consistent with the statement about the usefulness of the model. The third difference concerned the dependency of decision support systems on data quality, where a difference was noted: **H(3) = 9.40, p = .24, d = 0.52**. Agreement tended to be higher in the 250+ group than in the 10–49 and 50–249 groups. Descriptively, this also appeared to be true for the 1–9 group, but the differences with respect to this group were not shown to be statistically significant. It can be concluded that the quality of data in decision support system is most important in companies with 250+ employees. H_1: *There are differences in data quality, a digital twin and decision support in terms of management level, company size and industry.* **Conclusion: Accept** H_1

RQ 2 What could a theoretical model look like that relies on a digital twin for decision-making while focusing on data quality?

Based on the literature review, a theoretical DTDDMM was developed (shown in Figure 7.1 and summarized in Table 2.4), and defined as *"A process digital twin, with usable data through data quality management, analytics and the visualization in decision support systems"*. In this context, the implementation level played a crucial role where 84% of managers (N = 122) said they had either implemented digital twin, data quality management and decision support systems already or would do so within the next three years. Here, the theoretical DTDDMM could only be implemented if data quality management, digital twin, and decision support systems had been fully implemented, which was confirmed with *Mdn* = 4.00 [3.00, 5.00]. Figure 6.1 compares the preliminary and main study, where a shorter implementation period of the digital twin from five years (PS) to three years (MS) could be observed, which was due to the focus on digital twin experts (quality Score 3) in the main study.

For H_2, it was important to consider whether data quality management is seen as a basic requirement of digital twins, as data quality management will be implemented by 84% of companies within the next 3 years. For this reason the result of the preliminary study: z = 6.59, <.001, d = 1.54 with *Mdn* = 4.00 [3.00, 5.00] and the result of the main study: z = 7.20, p < .001, d = 1.71 with *Mdn* =

4.00 [3.00, 5.00] corresponded closely. Therefore, data quality management can be considered a basic requirement, and that without it a theoretical DTDDMM would have no practical use. So, regarding data quality for the model, corporate data quality management must be implemented with *Mdn* = 4.00 [3.00, 5.00]. Again, agreement in companies with 250 or more employees tended to be higher than in companies with fewer employees. Concerning the relationship between process digital twin and data quality, with *Mdn* = 4.00 [3.00, 5.00], this applies to all company sizes as well as decision support systems and data quality, with *Mdn* = 4.00 [3.00, 5.00], which tended to have a higher level of agreement in companies with 250+ employees. On this basis, data quality is an essential part of the theoretical DTDDMM, which means that a continuous corporate data quality management must be present, specifically for companies with 250 or more employees, because both the process digital twin and decision support system depend on the supplied data quality. If this were not the case, the theoretical DTDDMM would have no practical use because the data it uses would not be correct (data quality-proved). Due to the average data quality score of only 65%, it is extremely necessary to improve data quality, even if data quality management has already been implemented. *H_2: Data quality management is a basic requirement for a digital twin.* **Conclusion: Accept** H_2

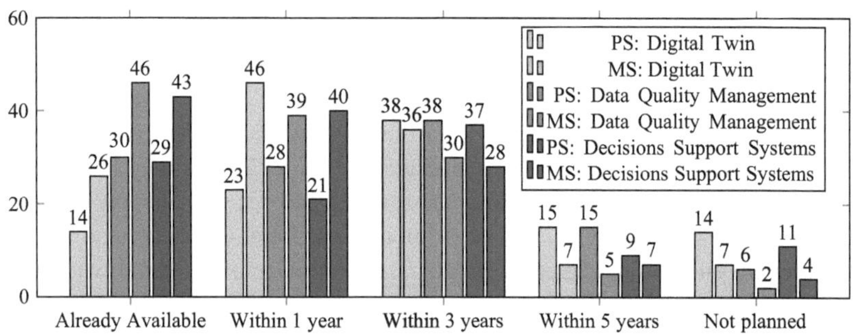

Figure 6.1 Implementation level comparison of the preliminary and main study. (Source: Own Figure)

For H_3, it was important to consider whether digital twins are seen as a competitive opportunity, as they will be implemented by 84% of companies within the next three years. For this reason, the result of the preliminary study: $z = 5.98$, $p < .001$, $d = 1.45$ with *Mdn* = 4.00 [3.00, 5.00] and the result of the main study: $z = 5.82$, $p < .001$, $d = 1.23$ with *Mdn* = 4.00 [3.00, 5.00] corresponded closely. On this basis, the digital twin can be considered a competitive opportunity, whereby there was a difference in the preliminary as well as the main study, with the level of agreement in companies with 250 or more employees tending to be higher than in companies with fewer employees. However, this does not mean that companies with fewer employees did not perceive the competitive opportunity provided by digital twins; otherwise, they would not consider it worthwhile to integrate a digital twin within the next three years. H_3*: The implementation of a digital twin is a competitive opportunity.* **Conclusion: Accept** H_3

For H_4, it was important to consider whether the decision support systems were improved by digital twins, as decision support systems will be implemented by the majority of companies within the next three years. For this reason, the results of the preliminary study: $z = 5.11$, $p < .001$, $d = 1.14$ with $Mdn = 4.00$ [3.00, 5.00] and the results of the main study: $z = 7.32$, $p < .001$, $d = 1.76$ with $Mdn = 4.00$ [3.00, 5.00] corresponded closely. Accordingly, decision support systems are improved by digital twins. Decision support systems can be implemented into the five-dimension digital twin as the service layer (Figure 2.8), which interacts with users directly. If this were not the case, the theoretical DTDDMM would have no practical use since decision support systems would not choose a process digital twin in model management to generate an enterprise-level view and provide end-to-end visibility for process transformation. H_4*: Decision support systems are improved by digital twins.* **Conclusion: Accept** H_4

For the DTDDMM, the theoretical implementation requirements and benefits are important. For this reason, the results of the main study concluded that the top five requirements for DTDDMM were timeliness, consistency, accuracy, integration and update and that the top five benefits were process monitoring, time reduction, process diagnosis, new insights and transparency. Accordingly, data quality is an essential requirement, as are the benefits to processes (process digital twin). If this were not the case, the theoretical DTDDMM would have no practical use because the top three requirements: timeliness, consistency and accuracy, relate to data quality management, and of the top three benefits, two relate to processes, with process monitoring (process digital twin) forming the core of the model. This can be regarded as an initial prioritization of requirements and benefits, which should then match the descriptions from the literature review. However, requirements may vary from use case to use case, and benefits should be taken as needed. Furthermore, it is important to consider whether the theoretical DTDDMM increases effectiveness.

RQ 3 Does the theoretical model, using digital twins for decision-making and focusing on data quality, increase operational effectiveness?

For H_5, it was important to consider whether the DTDDMM increases operational effectiveness. Here, the managers needed to analyse (**certainty**) the facts, such as risks, options and programs, which could be supported by digital twins. The important factor in the context of uncertainty, is the improvement of certainty, so that unstructured decisions become structured decisions through transparency, new insights and what-if analyses. The DTDDMM reduced the proportion of unstructured decisions in the company from 48.68% to 37.32%, which meant that unstructured decisions decreased by 11.36%. Furthermore, the manager had to allocate (**efficiency**) opportunities and resources, which could be supported by digital twins. The DTDDMM improved the efficiency of decisions through reduced time-to-market, process monitoring, process diagnostics, time reduction, cost reduction, predictive maintenance and product improvement in the company from 57.77% to 69.59%, which meant that decision-making efficiency increased by 11.83%. Finally, the managers had to evaluate quality based on the analysis (**certainty**) and the allocation of resources (**efficiency**) that could be supported by digital twins. The DTDDMM improved the quality of decisions in the company from 58.23% to 69.37%, which meant that decision quality, and thus **operational effectiveness**, increased by 11.13%, as shown in Figure 5.5. Therefore, the DTD-DMM increased the certainty of unstructured decisions by 11.36%, the efficiency of decisionmaking by 11.83% and the quality of decision-making by **11.13%**, which all to an increase in operational effectiveness. If this were not the case, the model would have no practical use because it should increase effectiveness to justify the implementation. *H_5: A theoretical DTDDMM increases effectiveness by 10%.* **Conclusion: Accept** H_5.

6.2 Recommendations

Due to the quality score of 3, only managers in the main study who were familiar with all three topics were included. However, the awareness levels from the preliminary study should still be considered due to the implementation of the digital twin, data quality management and decision support systems. For strategic positioning, and due to the results of H_3, digital twins should be added and anchored in the industry 4.0 digitization strategy of companies with 250+ employees, although companies with fewer employees should also consider implementation.

Due to the average data quality score of 65%, it is urgently necessary to address and improve data quality, even if data quality management has already been implemented. Both can be achieved by raising awareness and addressing digital twins and data quality through seminars, education and training from experts. Therefore, the recommendation of this paper is as follows:

- Companies should add and anchor digital twins as part of the Industry 4.0 digitization strategy.
- Companies should be aware of, and engage with, digital twins, as well as data quality, through seminars, training and educational programs with experts.

In addition, as only 84% of managers *(N = 122)* said they had either implemented already or would do so within the next 3 years full implementation may need to be carried out, with new and consistent organizational structures, processes and methods, architectures and application systems. Therefore:

- Companies should fully implement digital twins, data quality management and decision support systems, if necessary, with new and consistent organizational structures, processes and methods, architectures and application systems.
- Companies should undertake the practical and technical implementation of a DTDDMM with new and consistent organizational structures, processes and methods, architectures and application systems.

Due to the usefulness of a DTDDMM, especially for companies with 250 or more employees, the DTDDMM should be integrated into existing information systems and digitizing and linking processes to increase operational effectiveness. Whereby all relevant data (quality-proved) is integrated and updated through consistent corporate data quality management. In addition, a process digital twin should be fully integrated to enable real-time representation of processes for monitoring and diagnostics in the model management of decision support systems. Here, automatic model generation and updating for specific decision situations and the application of self-learning and controlling algorithms in the model management of decision support systems are particularly important. Therefore:

- A DTDDMM should be integrated into the existing information systems and digitization and linking of processes.
- All relevant data (quality-proved), through consistent corporate data quality management should be updated and integrated.
- A process digital twin enabling real-time representation of processes for monitoring and di agnosis in the model management of decision support systems should be integrated.

- Automatic model generation and updating for specific decision situations in decision support systems should be integrated.
- Self-learning and control algorithms for the model management of decision support systems should be applied.

6.3 Practical Implications

The practical implications of digital twins have already been discussed in 2.3.5 which identified 46 potential industries. Accordingly, Siemens AG, PTC Inc, Dassault Systèmes, IBM, Microsoft Azure, SAP and General Electric have already built a corresponding industrial IoT-platform for digital twins. However, the connection to data quality management, specifically data quality and digital twin for decision making, is also necessary to set up a DTDDMM. Regarding data quality management, Lünendonk & Hossenfelder have shown that although data quality in 155 companies has increased over the last five years, the average **data quality score** is only 60% (Zillmann, 2017), which is consistent with the results of a 64.88% industry-wide data quality score. Although companies are aware that poor data quality affects efficiency and is an important success criterion, Harvard Business Review surveyed 75 managers to determine data quality levels and discovered that, on average, 47% of newly created records had at least one critical error, and 3% were considered acceptable only by the loosest standards (Nagle et al., 2017). This dissertation also used the Friday Afternoon Measurement method (T. C. Redman, 2017) (The corresponding data can be viewed in Appendix Figure 4 in the electronic supplementary material), showing that on average 35% of newly created records had at least one critical error, showing an increase in industry-wide data quality. To achieve the improvement of data quality, the implementation of continuous data quality management in the form of corporate-level data quality management is recommended for companies using a DTDDMM. With regard to **decision making**, McKinsey & Company conducted a survey with 809 managers titled, *"Decision Making in the Age of Urgency"* (Aminov, 2019). Regarding speed and thus efficiency, only 48% of respondents agreed that their organizations made decisions quickly (Aminov, 2019), which is not quite consistent with the results of 57.77%. The difference, however, can be explained in that only time was considered and not the costs. To achieve efficiency in decision making, a DTDDMM is recommended, as it increases efficiency by 11.83%. In terms of the quality of decision making, 57% of respondents believed that their companies consistently made high-quality decisions (Aminov, 2019), which is consistent with the results of 58.23%. To achieve quality of decision making, a DTDDMM is also recommended, as it increases quality by 11.13%. As managers spend 37% of their time making decisions, of which 18.5% are ineffective[1] (Aminov, 2019) a DTDDMM is recommended to counteract this and effectively use time and minimize costs. The remaining % should be analysed and offset with other measures. Based on the results of the above studies, which were strengthened and confirmed by the preliminary and main studies of this dissertation, the implementation of a DTDDMM as a virtual model of a process digital twin, with usable data by data quality management, analytics, and the visualization in a decision support system (Figure 7.1), is recommended, as it increases operational effectiveness by 11.13%. The financial cost of bad data quality (the rule of ten) in Equation 6.1 (Nagle et al., 2017) should be kept in mind.

$$\begin{aligned} 100\%\ DQScore &: 100\$ * 1\$ = 100\$ \\ HBR : 53\%\ DQScore &: 53\$ * 1\$ + 47\$ * 10\$ = 523\$ \\ Dissertation : 65\%\ DQScore &: 67\$ * 1\$ + 35\$ * 10\$ = 417\$ \end{aligned} \tag{6.1}$$

6.4 Limitations

Three aspects of this dissertation were affected by limitations. Firstly, the theoretical DTDDMM; secondly, the sample size; and thirdly, the methods used. In connection with the theoretical DTDDMM, it is important to mention that the elaborated dimensions, requirements, characteristics and benefits were theoretical, which may vary from use case to use case and from company to company. In addition, there are no widely accepted standards and specifications, so combining data from different sources with different interfaces and data formats was[1] a major challenge (Adamenko et al., 2020). This limited the ways of closing the information loop between digital physical entities and virtual entities, as shown in Figure 2.8 (Durão et al., 2018). Regarding the sample size, it should be noted that both studies focused on managers in the automotive, healthcare, retail, transport, construction, computer, and food industries. To validate the survey of the preliminary and main studies, ten managers were previously interviewed, and there was consistently positive feedback concerning the relevance of the topic, the theoretical DTDDMM, and the conciseness of the survey. As a result, the number of managers surveyed for the preliminary study with (N = 144) (The corresponding data can be viewed in Appendix Figure 3 in the electronic supplementary

[1] Fortune 500 companies: 53,001 days work time and ~ \$250 labour costs per year lost

material) (average processing time: 5 minutes), and main study with (N = 122) (The corresponding data can be viewed in Appendix Figure 4 in the electronic supplementary material) (average completion time: 15 minutes), was due to the relevance of the topic and the simplicity of the surveys.

Furthermore, the 3.16 million managerial positions in Germany (CRIF, 2018) meant a margin of error for the preliminary study of 8% (confidence level of 95%) and for the main study of 9% (confidence level of 95%), which was acceptable. However, the number of managers and the selection of the automotive and retail industries were due to the fact that the author's direct network consisted mainly of managers from these industries. Furthermore, only German-speaking managers were involved—English-speaking managers were not represented in the samples, so the questions were not answered in English. Furthermore, with regard to percentage points, it should be mentioned that some managers answered the questions with percentage points instead of percentage values and others with percentage values instead of percentage points; here, no clear pattern emerged from the evaluation. In retrospect, it was not possible to clearly differentiate which managers thought in percentage values and which in percentage points. For this reason, the author made the assumptions 1–3 in Section 4.3 so that the results could be standardized. It is also important to note, in this context, that the focus lay exclusively on unstructured decisions and their share in a company. Thus, the focus was on increasing the certainty of unstructured decisions with high uncertainty. Note that unstructured decisions were answered with 50%. The remaining 50% may have referred to structured or semi-structured decisions where a clear assignment was not possible.

New Scientific Results

7

This chapter outlines the scientific results of this dissertation. Although this dissertation is not the first publication to address this issue (Figure 3.1), its novelty lies in the combination of topics that have either not been considered at all or have been considered in an undifferentiated manner in previous research. It empirically obtained the following six new results:

1. The development and validation of a theoretical DTDDMM (Figure 7.1) for the automotive, healthcare, retail, transport, construction, computer and food industries, and potentially for 39 other industries (Table 2.3).
2. The identification and analysis of differences between the industries. This revealed a lower awareness level in the retail industry and a higher acceptance level in companies with 250 or more employees. The acceptance level concerned the following areas: the competitive opportunity provided by digital twins; data quality management as a basic requirement for digital twins; the implementation level of decision support systems; the improvement of decision support systems through digital twin implementation; the usefulness of; the implementation of corporate data quality management for the model; and the dependency of decision support systems on data quality.
3. The identification and analysis of the implementation level of 84% managers

F. Blaschke, *Implementation and Benefits of Digital Twin on Decision Making and Data Quality Management*, https://doi.org/10.1007/978-3-658-44453-2_7

who reported that they had either implemented digital twins, data quality management and decision support systems already or would do so within the next three years, recognizing that this was a basic requirement of DTDDMM.

4. The identification and definition of the DTDDMMs top five requirements—timeliness, consistency, accuracy, integration, and update—and the top five benefits—process monitoring, time savings, process diagnostics, new insights, and transparency.
5. The identification of a potential increase of 11.13% in operational effectiveness by combining and using the benefits of digital twins.
6. The identification of 65% average data quality score in automotive, healthcare, retail, transport, construction, computers and food industries.

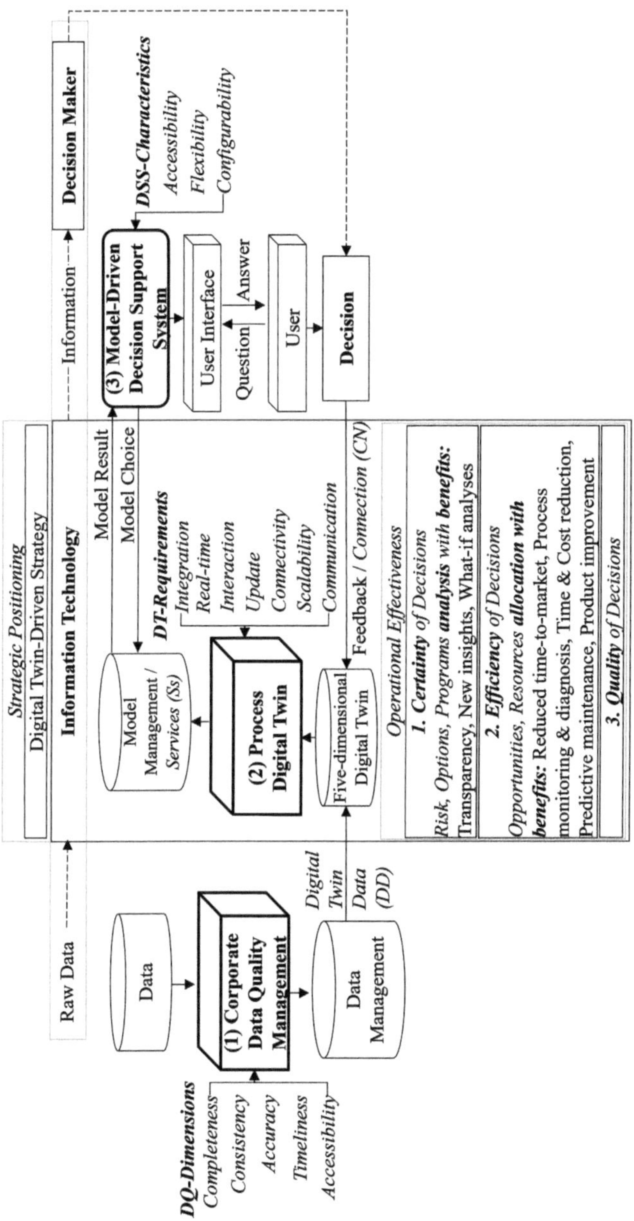

Figure 7.1 The Digital Twin-Driven Decision-Making Model. (Source: Own Figure)

8 Summary

Based on the literature review, a theoretical DTDDMM was developed. It is important to research digital twins as they offer promising technologies for strategic positioning and the realization of Industry 4.0 using cyber-physical systems (CPS) and information technology. CPS form the backbone to support the creation of a network for decentralized and autonomous **decision-making**. The design principles for Industry 4.0 serve as guidelines for digital twins: these provide a virtual copy of the physical world in order to collect data and monitor processes. The theoretical model of this dissertation revealed differences within and across management levels, company size and industry, focusing on the automotive, healthcare, retail, transport, construction, computer and food industries. These results will help managers understand the differences between data quality management, digital twins and decision support systems for **strategic positioning**. To an extent, these differences are a result of varying levels of digital twin awareness: this being lower in the retail industry. However, the primary factor is company size, with a higher acceptance level in companies with 250 or more employees.

These largely recognize and accept digital twin implementation as a competitive opportunity, and they acknowledge that data quality management is a basic requirement for digital twins, as is the implementation level of decision support systems. There is additionally considerable acceptance level of the extent to which decision support systems are improved by digital twin implementation, the usefulness of a DTDDMM, the need for corporate-level data quality management for the model, and the dependency of decision support systems on data

Supplementary Information The online version contains supplementary material available at https://doi.org/10.1007/978-3-658-44453-2_8.

F. Blaschke, *Implementation and Benefits of Digital Twin on Decision Making and Data Quality Management*, https://doi.org/10.1007/978-3-658-44453-2_8

quality. Due to an average data quality score of only 65%, it is imperative that this be addressed and improved, even if data quality management has already been implemented, ignoring can be very expensive for companies (rule of ten). A theoretical model was developed by combining corporate data quality management, a process digital twin and model-driven decision support systems. The model creates, tests, and builds a process in the virtual world to support decision-making by combining data, analytics, and visualization of insights. It prioritizes 14 requirements—the top five being timeliness, consistency, accuracy, integration, and update—all highlighting the importance of the relationship between digital twins and data quality. It also prioritizes 10 benefits, the top five being process monitoring, time reduction, process diagnostics, new insights, and transparency, all highlighting the importance of the relationship between digital twins and processes. The model identified the data quality dimensions of accuracy, completeness, consistency, timeliness, accessibility (The corresponding data can be viewed in Appendix Table 3 in the electronic supplementary material), real-time properties, integration, interaction, communication, connectivity, update and scalability for digital twin (The corresponding data can be viewed in Appendix Table 4 in the electronic supplementary material), and accessibility, flexibility and configurability for decision support systems. The benefits generated by digital twins for the model were projected onto decision-making (The corresponding data can be viewed in Appendix Figure 4 in the electronic supplementary material).

Through realistic process models, digital twins enable the linking of large amounts of data with rapid simulations for the early and efficient evaluation of the impact, performance, and quality of decisions (Tao, M. Zhang, and Nee, 2019b; Hao Zhang et al., 2017) identifying reduced time-to-market, process monitoring, process diagnosis, time reduction, cost reduction, predictive maintenance and product improvement as beneficial factors in efficient decision-making. Conversely, the quality of decision-making is negatively affected by a longer decision-making time, decisions made by the wrong people, in the wrong part of the organization, or with the wrong information (Blenko et al., 2010). Using risk avoidance to gain certainty with the above mentioned benefits of digital, allocating resources and opportunities efficiently, and using the above mentioned benefits of digital twins all improve decision quality and thus operational effectiveness. To conclude, the model improves certainty in unstructured decisions by 11.36%, the efficiency of decision-making by 11.83%, and the quality of decision-making by **11.13%**, and thus **operational effectiveness**.

The task of future research is to first implement data quality management, digital twins and decision support systems and to practically link these three topics. In addition, it is necessary to validate the 39 other industries (Figure 2.10) in terms of data quality management, digital twins and decision support systems to assess whether the theoretical model is also relevant. The second task of future research is the practical implementation of the model (Figure 7.1), so that all organizational and technical challenges of data quality management, digital twins and decision support systems can be further explored.

References

3DS (2021). *Manufacturing with Real-Time View: How Digital Twin Improves Visibility*. URL: https://www.3ds.com/manufacturing/connected-industry/manufacturing/digital-twin-improving-process-visibility.

Ada, Şükrü and Mohsen Ghaffarzadeh (2015). "Decision Making Based On Management Information System and Decision Support System". In: *European Researcher* 93.4, pp. 260–269. ISSN: 22198229. DOI: https://doi.org/10.13187/er.2015.93.260.

Adamenko, Dmytro, Steffen Kunnen, Robin Pluhnau, André Loibl, and Arun Nagarajah (2020). "Review and comparison of the methods of designing the Digital Twin". In: *Procedia CIRP* 91. Enhancing design through the 4th Industrial Revolution Thinking, pp. 27–32. ISSN: 2212–8271. DOI: https://doi.org/10.1016/j.procir.2020.02.146.

Afazov, Shukri and Daniele Scrimieri (Sept. 2020). "Chatter model for enabling a digital twin in machining". In: *The International Journal of Advanced Manufacturing Technology* 110, pp. 1–6. DOI: https://doi.org/10.1007/s00170-020-06028-9.

Agostino, Ícaro Romolo Sousa, Eike Broda, Enzo M. Frazzon, and Michael Freitag (2020). "Using a Digital Twin for Production Planning and Control in Industry 4.0". In: *Scheduling in Industry 4.0 and Cloud Manufacturing*. Ed. by Boris Sokolov, Dmitry Ivanov, and Alexandre Dolgui. Cham: Springer International Publishing, pp. 39–60. DOI: https://doi.org/10.1007/978-3-030-43177-8_3.

Ala-Laurinaho, Riku, Juuso Autiosalo, Anna Nikander, Joel Mattila, and Kari Tammi (Dec. 2020). "Data Link for the Creation of Digital Twins". In: *IEEE Access* 8, pp. 228675–228684. DOI: https://doi.org/10.1109/ACCESS.2020.3045856.

Alam, Kazi Masudul and Abdulmotaleb El Saddik (Jan. 2017). "C2PS: A Digital Twin Architecture Reference Model for the Cloud-Based Cyber-Physical Systems". In: *IEEE Access* PP, pp. 1–1. DOI: https://doi.org/10.1109/ACCESS.2017.2657006.

Allen, Mark and Dalton Cervo (Dec. 2015). "Data Quality Management". In: pp. 131–160. DOI: https://doi.org/10.1016/B978-0-12-800835-5.00009-9.

Aminov, Iskandar (2019). *Decision making in the age of urgency*. URL: https://www.Mckinsey.com/business-functions/people-and-organizational-performance/our-insights/decision-making-in-the-age-of-urgency.

Anagnostopoulos, Christos (Dec. 2016). "Quality-optimized predictive analytics". In: *Applied Intelligence* 45. DOI: https://doi.org/10.1007/s10489-016-0807-x.

F. Blaschke, *Implementation and Benefits of Digital Twin on Decision Making and Data Quality Management*, https://doi.org/10.1007/978-3-658-44453-2

Apte, Puskhar P. and Costas J. Spanos (2021). *The Digital Twin Opportunity*. URL: https://sloanreview.mit.edu/article/the-digital-twin-opportunity/.

Apuke, Oberiri (Oct. 2017). "Quantitative Research Methods : A Synopsis Approach". In: *Arabian Journal of Business and Management Review (kuwait Chapter)*. 6, pp. 40–47. DOI: https://doi.org/10.12816/0040336.

Aqel, Musbah, Omar Nakshabandi, Ayodeji Adeniyi, Musbah Firstauthor, and Aqel (Aug. 2019). "Decision Support Systems Classification in Industry". In: *Periodicals of Engineering and Natural Sciences (PEN)* 7, pp. 774–785. DOI: https://doi.org/10.21533/pen.v7i2.550.

Arrichiello, Vincenzo and Paola Gualeni (Mar. 2020). "Systems engineering and digital twin: a vision for the future of cruise ships design, production and operations". In: *International Journal on Interactive Design and Manufacturing (IJIDeM)* 14. DOI: https://doi.org/10.1007/s12008-019-00621-3.

Augustine, Peter (Jan. 2019). "The industry use cases for the Digital Twin idea". In: ISBN: 9780128187562. DOI: https://doi.org/10.1016/bs.adcom.2019.10.008.

Avison, David, Steve Elliot, John Krogstie, and Jan Pries-Heje (Jan. 2006). *The Past and Future of Information Systems: 1976–2006 and Beyond: IFIP 19th World Computer Congress, TC-8, Information System Stream, August 21–23, 2006, Santiago, Chile*. Vol. 214. DOI: https://doi.org/10.1007/978-0-387-34732-5.

Awino, Zachary (Feb. 2013). "Top Management Team Diversity, Quality Decisions and Organizational Performance in the Service Industry". In: *Journal of Management and Strategy* 4. DOI: https://doi.org/10.5430/jms.v4n1p113.

Azevedo, Miguel, Sérgio Tavares, and António Soares (Nov. 2020). "The Digital Twin as a Knowledge-Based Engineering Enabler for Product Development". In: pp. 450–459. ISBN: 978-3-030-62411-8. DOI: https://doi.org/10.1007/978-3-030-62412-5_37

Babu, M. and Hanumanth Sastry (June 2014). "Big data and predictive analytics in ERP systems for automating decision making process". In: pp. 259–262. DOI: https://doi.org/10.1109/ICSESS.2014.6933558.

Barricelli, Barbara, Elena Casiraghi, and Daniela Fogli (Nov. 2019). "A Survey on Digital Twin: Definitions, Char acteristics, Applications, and Design Implications". In: *IEEE Access* PP, pp. 1–1. DOI: https://doi.org/10.1109/ACCESS.2019.2953499.

Batini, Carlo, Cinzia Cappiello, Chiara Francalanci, and Andrea Maurino (July 2009). "Methodologies for Data Quality Assessment and Improvement". In: *ACM Comput. Surv.* 41.3. DOI: https://doi.org/10.1145/1541880.1541883.

Batini, Carlo and Monica Scannapieco (Jan. 2006). *Data Quality: Concepts, Methodologies and Techniques*. DOI: https://doi.org/10.1007/3-540-33173-5.

Batini, Carlo and Monica Scannapieco (2016). "Data and information quality". In: *Cham, Switzerland: Springer International Publishing. Google Scholar* 43. DOI: https://doi.org/10.1007/978-3-319-24106-7.

Bellatreche, Ladjel et al. (Aug. 2020). *ADBIS, TPDL and EDA 2020 Common Workshops and Doctoral Consortium International Workshops: DOING, MADEISD, SKG, BBIGAP, SIMPDA, AIMinScience 2020 and Doctoral Consortium, Lyon, France, August 25–27, 2020, Proceedings: International Workshops: DOING, MADEISD, SKG, BBIGAP, SIMPDA, AIMinScience 2020 and Doctoral Consortium, Lyon, France, August 25–27, 2020, Proceedings*. DOI: https://doi.org/10.1007/978-3-030-55814-7.

Biewendt, Marcel, Florian Blaschke, and Arno Böhnert (Jan. 2020). "An Evaluation of Corporate Sustainability In Context of the Jevons Paradox". In: *SocioEconomic Challenges* 4, pp. 46–65. DOI: https://doi.org/10.21272/sec.4(3).46-65.2020.

Blaschke, Florian, Marcel Biewendt, and Arno Böhnert (Feb. 2021). "The Repercussions of the Digital Twin in the Automotive Industry on the New Marketing Logic". In: *European Journal of Marketing and Economics* 3. DOI: https://doi.org/10.26417/229eim64f.

Blenko, Marcia W., Michael C. Mankins, and Paul Rogers (2010). *Decide & deliver: 5 steps to breakthrough performance in your organization / Marcia W. Blenko, Michael C. Mankins, and Paul Rogers ; with John Case and Jenny Davis-Peccoud*. Boston, Mass.: Harvard Business Review and London: McGraw-Hill [distributor]. ISBN: 978-1422147573.

Boschert, Stefan, Christoph Heinrich, and R. Rosen (May 2018). "Next Generation Digital Twin". In. Boschert, Stefan and Roland Rosen (2016). "Digital Twin—The Simulation Aspect". In: *Mechatronic Futures: Challenges and Solutions for Mechatronic Systems and their Designers*. Ed. by Peter Hehenberger and David Bradley. Cham: Springer International Publishing, pp. 59–74. DOI: https://doi.org/10.1007/978-3-319-32156-1.

Bousquet, Françoise, Vladislav Fomin, and Dominique Drillon (Jan. 2011). "Anticipatory Standards Development and Competitive Intelligence". In: *IJBIR* 2, pp. 16–30. DOI: https://doi.org/10.4018/jbir.2011010102.

Brüggemann, Stefan and Fabian Grüning (2009). "Using Ontologies Providing Domain Knowledge for Data Quality Management". In: *Networked Knowledge—Networked Media: Integrating Knowledge Management, New Media Technologies and Semantic Systems*. Ed. by Tassilo Pellegrini, Sóren Auer, Klaus Tochtermann, and Sebastian Schaffert. Berlin, Heidelberg: Springer Berlin Heidelberg, pp. 187–203. DOI: https://doi.org/10.1007/978-3-642-02184-8_13.

Bruynseels, Koen, Filippo Santoni de Sio, and Jeroen van den Hoven (2018). "Digital Twins in Health Care: Ethical Implications of an Emerging Engineering Paradigm". In: *Frontiers in genetics* 9, p. 31. ISSN: 1664-8021. DOI: https://doi.org/10.3389/fgene.2018.00031.

Burstein, Frada and Clyde W. Holsapple, eds. (2008). *Handbook on Decision Support Systems 1*. Berlin, Heidelberg: Springer Berlin Heidelberg. ISBN: 978-3-540-48712-8. DOI: https://doi.org/10.1007/978-3-540-48713-5.

Cai, Hongxia, Wei Zhang, and Zheng Zhu (2019). "Quality Management and Analysis of Aircraft Final Assembly Based on Digital Twin". In: *2019 11th International Conference on Intelligent Human-Machine Systems and Cybernetics (IHMSC)*. Vol. 1, pp. 202–205. DOI: https://doi.org/10.1109/IHMSC.2019.00054.

Cai, Li and Yangyong Zhu (2015). "The Challenges of Data Quality and Data Quality Assessment in the Big Data Era". In: 14. DOI: https://doi.org/10.5334/dsj-2015-002.

Canedo, Arquimedes (Oct. 2016). "Industrial IoT lifecycle via digital twins". In: pp. 1–1. DOI: https://doi.org/10.1145/2968456.2974007.

Chatti, Sami and Tullio Tolio, eds. (2019). *CIRP Encyclopedia of Production Engineering*. Berlin, Heidelberg: Springer Berlin Heidelberg. ISBN: 978-3-642-35950-7. DOI: https://doi.org/10.1007/978-3-642-35950-7.

Chen, Qiuan, Zhenwei Zhu, Shubin Si, and Zhiqiang Cai (Dec. 2020). "Intelligent Maintenance of Complex Equipment Based on Blockchain and Digital Twin Technologies". In: pp. 908–912. DOI: https://doi.org/10.1109/IEEM45057.2020.9309898.

Cohen, Barry H. (2008). *Explaining psychological statistics*. 3rd ed. Hoboken, N.J.: John Wiley & Sons. ISBN: 978-0470007181.

Cohen, Jacob (1988). *Statistical power analysis for the behavioral sciences*. 2nd ed. Hillsdale, N.J.: L. Erlbaum Associates. ISBN: 9780805802832.

Conejos Fuertes, P., F. Martínez Alzamora, M. Hervás Carot, and J. C. Alonso Campos (2020). "Building and exploiting a Digital Twin for the management of drinking water distribution networks". In: *Urban Water Journal* 17.8, pp. 704–713. ISSN: 1573-062X. DOI: https://doi.org/10.1080/1573062X.2020.1771382.

Cortés, Daniel, José Ramírez, Luis Villagómez, Rafael Batres, Virgilio López, and Arturo Molina (June 2020). "Digital Pyramid: an approach to relate industrial automation and digital twin concepts". In: pp. 1–7. DOI: https://doi.org/10.1109/ICE/ITMC49519.2020.9198643.

Creswell, John W (2002). "Educational research: Planning, conducting, and evaluating quantitative". In: *Prentice Hall Upper Saddle River, NJ*. ISSN: 9780131367395.

Creswell, John W. (2003). *Research design: Qualitative, quantitative, and mixed methods approaches / John W. Creswell*. 2nd ed. Thousand Oaks, Calif. and London: Sage. ISBN: 9780761924425.

CRIF (Sept. 2018). *Verteilung der Führungskräfte in Deutschland nach Altersgruppen im Jahr 2018*. URL: https://de.statista.com/statistik/daten/studie/182538.

Datta, Shoumen Palit Austin (2017). "Emergence of Digital Twins—Is this the march of reason?" In: *Journal of Innovation Management* 5.3, pp. 14–33. DOI: https://doi.org/10.24840/2183-0606_005.003_0003.

DebRoy, T., W. Zhang, J. Turner, and S. S. Babu (2017). "Building digital twins of 3D printing machines". In: *Scripta Materialia* 135, pp. 119–124. ISSN: 1359–6462. DOI: https://doi.org/10.1016/j.scriptamat.2016.12.005.

Deryabin, Sergey, Igor Temkin, and Sergey Zykov (Jan. 2020). "About some issues of developing Digital Twins for the intelligent process control in quarries". In: *Procedia Computer Science* 176, pp. 3210–3216. DOI: https://doi.org/10.1016/j.procs.2020.09.128.

Dong, Xinhua, Heng He, Chao Li, Yongchuan Liu, and Houbo Xiong (2018). "Scene-Based Big Data Quality Management Framework". In: *Data Science*. Ed. by Qinglei Zhou, Yong Gan, Weipeng Jing, Xianhua Song, Yan Wang, and Zeguang Lu. Singapore: Springer Singapore, pp. 122–139. DOI: https://doi.org/10.1007/978-981-13-2203-7_10.

Drucker, P. F. (1963). *Managing for business effectiveness*. URL: https://hbr.org/1963/05/managing-for-business-effectiveness.

Durão, Luiz, Sebastian Haag, Reiner Anderl, Klaus Schützer, and Eduardo Zancul (July 2018). "Digital Twin Requirements in the Context of Industry 4.0: 15th IFIP WG 5.1 International Conference, PLM 2018, Turin, Italy, July 2–4, 2018, Proceedings". In: pp. 204–214. DOI: https://doi.org/10.1007/978-3-030-01614-2_19.

Erol, Tolga, Arif Mendi, and Dilara Dogan (Oct. 2020). "Digital Transformation Revolution with Digital Twin Technology". In: pp. 1–7. DOI: https://doi.org/10.1109/ISMSIT50672.2020.9254288.

Errandonea, Itxaro, Sergio Beltrán, and Saioa Arrizabalaga (2020). "Digital Twin for maintenance: A literature review". In: *Computers in Industry* 123, p. 103316. ISSN: 0166–3615. DOI: https://doi.org/10.1016/j.compind.2020.103316.

Even, Adir, G. Shankaranarayanan, and Paul D. Berger (2010). "Evaluating a model for cost-effective data quality management in a real-world CRM setting". In: *Decision Support*

Systems 50.1, pp. 152–163. ISSN: 0167–9236. DOI: https://doi.org/10.1016/j.dss.2010.07.011.

Fatimah, Sidi, Payam Hassany Shariat Panahy, Suriani Affendey Lilly, Marzanah A. Jabar, Hamidah Ibrahim, and Aida Mustapha (2012). "Data quality: A survey of data quality dimensions". In: *2012 International Conference on Information Retrieval Knowledge Management*, pp. 300–304. DOI: https://doi.org/10.1109/InfRKM.2012.6204995.

Feldt geb. Wagner, Julia, Thanos Kourouklis, Henning Kontny, and Axel Wagenitz (Jan. 2020). "Digital twin: revealing potentials of real-time autonomous decisions at a manufacturing company". In: *Procedia CIRP* 88, pp. 185–190. DOI: https://doi.org/10.1016/j.procir.2020.05.033.

Fielder, Andrew, Emmanouil Panaousis, Pasquale Malacaria, Chris Hankin, and Fabrizio Smeraldi (2016). "Decision support approaches for cyber security investment". In: *Decision Support Systems* 86, pp. 13–23. ISSN: 0167-9236. DOI: https://doi.org/10.1016/j.dss.2016.02.012.

Fritz, Catherine, Peter Morris, and Jennifer Richler (Aug. 2011). "Effect Size Estimates: Current Use, Calculations, and Interpretation". In: *Journal of experimental psychology. General* 141, pp. 2–18. DOI: https://doi.org/10.1037/a0024338.

Fuller,Aidan, Zhong Fan, Charles Day, and Chris Barlow (May 2020). "Digital Twin: Enabling Technologies, Challenges and Open Research". In: *IEEE Access* PP, pp. 1–1. DOI: https://doi.org/10.1109/ACCESS.2020.2998358.

Fürber,Christian (2016). *Semantic Technologies*. Springer, pp. 56–68. DOI: https://doi.org/10.1007/978-3-658-12225-6.

Fürber,Christian and Martin Hepp (2010). "Using Semantic Web Resources for Data Quality Management". In: *Knowledge Engineering and Management by the Masses*. Ed. by Philipp Cimiano and H. Sofia Pinto. Berlin, Heidelberg: Springer Berlin Heidelberg, pp. 211–225. DOI: https://doi.org/10.1007/978-3-642-16438-5_15.

Fürber, Christian and Martin Hepp (Feb. 2013). "Using Semantic Web Technologies for Data Quality Management". In: *Handbook of Data Quality: Research and Practice*, pp. 141–161. DOI: https://doi.org/10.1007/978-3-642-36257-6_7.

Ganguli, R. and S. Adhikari (2020). "The digital twin of discrete dynamic systems: Initial approaches and future challenges". In: *Applied Mathematical Modelling* 77, pp. 1110–1128. ISSN: 0307-904X. DOI: https://doi.org/10.1016/j.apm.2019.09.036.

Gartner (2017a). *Gartner's Top 10 Strategic Technology Trends for 2017*. URL: https://www.gartner.com/smarterwithgartner/gartners-top-10-technology-trends-2017/.

Gartner (2017b). *Prepare for the Impact of Digital Twins*. URL: https://www.gartner.com/smarterwithgartner/prepare-for-the-impact-of-digital-twins.

Gartner (2018). *Gartner's Top 10 Strategic Technology Trends for 2018*. URL: https://www.gartner.com/smarterwithgartner/gartner-top-10-strategic-technology-trends-for-2018/.

Gartner (2019). *Gartner's Top 10 Strategic Technology Trends for 2019*. URL: https://www.gartner.com/smarterwithgartner/gartner-top-10-strategic-technology-trends-for-2019/.

Gartner (2020). *Gartner's Top 10 Strategic Technology Trends for 2020*. URL: https://www.gartner.com/smarterwithgartner/gartner-top-10-strategic-technology-trends-for-2020/.

GE (2021). *Digital Twin*. URL: https://www.ge.com/digital/applications/digital-twin.

Geerdink, Bas (Dec. 2013). "A reference architecture for big data solutions introducing a model to perform predictive analytics using big data technology". In: pp. 71–76. DOI: https://doi.org/10.1109/ICITST.2013.6750165.

Glaessgen, Edward and David Stargel (Apr. 2012). "The digital twin paradigm for future NASA and U.S. air force vehicles". In: ISBN: 978-1-60086-937-2. DOI: https://doi.org/10.2514/6.2012-1818.

Glowalla, Paul, Patryk Balazy, Dirk Basten, and Ali Sunyaev (Jan. 2014). "Process-Driven Data Quality Manage ment—An Application of the Combined Conceptual Life Cycle Model". In: DOI: https://doi.org/10.1109/HICSS.2014.575.

Glowalla, Pauland Ali Sunyaev (Dec. 2013). "Process-Driven Data Quality Management Through Integration of Data Quality into Existing Process Models". In: *Business Information Systems Engineering* 5, pp. 433–448. DOI: https://doi.org/10.1007/s12599-013-0297-x.

Grieves, Michael (Mar. 2015). "Digital Twin: Manufacturing Excellence through Virtual Factory Replication". In. Grieves, Michael (Aug. 2016). *Origins of the Digital Twin Concept.* DOI: https://doi.org/10.13140/RG.2.2.26367.61609.

Grieves, Michael and John Vickers (Aug. 2017). "Digital Twin: Mitigating Unpredictable, Undesirable Emergent Behavior in Complex Systems". In: pp. 85–113. DOI: https://doi.org/10.1007/978-3-319-38756-7_4.

Guo, Jiapeng, Ning Zhao, Lin Sun, and Saipeng Zhang (2019). "Modular based flexible digital twin for factory design". In: *Journal of Ambient Intelligence and Humanized Computing* 10.3, pp. 1189–1200. ISSN: 1868-5137. DOI: https://doi.org/10.1007/s12652-018-0953-6.

Gupta, M., A. Serebrenik, and P. Jalote (2017). "Improving Software Maintenance Using Process Mining and Predictive Analytics". In: *2017 IEEE International Conference on Software Maintenance and Evolution (ICSME)*, pp. 681–686. DOI: https://doi.org/10.1109/ICSME.2017.39.

Haag, Sebastian and Reiner Anderl (Feb. 2018). "Digital Twin—Proof of Concept". In: *Manufacturing Letters* 15. DOI: https://doi.org/10.1016/j.mfglet.2018.02.006.

Helmy Ismail Abdelaal, Mariam, Mohamed Khater, and Mohamed Zaki (Jan. 2018). "Digital Business Transformation and Strategy: What Do We Know So Far?" In: DOI: https://doi.org/10.13140/RG.2.2.36492.62086.

Hermann, Mario, Tobias Pentek, and Boris Otto (Jan. 2015). *Design Principles for Industrie 4.0 Scenarios: A Literature Review.* DOI: https://doi.org/10.13140/RG.2.2.29269.22248.

Hernes, Marcin, Andrzej Bytniewski, Karolina Maten´czuk, Artur Rot, Szymon Dziuba, Marcin Fojcik, Tran Nguyet, Pawel Golec, and Agata Kozina (Nov. 2020). "Data Quality Management in ERP Systems—Accounting Case". In: pp. 353–362. DOI: https://doi.org/10.1007/978-3-030-63119-2_29.

Hofmann, Wladimir and Fredrik Branding (Jan. 2019). "Implementation of an IoT- and Cloud-based Digital Twin for Real-Time Decision Support in Port Operations". In: *IFAC-PapersOnLine* 52, pp. 2104–2109. DOI: https://doi.org/10.1016/j.ifacol.2019.11.516.

Hogenboom, Frederik, Flavius Frasincar, Uzay Kaymak, Franciska de Jong, and Emiel Caron (2016). "A Survey of event extraction methods from text for decision support systems". In: *Decision Support Systems* 85, pp. 12–22. ISSN: 0167-9236. DOI: https://doi.org/10.1016/j.dss.2016.02.006.

Holsapple, Clyde and Mark Sena (Aug. 2003). "The Decision-Support Characteristics of ERP Systems". In: *Int. J. Hum. Comput. Interaction* 16, pp. 101–123. DOI: https://doi.org/10.1207/S15327590IJHC1601_7.

Hopkins, Sarah, Joseph Dettori, and Jens Chapman (June 2018). "Parametric and Nonparametric Tests in Spine Research: Why Do They Matter?" In: *Global Spine Journal* 8, p. 219256821878267. DOI: https://doi.org/10.1177/2192568218782679.

Hosack, Bryan, Dianne Hall, David Paradice, and James Courtney (May 2012). "A Look Toward the Future: Decision Support Systems Research is Alive and Well". In: *Journal of the Association for Information Systems* 13, pp. 315–340. DOI: https://doi.org/10.17705/1jais.00297.

Howard, Ronald A. (1988). "Decision Analysis: Practice and Promise". In: *Management Science* 34.6, pp. 679–695. ISSN: 0025-1909. DOI: https://doi.org/10.1287/mnsc.34.6.679.

Husamaldin, Laden and Nagham Saeed (2020). "Big Data Analytics Correlation Taxonomy". In: *Information* 11.1. ISSN: 2078-2489. DOI: https://doi.org/10.3390/info11010017. URL: https://www.mdpi.com/2078-2489/11/1/17.

IBM (2021). *What is a digital twin?* URL: https://www.ibm.com/topics/what-is-a-digital-twin.

Infiniti (2021). *Digital Twin Market by End-user, Deployment, and Geography—Forecast and Analysis 2021–2025.* URL: https://www.technavio.com/report/digital-twin-market-size-industry-analysis.

ISO (2015). *ISO 9000:2015(en) Quality management systems.* URL: https://www.iso.org/standard/45481.html.

Jaensch, Florian, Akos Csiszar, Christian Scheifele, and Alexander Verl (Nov. 2018). "Digital Twins of Manufacturing Systems as a Base for Machine Learning". In: pp. 1–6. DOI: https://doi.org/10.1109/M2VIP.2018.8600844.

Jaya, Izham, Fatimah Sidi, Iskandar Ishak, Lilly Affendey, and Marzanah A. Jabar (June 2017). "A review of data quality research in achieving high data quality within organization". In: *Journal of Theoretical and Applied Information Technology* 95, pp. 2647–2657. ISSN: 1992-8645.

Jiang, Haifan, Shengfeng Qin, Jianlin Fu, Jian Zhang, and Guofu Ding (2020). "How to model and implement connections between physical and virtual models for digital twin application". In: *Journal of Manufacturing Systems.* DOI: https://doi.org/10.1016/j.jmsy.2020.05.012.

Jiang, Hao, Jia-xin Liu, Yi Zhang, and Chun-hua Yu (Jan. 2013). "An Exploration of Data Quality Management Based on Allocation Efficiency Model". In: pp. 943–953. DOI: https://doi.org/10.1007/978-3-642-40072-8_94.

Jiang, Lizheng and Jiantao Zhao (Oct. 2012). "An empirical study on risk data quality management". In: pp. 511–514. DOI: https://doi.org/10.1109/ICIII.2012.6339714.

Kahn, Beverly, Diane Strong, and Richard Wang (Apr. 2002). "Information Quality Benchmarks: Product and Service Performance". In: *Commun. ACM* 45, pp. 184–192. DOI: https://doi.org/10.1145/505999.506007.

Kamath, Vignesh, Jeff Morgan, and Muhammad Intizar Ali (June 2020). "Industrial IoT and Digital Twins for a Smart Factory : An open source toolkit for application design and benchmarking". In: pp. 1–6. DOI: https://doi.org/10.1109/GIOTS49054.2020.9119497.

Karkouch, Aimad, Hajar Mousannif, Hassan Al Moatassime, and Thomas Noël (May 2016). "A model-driven architecture-based data quality management framework for the internet of Things". In: pp. 252–259. DOI: https://doi.org/10.1109/CloudTech.2016.7847707.

Katz, Daniel and Robert Louis Kahn (1978). *The social psychology of organizations*. 2nd ed. New York and Chichester: Wiley. ISBN: 978-0471023555.

Kaur, Maninder, Ved P Mishra, and Piyush Maheshwari (Jan. 2020). “The Convergence of Digital Twin, IoT, and Machine Learning: Transforming Data into Action”. In: pp. 3–17. DOI: https://doi.org/10.1007/978-3-030-18732-3_1.

Keefer, Donald L., Craig W. Kirkwood, and James L. Corner (2004). “Perspective on Decision Analysis Applications, 1990–2001”. In: *Decision Analysis* 1.1, pp. 4–22. ISSN: 1545-8490. DOI: https://doi.org/10.1287/deca.1030.0004.

Khan,Samir, Michael Farnsworth, Richard McWilliam, and John Erkoyuncu (2020). “On the requirements of digital twin-driven autonomous maintenance”. In: *Annual Reviews in Control* 50, pp. 13–28. ISSN: 1367-5788. DOI: https://doi.org/10.1016/j.arcontrol.2020.08.003.

Kiritsis, Dimitris (May 2011). “Closed-Loop PLM for intelligent products in the era of the Internet-Of-Things”. In: *Computer-Aided Design* 43, pp. 479–501. DOI: https://doi.org/10.1016/j.cad.2010.03.002.

Kong, Leo Chi Wai, Sam Harper, Daniel Mitchell, Jamie Blanche, Theodore Lim, and David Flynn (2020). “Interactive Digital Twins Framework for Asset Management Through Internet”. In: *2020 IEEE Global Conference on Artificial Intelligence and Internet of Things (GCAIoT)*, pp. 1–7. DOI: https://doi.org/10.1109/GCAIoT51063.2020.9345890.

Konstantinov, Sergey, Mussawar Ahmad, Karthik Ananthanarayan, and Robert Harrison (Dec. 2017). “The Cyber- physical E-machine Manufacturing System: Virtual Engineering for Complete Lifecycle Support”. In: *Procedia CIRP* 63, pp. 119–124. DOI: https://doi.org/10.1016/j.procir.2017.02.035.

Kopáčková, Hana and Markéta Škrobáčková (2006). “Decision support systems or business intelligence : what can help in decision making?” In. Kraemer, Kenneth L. (1991). *The information systems research challenge: Survey research methods : Methodology colloquium on survey research : Papers. Vol 3, Survey Research Methods*. Vol. vol 3. Harvard Business School research colloquium. Boston: Harvard Business School. ISBN: 9780875842592.

Kritzinger, Werner, Matthias Karner, Georg Traar, Jan Henjes, and Wilfried Sihn (Jan. 2018). “Digital Twin in manufacturing: A categorical literature review and classification”. In: *IFAC-PapersOnLine* 51, pp. 1016–1022. DOI: https://doi.org/10.1016/j.ifacol.2018.08.474.

Kruskal, William H. and W. Allen Wallis (1952). “Use of Ranks in One-Criterion Variance Analysis”. In: *Journal of the American Statistical Association* 47.260, p. 583. ISSN: 0162-1459. DOI: https://doi.org/10.2307/2280779.

Kumar, Rohit (Nov. 2017). “Predictive Analytics”. In: pp. 75–97. DOI: https://doi.org/10.1007/978-1-4842-3069-5_6.

Kunath, Martin and Herwig Winkler (June 2018). “Integrating the Digital Twin of the manufacturing system into a decision support system for improving the order management process”. In: *Procedia CIRP* 72. DOI: https://doi.org/10.1016/j.procir.2018.03.192.

Lee, Edward (June 2008). “Cyber Physical Systems: Design Challenges”. In: pp. 363–369. ISBN: 978-0-7695-3132-8. DOI: https://doi.org/10.1109/ISORC.2008.25.

Lee, Ming-Xuan, Yen-Chun Lee, and Chiyang James Chou (2017). “Essential Implications of the Digital Transformation in Industry 4.0”. In: *Journal of Scientific & Industrial Research* 76, pp. 465–467.

Leedy, Paul D. and Jeanne Ellis Ormrod (2001). *Practical research: Planning and design / Paul D. Leedy, Jeanne Ellis Ormrod ; with contributions by Timothy J. Newby and Peggy A. Ertmer*. 7th ed. Upper Saddle River, N.J.: Merrill. ISBN: 9780536859570.

Li, Chenzhao, Sankaran Mahadevan, You Ling, Liping Wang, and Sergio Choze (Jan. 2017). "A dynamic Bayesian network approach for digital twin". In: DOI: https://doi.org/10.2514/6.2017-1566.

Lim, Kendrik Yan Hong, Pai Zheng, and Chun-Hsien Chen (Aug. 2020). "A state-of-the-art survey of Digital Twin: techniques, engineering product lifecycle management and business innovation perspectives". In: *Journal of Intelligent Manufacturing*. DOI: https://doi.org/10.1007/s10845-019-01512-w.

Lipshitz, Raanan and Orna Strauss (1997). "Coping with Uncertainty: A Naturalistic Decision-Making Analysis". In: *Organizational Behavior and Human Decision Processes* 69.2, pp. 149–163. ISSN: 07495978. DOI: https://doi.org/10.1006/obhd.1997.2679.

Liu, Mengnan, Fang Shuiliang, Huiyue Dong, and Cunzhi Xu (July 2020). "Review of digital twin about concepts, technologies, and industrial applications". In: *Journal of Manufacturing Systems* 58. DOI: https://doi.org/10.1016/j.jmsy.2020.06.017.

Liu, Xiaojun, Jinfeng Liu, Honggen Zhou, and Zhonghua Ni (Jan. 2020). "Digital twin driven process design evaluation". In: pp. 309–332. ISBN: 9780128189184. DOI: https://doi.org/10.1016/B978-0-12-818918-4.00012-9.

Liu, Zhifeng, Wei Chen, Caixia Zhang, Congbin Yang, and Hongyan Chu (Dec. 2019). "Data Super-Network Fault Prediction Model and Maintenance Strategy for Mechanical Product Based on Digital Twin". In: *IEEE Access* PP, pp. 1–1. DOI: https://doi.org/10.1109/ACCESS.2019.2957202.

Löcklin, Andreas, Manuel Müller, Tobias Jung, Nasser Jazdi, Dustin White, and Michael Weyrich (Sept. 2020). "Digital Twin for Verification and Validation of Industrial Automation Systems a Survey". In: DOI: https://doi.org/10.1109/ETFA46521.2020.9212051.

Lu, Yuqian, Chao Liu, Kevin Wang, Huiyue Huang, and Xun Xu (Aug. 2019). "Digital Twin-driven smart manufacturing: Connotation, reference model, applications and research issues". In: *Robotics and Computer-Integrated Manufacturing* 61. DOI: https://doi.org/10.1016/j.rcim.2019.101837.

Lutters, Eric and Roy Damgrave (2019). "The development of Pilot Production Environments based on Digital Twins and Virtual Dashboards". In: *Procedia CIRP* 84, pp. 94–99. ISSN: 2212-8271. DOI: https://doi.org/10.1016/j.procir.2019.04.228.

Mabkhot, Mohammed, Abdulrahman Al-Ahmari, Bashir Salah, and Hisham Alkhalefah (2018). "Requirements of the Smart Factory System: A Survey and Perspective". In: *Machines* 6.2, p. 23. DOI: https://doi.org/10.3390/machines6020023.

Madni, Azad, Carla Madni, and Scott Lucero (2019). "Leveraging Digital Twin Technology in Model-Based Systems Engineering". In: *Systems* 7.1, p. 7. DOI: https://doi.org/10.3390/systems7010007.

Makarov, V.V., Ye.B. Frolov, I. Parshina, and M.V. Ushakova (Oct. 2019). "The Design Concept of Digital Twin". In: pp. 1–4. DOI: https://doi.org/10.1109/MLSD.2019.8911091.

Mandl, Ulrike, Adriaan Dierx, and Fabienne Ilzkovitz (Jan. 2008). "The effectiveness and efficiency of public spending". In: *Directorate General Economic and Monetary Affairs, European Commission, European Economy—Economic Papers*.

Mao, Xu, Bowen Gong, Fei Su, Kaicheng Xu, Kuitong Xian, Donghua Liu, and Hua Guo (Jan. 2019). "Data Quality Management and Measurement: Proceedings of the 4th International Conference on Signal and Information Processing, Networking and Computers (ICSINC)". In: pp. 229–236. DOI: https://doi.org/10.1007/978-981-13-1733-0_28.

MarketsandMarkets (2020). *Digital Twin Market by Technology, Type (Product, Process, and System), Application (predictive maintenance, and others), Industry (Aerospace Defense, Automotive Transportation, Healthcare, and others), and Geography—Global Forecast to 2026*. URL: https://www.marketsandmarkets.com/Market-Reports/digital-twin-market-225269522.html.

Marsh, Richard (Jan. 2005). "Drowning in dirty data? It's time to sink or swim: A four-stage methodology for total data quality management". In: *The Journal of Database Marketing Customer Strategy Management* 12, pp. 105–112. DOI: https://doi.org/10.1057/palgrave.dbm.3240247.

Mathupriya, S., S. Saira Banu, S. Sridhar, and B. Arthi (2020). "Digital twin technology on IoT, industries other smart environments: A survey". In: *Materials Today: Proceedings*. ISSN: 2214-7853. DOI: https://doi.org/10.1016/j.matpr.2020.11.358.

Mccarthy, Richard, Mary McCarthy, Wendy Ceccucci, and Leila Halawi (Jan. 2019). "Introduction to Predictive Analytics: Finding Value in Data". In: pp. 1–25. DOI: https://doi.org/10.1007/978-3-030-14038-0_1.

McGregor, Lynn (Dec. 2001). "Improving the quality and speed of decision making". In: *Journal of Change Management* 2, pp. 344–356. DOI: https://doi.org/10.1080/714042513.

Meierhofer, Jürg and Shaun West (June 2020). "Data-Driven Decision Support by Digital Twins in Manufacturing". In: *Proceedings of the IEEE*. DOI: https://doi.org/10.1109/SDS49233.2020.00019.

Melesse, Tsega, Valentina Di Pasquale, and Stefano Riemma (Apr. 2020). "Digital Twin Models in Industrial Operations: A Systematic Literature Review". In: vol. 42. DOI: https://doi.org/10.1016/j.promfg.2020.02.084.

Microsoft (2021). *Azure Digital Twins—Use IoT spatial intelligence to create models of physical environments*. URL: https://azure.microsoft.com/en-us/services/digital-twins/#overview.

Mircioiu, Constantin and Jeffrey Atkinson (May 2017). "A Comparison of Parametric and Non-Parametric Methods Applied to a Likert Scale". In: *Pharmacy* 5, p. 26. DOI: https://doi.org/10.3390/pharmacy5020026.

Mitra, S. and Pramod Pathak (Dec. 1984). "The Nature of Simple Random Sampling". In: *The Annals of Statistics* 12. DOI: https://doi.org/10.1214/aos/1176346810.

Moher, David, Alessandro Liberati, Jennifer Tetzlaff, and Douglas G. Altman (2009). "Preferred reporting items for systematic reviews and meta-analyses: the PRISMA statement". In: *PLoS medicine* 6.7, e1000097. DOI: https://doi.org/10.1371/journal.pmed.1000097.

Morana, Stefan, Silvia Schacht, Ansgar Scherp, and Alexander Maedche (May 2017). "A review of the nature and effects of guidance design features". In: *Decision Support Systems* 97, pp. 31–42. DOI: https://doi.org/10.1016/j.dss.2017.03.003.

Nagle, Tadhg, Thomas C. Redman, and David Sammon (2017). *Only 3% of Companies' Data Meets Basic Quality Standards*. URL: https://hbr.org/2017/09/only-3-of-companies-data-meets-basic-quality-standards.

Negulescu, Oriana and Elena Doval (Dec. 2014). "The Quality of Decision Making Process Related to Organiza tions' Effectiveness". In: *Procedia Economics and Finance* 15. DOI: https://doi.org/10.1016/S2212-5671(14)00548-6.

Nikolaev, S., M. Gusev, D. Padalitsa, E. Mozhenkov, S. Mishin, and I. Uzhinsky (2018). "Implementation of "Digital Twin" Concept for Modern Project-Based Engineering Education". In: *Product Lifecycle Management to Support Industry 4.0*. Ed. by Paolo Chiabert, Abdelaziz Bouras, Frédéric Noël, and José Ríos. Vol. 540. IFIP Advances in Information and Communication Technology. Cham: Springer International Publishing, pp. 193–203. ISBN: 978-3-030-01613-5. DOI: https://doi.org/10.1007/978-3-030-01614-2_18.

Ongsulee, Pariwat, Veena Chotchaung, Eak Bamrungsi, and Thanaporn Rodcheewit (Nov. 2018). "Big Data, Predictive Analytics and Machine Learning". In: pp. 1–6. DOI: https://doi.org/10.1109/ICTKE.2018.8612393.

Oo, Myat Cho Mon and Thandar Thein (2019). "An efficient predictive analytics system for high dimensional big data". In: *Journal of King Saud University—Computer and Information Sciences*. ISSN: 1319-1578. DOI: https://doi.org/10.1016/j.jksuci.2019.09.001.

Otto, Boris and Hubert Oesterle (Dec. 2015). *Corporate Data Quality: Prerequisite for Successful Business Models*. ISBN: 978-3-7375-7593-5.

Otto, Boris, Kristin Weber, Alexander Schmidt, and Philipp Osl (Dec. 2007). "Towards a Framework for Corporate Data Quality Management". In: *ACIS Proceedings* 109. URL: https://aisel.aisnet.org/acis2007/109/.

Papanagnou, Christos (Jan. 2020). "A Digital Twin Model for Enhancing Performance Measurement in Assembly Lines". In: pp. 53–66. DOI: https://doi.org/10.1007/978-3-030-18732-3_4.

Park, Heejong, Arvind Easwaran, and Sidharta Andalam (2019). "Challenges in Digital Twin Development for Cyber-Physical Production Systems". In: *Cyber Physical Systems. Model-Based Design*. Ed. by Roger Chamberlain, Walid Taha, and Martin Törngren. Vol. 11615. Lecture Notes in Computer Science. Cham: Springer International Publishing, pp. 28–48. ISBN: 978-3-030-23702-8. DOI: https://doi.org/10.1007/978-3-030-23703-5_2.

Parmar, Rashik, Aija Leiponen, and Llewellyn Thomas (Aug. 2020). "Building an organizational digital twin". In: *Business Horizons*. DOI: https://doi.org/10.1016/j.bushor.2020.08.001.

Pavlovich, Tatyana and Elena Dron (Jan. 2020). "Data Quality and Digital Twins in Decision Support Systems of Oil and Gas Companies". In: DOI: https://doi.org/10.2991/aisr.k.201029.028.

Perno, Matteo, Lars Hvam, and Anders Haug (Dec. 2020). "Enablers and Barriers to the Implementation of Digital Twins in the Process Industry: A Systematic Literature Review". In: pp. 959–964. DOI: https://doi.org/10.1109/IEEM45057.2020.9309745.

Persson, Anders and Iordanis Kavathatzopoulos (Oct. 2017). "How to make decisions with algorithms". In: *ORBIT Journal* 1. DOI: https://doi.org/10.29297/orbit.v1i2.44.

Pires, Flávia, Ana Cachada, José Barbosa, António Paulo Moreira, and Paulo Leitão (2019). "Digital Twin in Industry 4.0: Technologies, Applications and Challenges". In: *2019 IEEE 17th International Conference on Industrial Informatics (INDIN)*. Vol. 1, pp. 721–726. DOI: https://doi.org/10.1109/INDIN41052.2019.8972134.

Platenius-Mohr, Marie, Somayeh Malakuti, Sten Grüner, Johannes Schmitt, and Thomas Goldschmidt (2020). "File- and API-based interoperability of digital twins by model transformation: An IIoT case study using asset administration shell". In: *Future Generation Computer Systems* 113, pp. 94–105. ISSN: 0167-739X. DOI: https://doi.org/10.1016/j.future.2020.07.004.

Porter, Michael E. (1996). *What Is Strategy?* URL: https://hbr.org/1996/11/what-is-strategy.

Power, Daniel (Mar. 2008). "Understanding Data-Driven Decision Support Systems". In: *IS Management* 25, pp. 149–154. DOI: https://doi.org/10.1080/10580530801941124.

Power, Daniel J. (2002). *Decision support systems: Concepts and resources for managers / Daniel J. Power*. Westport, Conn. and London: Quorum Books. ISBN: 978-1567204971.

Power, Daniel J. (2003). "A brief history of decision support systems". In: *DSSResources.COM, World Wide Web*. URL: http://dssresources.com/history/dsshistoryv28.html.

Power, Daniel J. and Ramesh Sharda (2007). "Model-driven decision support systems: Concepts and research directions". In: *Decision Support Systems* 43.3, pp. 1044–1061. ISSN: 0167-9236. DOI: https://doi.org/10.1016/j.dss.2005.05.030.

Prescient and Strategic (2020). *Digital Twin Market Research Report*. URL: https://www.psmarketresearch.com/market-analysis/digital-twin-market.

PTC (2021). *What is a digital twin?* URL: https://www.ptc.com/en/industry-insights/digital-twin.

Qi,Qinglin and Fei Tao (2018). "Digital Twin and Big Data Towards Smart Manufacturing and Industry 4.0: 360 Degree Comparison". In: *IEEE Access* 6, pp. 3585–3593. ISSN: 2169-3536. DOI: https://doi.org/10.1109/ACCESS.2018.2793265.

Qi, Qinglin, Fei Tao, Tianliang Hu, Nabil Anwer, Ang Liu, Yongli Wei, Lihui Wang, and Andrew Nee (Oct. 2019). "Enabling technologies and tools for digital twin". In: *Journal of Manufacturing Systems*. DOI: https://doi.org/10.1016/j.jmsy.2019.10.001.

Qi, Qinglin, Fei Tao, Ying Zuo, and Dongming Zhao (2018). "Digital Twin Service towards Smart Manufacturing". In: *Procedia CIRP* 72, pp. 237–242. ISSN: 2212-8271. DOI: https://doi.org/10.1016/j.procir.2018.03.103.

Qianzhe, Qiao, Jinjiang Wang, Lunkuan Ye, and Robert Gao (Jan. 2019). "Digital Twin for Machining Tool Condition Prediction". In: *Procedia CIRP* 81, pp. 1388–1393. DOI: https://doi.org/10.1016/j.procir.2019.04.049.

Raghunathan, Srinivasan (1999). "Impact of information quality and decision-maker quality on decision quality: a theoretical model and simulation analysis". In: *Decision Support Systems* 26.4, pp. 275–286. ISSN: 0167-9236. DOI: https://doi.org/10.1016/s0167-9236(99)00060-3.

Rahm, Erhard and Hong Hai Do (2000). *Data Cleaning: Problems and Current Approaches*.

Raj, Pethuru and Chellammal Surianarayanan (2020). "Chapter Twelve—Digital twin: The industry use cases". In: *The Digital Twin Paradigm for Smarter Systems and Environments: The Industry Use Cases*. Ed. by Pethuru Raj and Preetha Evangeline. Vol. 117. Advances in Computers 1. Elsevier, pp. 285–320. DOI: https://doi.org/10.1016/bs.adcom.2019.09.006.

Rajratnakharat, Vikas Bavane, Santosh Jadhao, and Roshan Marode (Nov. 2018). "DIGITAL TWIN: MANUFACTURING EXCELLENCE THROUGH VIRTUAL FACTORY REPLICATION". In: DOI: https://doi.org/10.5281/zenodo.1493930.

Rashidi, Maria, Maryam Ghodrat, Bijan Samali, and Masoud Mohammadi (Oct. 2018). "Decision Support Systems". In: pp. 19–38. ISBN: 978-1-78984-197-8. DOI: https://doi.org/10.5772/intechopen.79390.

Rashidi, Maria and Brett Lemass (2011). “A Decision Support Methodology for Remediation Planning of Concrete Bridges”. In: *Journal of Construction Engineering and Project Management* 1.2, pp. 1–10. DOI: https://doi.org/10.6106/JCEPM.2011.1.2.001.

Redman, Thomas (Jan. 2013). “Data quality management past, present, and future: Towards a management system for data”. In: pp. 15–40. DOI: https://doi.org/10.1007/978-3-642-36257-6_2.

Redman, Thomas C. (2001). *Data Quality: The Field Guide.* USA: Digital Press. DOI: https://doi.org/10.5555/362427.

Redman, Thomas C. (2017). *Assess Whether You Have a Data Quality Problem.* URL: https://hbr.org/2016/07/assess-whether-you-have-a-data-quality-problem.

Reis, João, Marlene Amorim, Nuno Melao, and Patrícia Matos (Mar. 2018). “Digital Transformation: A Literature Review and Guidelines for Future Research”. In: pp. 411–421. DOI: https://doi.org/10.1007/978-3-319-77703-0_41.

Research and Markets (2020). *Digital Twin Market: Global Opportunity and Trend Analysis, 2020–2035.* URL: https://www.researchandmarkets.com/reports/5023844/digital-twin-market-global-opportunity-and-trend?utm_source=dynamic&utm_medium=GNOM&utm_code=kqqw3d&utm_campaign=1387608+-+Global+Digital+Twin+Market+(2020+to+2035)+-+Opportunity+and+Trend+Analysis&utm_exec=jamu273gnomd.

Rodič, Blaž (2017). “Industry 4.0 and the New Simulation Modelling Paradigm”. In: *Organizacija* 50.3, pp. 193–207. DOI: https://doi.org/10.1515/orga-2017-0017.

Rossouw, Jannie (Sept. 2013). “A small note about a big difference: Percentage change compared to percentage point change”. In: *Tydskrif vir Geesteswetenskappe* 53, pp. 481–491.

Roy, Sanjiban Sekhar, Pijush Samui, Ravinesh Deo, and Stavros Ntalampiras (2018). *Big Data in Engineering Applications.* 1st. Springer Publishing Company, Incorporated. DOI: https://doi.org/10.5555/3238243.

Sadun, Raffaella, Nicholas Bloom, and John van Reenen (2017). *Why Do We Undervalue Competent Management?* URL: https://hbr.org/2017/09/why-do-we-undervalue-competent-management.

Salehi, Keyvan (Apr. 2015). *Using Mixed Methods in Research Studies: An Opportunity with its Challenges.* DOI: https://doi.org/10.5172/mra.2010.4.3.186.

Samitsch, Christoph (Jan. 2015). *Data Quality and its Impacts on Decision-Making: How Managers can benefit from Good Data*, pp. 1–59. ISBN: 978-3-658-08199-7. DOI: https://doi.org/10.1007/978-3-658-08200-0.

SAP (2021). *Digital Twin.* URL: https://www.sap.com/products/supply-chain-management/digital-twin.html.

Schleich, Benjamin, Nabil Anwer, Luc Mathieu, and Sandro Wartzack (Apr. 2017). “Shaping the digital twin for design and production engineering”. In: *CIRP Annals—Manufacturing Technology* 66, pp. 141–144. DOI: https://doi.org/10.1016/j.cirp.2017.04.040.

Schroeder, Greyce, Charles Steinmetz, Carlos Pereira, and Danúbia Espíndola (Dec. 2016). “Digital Twin Data Modeling with Automation ML and a Communication Methodology for Data Exchange”. In: *IFAC-PapersOnLine* 49. DOI: https://doi.org/10.1016/j.ifacol.2016.11.115.

Schwartz, Evan I. (2001). *Digital Darwinism: 7 Breakthrough Business Strategies for Surviving in the Cutthroat Web Economy.* Broadway Books. ISBN: 076790334X.

Shankaranarayanan, Ganesan and Yu Cai (Oct. 2006). "Supporting data quality management in decision-making". In: *Decision Support Systems* 42, pp. 302–317. DOI: https://doi.org/10.1016/j.dss.2004.12.006.

Shao, Guodong and Moneer Helu (Apr. 2020). "Framework for a Digital Twin in Manufacturing: Scope and Requirements". In: *Manufacturing Letters* 24. DOI: https://doi.org/10.1016/j.mfglet.2020.04.004.

Sheskin, David (2000). *Handbook of parametric and nonparametric statistical procedures.* 2nd ed. Boca Raton: Chapman & Hall/CRC Press. ISBN: 9781584881339.

Shi, Xiaohua, Zhuoyuan Xing, and Hongtao Lu (2019). "Data Quality Management in Institutional Research Output Data Center". In: *Database Systems for Advanced Applications.* Ed. by Guoliang Li, Jun Yang, Joao Gama, Juggapong Natwichai, and Yongxin Tong. Cham: Springer International Publishing, pp. 142–157. DOI: https://doi.org/10.1007/978-3-030-18590-910.

Shurrab, Hafez (Oct. 2014). *Informatics for Socially Sustainable Manufacturing and Production Workplaces.* DOI: https://doi.org/10.13140/RG.2.2.17725.56805.

Siemens (2021). *Digital Twin.* URL: https://new.siemens.com/global/en/company/stories/research-technologies/digitaltwin/digital-twin.html.

Silva Souza, Vinicius da, Robson Cruz, Walmir e Silva, Sidney Lins, and Vicente Lucena Jr (Jan. 2019). "A Digital Twin Architecture Based on the Industrial Internet of Things Technologies". In: pp. 1–2. DOI: https://doi.org/10.1109/ICCE.2019.8662081.

Simon, Herbert A. (1977). *The new science of management decision.* Revised ed. Englewood Cliffs and London: Prentice-Hall. ISBN: 978-0-13-616136-3.

Sjarov, Martin, Tobias Lechler, Jonathan Fuchs, Matthias Brossog, Andreas Selmaier, Florian Faltus, Toni Donhauser, and Jörg Franke (Sept. 2020). "The Digital Twin Concept in Industry—A Review and Systematization". In: DOI: https://doi.org/10.1109/ETFA46521.2020.9212089.

Spetzler, Carl, Hannah Mannchen, and Jennifer Meyer (2016). *Decision Quality: Value Creation from Better Business Decisions.* Wiley online library. Hoboken, NJ, USA: Wiley. ISBN: 9781119176657. DOI: https://doi.org/10.1002/9781119176657. URL: http://onlinelibrary.wiley.com/book/10.1002/9781119176657.

Sprague, Ralph H. (1980). "A Framework for the Development of Decision Support Systems". In: *MIS Quarterly* 4.4, p 1. ISSN: 02767783. DOI: https://doi.org/10.2307/248957.

Srinivasan, Ananth, David Sundaram, and Joseph Davis (2000). *Implementing decision support systems: Methods, techniques, and tools.* Information systems series. London: McGraw-Hill. ISBN: 0077095081.

Stark, Rainer and Thomas Damerau (2019). "Digital Twin". In: *CIRP Encyclopedia of Production Engineering.* Ed. by Sami Chatti and Tullio Tolio. Berlin, Heidelberg: Springer Berlin Heidelberg, pp. 1–8. DOI: https://doi.org/10.1007/978-3-642-35950-7_16870-1.

Stojanovic, Nenad and Dejan Milenovic (Dec. 2018). "Data-driven Digital Twin approach for process optimization: an industry use case". In: pp. 4202–4211. DOI: https://doi.org/10.1109/BigData.2018.8622412.

Stolterman, Erik and Anna Croon Fors (2004). "Information Technology and the Good Life". In: *Information Systems Research: Relevant Theory and Informed Practice.* Ed. by Bonnie Kaplan, Duane P. Truex, David Wastell, A. Trevor Wood-Harper, and Janice I. DeGross. Boston, MA: Springer US, pp. 687–692. DOI: https://doi.org/10.1007/1-4020-8095-6_45.

Subbalakshmi, Sakineti and Prabhu Csr (Dec. 2018). "Protagonist of Big Data and Predictive Analytics using data analytics". In: pp. 276–279. DOI: https://doi.org/10.1109/CTEMS.2018.8769141.

Sukamolson, Suphat (2007). "Fundamentals of quantitative research". In: *Language Institute Chulalongkorn University* 1.3, pp. 1–20.

Sulistyo, Haidar Alvinanda, Tien Febrianti Kusumasari, and Ekky Novriza Alam (2020). "Implementation of Data Cleansing Null Method for Data Quality Management Dashboard using Pentaho Data Integration". In: *2020 3rd International Conference on Information and Communications Technology (ICOIACT)*, pp. 12–16. DOI: https://doi.org/10.1109/ICOIACT50329.2020.9332030.

Sundharam, Sakthivel Manikandan and Elke Pulvermueller (Sept. 2020). "Integrated Performance Tuning of an IIoT Digital Twin: Work-in-Progress". In: pp. 7–9. DOI: https://doi.org/10.1109/EMSOFT51651.2020.9244020.

Tao, Fei, Jiangfeng Cheng, Qinglin Qi, Meng Zhang, He Zhang, and Fangyuan Sui (Feb. 2018). "Digital twin- driven product design, manufacturing and service with big data". In: *The International Journal of Advanced Manufacturing Technology* 94. DOI: https://doi.org/10.1007/s00170-017-0233-1.

Tao, Fei and Qinglin Qi (2019). "New IT Driven Service-Oriented Smart Manufacturing: Framework and Characteristics". In: *IEEE Transactions on Systems, Man, and Cybernetics: Systems* 49.1, pp. 81–91. ISSN: 2168-2232. DOI: https://doi.org/10.1109/TSMC.2017.2723764.

Tao, Fei, Qinglin Qi, Lihui Wang, and A.Y.C. Nee (2019). "Digital Twins and Cyber–Physical Systems toward Smart Manufacturing and Industry 4.0: Correlation and Comparison". In: *Engineering* 5.4, pp. 653–661. ISSN: 2095–8099. DOI: https://doi.org/10.1016/j.eng.2019.01.014.

Tao, Fei, Fangyuan Sui, Ang Liu, Qinglin Qi, Meng Zhang, Boyang Song, Zirong Guo, Stephen C.-Y. Lu, and A. Y. C. Nee (2019). "Digital twin-driven product design framework". In: *International Journal of Production Research* 57.12, pp. 3935–3953. ISSN: 0020-7543. DOI: https://doi.org/10.1080/00207543.2018.1443229.

Tao, Fei and Meng Zhang (2017). "Digital Twin Shop-Floor: A New Shop-Floor Paradigm Towards Smart Manufacturing". In: *IEEE Access* 5, pp. 20418–20427. ISSN: 2169-3536. DOI: https://doi.org/10.1109/ACCESS.2017.2756069.

Tao, Fei, Meng Zhang, Yushan Liu, and A.Y.C. Nee (2018). "Digital twin driven prognostics and health management for complex equipment". In: *CIRP Annals* 67.1, pp. 169–172. ISSN: 0007-8506. DOI: https://doi.org/10.1016/J.CIRP.2018.04.055.

Tao, Fei, Meng Zhang, and Andrew Nee (Jan. 2019a). "Applications of Digital Twin". In: pp. 29–62. DOI: https://doi.org/10.1016/B978-0-12-817630-6.00002-3.

Tao, Fei, Meng Zhang, and Andrew Nee (Jan. 2019b). "Background and Concept of Digital Twin". In: pp. 3–28. ISBN: 9780128176306. DOI: https://doi.org/10.1016/B978-0-12-817630-6.00001-1.

Tao, Fei, Meng Zhang, and Andrew Nee (Jan. 2019c). "Five-Dimension Digital Twin Modeling and Its Key Technologies". In: pp. 63–81. ISBN: 9780128176306. DOI: https://doi.org/10.1016/B978-0-12-817630-6.00003-5.

Turban, E., J.E. Aronson, and R. Sharda (2007). *Decision Support and Business Intelligence Systems*. Pearson Prentice Hall. ISBN: 9780131986602.

Turban, Efraim and Jay E. Aronson (2001). *Decision support systems and intelligent systems.* 6th ed. / Efraim Turban, Jay E. Aronson with contributions by Narashima Bolloju. Upper Saddle River, N.J. and Great Britain: Prentice Hall. ISBN: 9780130894656.

Uhlemann, Thomas, Christoph Schock, Christian Lehmann, Stefan Freiberger, and Rolf Steinhilper (Dec. 2017). "The Digital Twin: Demonstrating the Potential of Real Time Data Acquisition in Production Systems". In: *Procedia Manufacturing* 9, pp. 113–120. DOI: https://doi.org/10.1016/j.promfg.2017.04.043.

Uhlemann, Thomas H.-J., Christian Lehmann, and Rolf Steinhilper (2017). "The Digital Twin: Realizing the Cyber-Physical Production System for Industry 4.0". In: *Procedia CIRP* 61, pp. 335–340. ISSN: 2212–8271. DOI: https://doi.org/10.1016/j.procir.2016.11.152.

Vassakis, Konstantinos, Emmanuel Petrakis, and Ioannis Kopanakis (Jan. 2018). "Big Data Analytics: Applications, Prospects and Challenges". In: pp. 3–20. DOI: https://doi.org/10.1007/978-3-319-67925-9_1.

Vijayakumar, D. Sudaroli (2020). "Digital twin in consumer choice modeling". In: *The Digital Twin Paradigm for Smarter Systems and Environments: The Industry Use Cases.* Vol. 117. Advances in Computers. Elsevier, pp. 265–284. ISBN: 9780128187562. DOI: https://doi.org/10.1016/bs.adcom.2019.09.010.

Volk, Matthias, Sascha Bosse, Dennis Bischoff, and Klaus Turowski (May 2019). "Decision-Support for Selecting Big Data Reference Architectures". In: pp. 3–17. DOI: https://doi.org/10.1007/978-3-030-20485-3_1.

Wadan, Rafi and Frank Teuteberg (May 2019). "Understanding Requirements and Benefits of the Usage of Predictive Analytics in Management Accounting: Results of a Qualitative Research Approach". In: pp. 100–111. DOI: https://doi.org/10.1007/978-3-030-20485-3_8.

Wagner, Raphael, Benjamin Schleich, Benjamin Haefner, Andreas Kuhnle, Sandro Wartzack, and Gisela Lanza (Jan. 2019). "Challenges and Potentials of Digital Twins and Industry 4.0 in Product Design and Production for High Performance Products". In: *Procedia CIRP* 84, pp. 88–93. DOI: https://doi.org/10.1016/j.procir.2019.04.219.

Walsh, John E. (1959). "Definition and Use of Generalized Percentage Points". In: *Sankhyā: The Indian Journal of Statistics (1933–1960)* 21.3/4, pp. 281–288. ISSN: 00364452. DOI: https://doi.org/10.2307/25048423. URL: http://www.jstor.org/stable/25048423.

Wanasinghe, Thumeera R., Leah Wroblewski, Bui K. Petersen, Raymond G. Gosine, Lesley Anne James, Oscar de Silva, George K. I. Mann, and Peter J. Warrian (2020). "Digital Twin for the Oil and Gas Industry: Overview, Research Trends, Opportunities, and Challenges". In: *IEEE Access* 8, pp. 104175–104197. ISSN: 2169–3536. DOI: https://doi.org/10.1109/ACCESS.2020.2998723.

Wand, Yair and Richard Y. Wang (1996). "Anchoring data quality dimensions in ontological foundations". In: *Communications of the ACM* 39.11, pp. 86–95. ISSN: 0001–0782. DOI: https://doi.org/10.1145/240455.240479.

Wang, Jinjiang, Lunkuan Ye, Robert X. Gao, Chen Li, and Laibin Zhang (2019). "Digital Twin for rotating machinery fault diagnosis in smart manufacturing". In: *International Journal of Production Research* 57.12, pp. 3920–3934. ISSN: 0020-7543. DOI: https://doi.org/10.1080/00207543.2018.1552032.

Wang, Richard Y. (Feb. 1998). "A Product Perspective on Total Data Quality Management". In: *Commun. ACM* 41.2, pp. 58–65. ISSN: 0001-0782. DOI: https://doi.org/10.1145/269012.269022.

Wang, Richard Y., M. P. Reddy, and Henry B. Kon (1995). "Toward quality data: An attribute-based approach". In: *Decision Support Systems* 13.3–4, pp. 349–372. ISSN: 0167-9236. DOI: https://doi.org/10.1016/0167-9236(93)E0050-N.

Wang, Richard Y. and Diane M. Strong (Mar. 1996). "Beyond Accuracy: What Data Quality Means to Data Consumers". In: *J. Manage. Inf. Syst.* 12.4, pp. 5–33. ISSN: 0742-1222. DOI: https://doi.org/10.1080/07421222.1996.11518099.

Wang, Yankai, Shilong Wang, Bo Yang, Lingzi Zhu, and Feng Liu (2020). "Big data driven Hierarchical Digital Twin Predictive Remanufacturing paradigm: Architecture, control mechanism, application scenario and benefits". In: *Journal of Cleaner Production* 248, p. 119299. ISSN: 0959-6526. DOI: https://doi.org/10.1016/j.jclepro.2019.119299.

Wärmefjord, Kristina, Rikard Söderberg, Lars Lindkvist, Björn Lindau, and Johan Carlson (Nov. 2017). "Inspection Data to Support a Digital Twin for Geometry Assurance". In: V002T02A101. DOI: https://doi.org/10.1115/IMECE2017-70398.

Waschull, Sabine, J. Wortmann, and Jos Bokhorst (Aug. 2020). "The Transformation Towards Smart(er) Factories: Integration Requirements of the Digital Twin". In: pp. 187–194. DOI: https://doi.org/10.1007/978-3-030-57993-7_22.

Wilcoxon, Frank (1945). "Individual Comparisons by Ranking Methods". In: *Biometrics Bulletin* 1.6, p. 80. ISSN:00994987. DOI: https://doi.org/10.2307/3001968.

Williams, Carrie (2007). "Research Methods". In: *Journal of Business & Economics Research (JBER)* 5(3). DOI: https://doi.org/10.19030/jber.v5i3.2532.

Wright, Louise and Stuart Davidson (Dec. 2020). "How to tell the difference between a model and a digital twin". In: *Advanced Modeling and Simulation in Engineering Sciences* 7. DOI: https://doi.org/10.1186/s40323-020-00147-4.

Wu, Jiaju, Yonghui Yang, XUN Cheng, and Hongfu Zuo (Nov. 2020). "The Development of Digital Twin Technology Review". In: pp. 4901–4906. DOI: https://doi.org/10.1109/CAC51589.2020.9327756.

Xu, Wenjun, Jia Cui, Lan Li, Bitao Yao, Sisi Tian, and Zude Zhou (July 2020). "Digital twin-based industrial cloud robotics: Framework, control approach and implementation". In: *Journal of Manufacturing Systems* 58. DOI: https://doi.org/10.1016/j.jmsy.2020.07.013.

Yang, Qiang and Geoffrey Webb (Jan. 2006). *PRICAI 2006: Trends in Artificial Intelligence, 9th Pacific Rim International Conference on Artificial Intelligence, Guilin, China, August 7–11, 2006, Proceedings*. Vol. 4099. DOI: https://doi.org/10.1007/978-3-540-36668-3.

Yoo, Youngjin, Ola Henfridsson, and Kalle Lyytinen (Dec. 2010). "The New Organizing Logic of Digital Innovation: An Agenda for Information Systems Research". In: *Information Systems Research* 21, pp. 724–735. DOI: https://doi.org/10.1287/isre.1100.0322.

Zhang, Chao, Guanghui Zhou, Junsheng Hu, and Jing Li (2020). "Deep learning-enabled intelligent process planning for digital twin manufacturing cell". In: *Knowledge-Based Systems* 191, p. 105247. ISSN: 0950-7051. DOI: https://doi.org/10.1016/j.knosys.2019.105247.

Zhang, Haijun, Qiong Yan, and Zhenghua Wen (Mar. 2020). "Information modeling for cyber-physical production system based on digital twin and AutomationML". In: *The International Journal of Advanced Manufacturing Technology* 107. DOI: https://doi.org/10.1007/s00170-020-05056-9.

Zhang, Hao, Qiang Liu, Xin Chen, Ding Zhang, and Jiewu Leng (2017). "A Digital Twin-Based Approach for Designing and Multi-Objective Optimization of Hollow Glass Production Line". In: *IEEE Access* 5, pp. 26901–26911. ISSN: 2169-3536. DOI: https://doi.org/10.1109/ACCESS.2017.2766453.

Zheng, Pai and Kendrik Yan Hong Lim (July 2020). "Product family design and optimization: a digital twin- enhanced approach". In: vol. 93. DOI: https://doi.org/10.1016/j.procir.2020.05.162.

Zheng, Pai, Zhiqian Sang, Ray Y Zhong, Yongkui Liu, Chao Liu, Khamdi Mubarok, Shiqiang Yu, Xun Xu, et al. (2018). "Smart manufacturing systems for Industry 4.0: Conceptual framework, scenarios, and future perspectives". In: *Frontiers of Mechanical Engineering* 13.2, pp. 137–150. DOI: https://doi.org/10.1007/s12652-018-0911-3.

Zheng, Xiaochen, Foivos Psarommatis, Pierluigi Petrali, Claudio Turrin, Jinzhi Lu, and Dimitris Kiritsis (2020). "A Quality-Oriented Digital Twin Modelling Method for Manufacturing Processes Based on A Multi-Agent Architecture". In: *Procedia Manufacturing* 51. 30th International Conference on Flexible Automation and Intelligent Manufacturing (FAIM2021), pp. 309–315. ISSN: 2351-9789. DOI: https://doi.org/10.1016/j.promfg.2020.10.044.

Zheng, Yu, Sen Yang, and Huanchong Cheng (Mar. 2019). "An application framework of digital twin and its case study". In: *Journal of Ambient Intelligence and Humanized Computing* 10. DOI: https://doi.org/10.1007/s12652-018-0911-3.

Zhuang, Cunbo, Jingcheng Gong, and Jianhua Liu (June 2020). "Digital twin-based assembly data management and process traceability for complex products". In: *Journal of Manufacturing Systems* 58. DOI: https://doi.org/10.1016/j.jmsy.2020.05.011.

Summary

Zhuang, Cunbo, Jianhua Liu, and Hui Xiong (2018). "Digital twin-based smart production management and control framework for the complex product assembly shop-floor". In: *The International Journal of Advanced Manufacturing Technology* 96.1–4, pp. 1149–1163. ISSN: 0268-3768. DOI: https://doi.org/10.1007/s00170-018-1617-6.

Zillmann, Mario (2017). *Revival of master data: Is poor data quality hindering the digital transformation?* URL: https://www.kps.com/assets/documents/Stammdatenstudie.pdf.

MIX
Papier aus verantwortungsvollen Quellen
Paper from responsible sources
FSC® C105338

If you have any concerns about our products,
you can contact us on
ProductSafety@springernature.com

In case Publisher is established outside the EU,
the EU authorized representative is:
Springer Nature Customer Service Center GmbH
Europaplatz 3, 69115 Heidelberg, Germany

Printed by Libri Plureos GmbH
in Hamburg, Germany